I0025488

TC 3-04.93 (FM 3-04.301)

Aeromedical Training for Flight Personnel

August 2009

DISTRIBUTION RESTRICTION: Approved for public release; distribution is unlimited.

Headquarters, Department of the Army

Published by Books Express Publishing
Books Express Publishing, 2011
ISBN 978-1-78039-952-2

Books Express publications are available from all good retail and online booksellers. For
publishing proposals and direct ordering please contact us at: info@books-express.com

Training Circular
No. 3-04.93 (FM 3-04.301)

Headquarters
Department of the Army
Washington, DC, 31 August 2009

Aeromedical Training for Flight Personnel

Contents

Figures

Tables

Preface

This manual is intended for use by all Army crewmembers in meeting requirements set forth in Army Regulation 95-1, Training Circular 1-210, and other appropriate aircrew training manuals.

Lessons learned from previous military conflicts and recent contingency operations have caused changes in Army aviation doctrine. With the development of more sophisticated aircraft and weapons systems, Army crewmembers must be capable of operating these systems around the clock, in austere environments, and under adverse conditions. The hazards of stress and fatigue in combat operations and concept of operations will eventually take a toll in aircrew performance and could jeopardize mission accomplishment unless crewmembers are trained to recognize and understand these hazards. Proper training prepares crewmembers and prevents stress and fatigue from reducing mission effectiveness, thereby increasing their chances of survival.

Training Circular 3-04.93 provides crewmembers with an understanding of the physiological responses that can occur in the aviation environment. It also describes the effects of the flight environment on individual mission accomplishment. In addition, this publication outlines essential aeromedical training requirements (in Chapter 1) that assist commanders and flight surgeons in conducting aeromedical education for Army crewmembers. Subject areas addressed are by no means all inclusive but are presented to assist crewmembers in increasing performance and efficiency.

This publication applies to the Active Army, the Army National Guard/Army National Guard of the United States, and the United States Army Reserve unless otherwise stated.

The proponent of this publication is Headquarters, U.S. Army Training and Doctrine Command. Send comments and recommendations on Department of the Army Form 2028 (Recommended Changes to Publications and Blank Forms) to Dean, U.S. Army School of Aviation Medicine, ATTN: MCCS-HA, Fort Rucker, AL 36362-5377.

The provisions of this publication are the subject of the following international agreement: Standardization Agreement 3114.

The use of trade names in this manual is for clarity only and does not constitute endorsement by the Department of Defense.

This publication has been reviewed for operations security considerations.

Chapter 1

The Training Program

This chapter outlines essential aeromedical training requirements needed for crewmembers. Aircrews must be trained and ready in peacetime to perform their missions in combat or other contingency operations. Therefore, leaders at all levels must understand, sustain, and enforce high standards of combat readiness. Tough, realistic training should be designed to challenge and develop Soldiers, leaders, and units. This chapter outlines the essential aeromedical training requirements needed for all crewmembers.

TRAINING OVERVIEW

1-1. The U.S. Army provides aeromedical training during initial flight training and during designated courses to all flight students at the U.S. Army Aviation Center of Excellence (USAACE), Fort Rucker, AL. In addition, unit commanders are responsible for aeromedical training at the unit level.

<table>
<tr><th colspan="2">Contents</th></tr>
<tr><td colspan="2"></td></tr>
</table>

AEROMEDICAL TRAINING IN SPECIFIC COURSES

1-2. Initial aeromedical training is conducted for all U.S. Army students in the Initial Entry Rotary Wing Course. Initial physiological training is performed according to the provisions of Standardization Agreement 3114 and U.S. Army Training and Doctrine Command programs of instruction (POIs) at USAACE. Aeromedical training is conducted for aviators receiving transition or advanced training at USAACE.

HYPOBARIC REFRESHER TRAINING

1-3. Fixed- or rotary-wing crewmembers who fly in pressurized aircraft or in aircraft that routinely exceed 10,000 feet mean sea level (MSL) must complete aeromedical refresher training every 5 years. Crewmembers are required to participate in a hypobaric (low pressure/high altitude) chamber exercise or a reduced oxygen breathing device (ROBD) exercise using the appropriate profile for the aircraft and mission requirements (see appendix A). Crewmembers who fly in pressurized aircraft also must complete a rapid decompression. Training will be conducted by an approved physiological training unit for crewmembers meeting these criteria, with the exception of personnel specified in paragraph 1-4.

1-4. Crewmembers with 240 months total operational flying duty credit (TOFDC) and four successful altitude chamber iterations must complete classroom training requirements but are exempt from the altitude chamber and rapid decompression practical exercise requirements. Department of the Army civilians (DACs) and contractors with documentation of prior Department of Defense-approved training may, upon approval from the Government flight representative, request exceptions through the unit standardization section. (DACs and contractors are required to complete annual altitude physiology training requirements.) All crewmembers who meet these requirements and provide the unit standardization section with documented proof of training may receive altitude physiology review classroom training at the unit level. See paragraph 1-20 for Department of the Army (DA) Form 759 (Individual Flight Record and Flight Certificate-Army) requirements.

1-5.   Refresher training consists of classroom instruction to review the essential materials presented in initial training. The minimum refresher training needed to meet the requirements of paragraph 1-3 are—

- Altitude physiology review.
- Altitude chamber orientation.
- Altitude chamber practical exercise.
- Rapid decompression practical exercise.

APPROVED PHYSIOLOGICAL TRAINING UNITS

1-6.   U.S. Air Force or U.S. Navy physiological training units may be used if aviators cannot attend aeromedical training, including hypobaric (low pressure/high altitude) chamber qualification, at the U.S. Army School of Aviation Medicine (USASAM), Fort Rucker, AL. Initial and refresher training conducted by other services meets U.S. Army requirements for renewal of aeromedical training currency for a 5-year period.

UNIT TRAINING

1-7.   The unit commander must develop an aeromedical training program that meets the unit's specific needs as part of the Aircrew Training Program governed by Training Circular (TC) 1-210. This training is crucial because most Army crewmembers are not required to attend the established refresher training courses described previously.

1-8.   The unit's mission and its wide range of operations are important factors for the commander to consider in developing an aeromedical training program. The program should include the various aeromedical factors that affect crewmember performance in different environments, during flight maneuvers, and while wearing protective gear. The unit aeromedical training program will contain, at a minimum, the continuation training described in paragraph 1-10.

1-9.   Because of the medical and technical nature of the aeromedical training program, the commander must involve the unit's supporting flight surgeons in developing the program. The flight surgeon will provide input for all aspects of unit aviation plans, operations, and training. Commanders can obtain further assistance in developing a unit aeromedical training program from the Dean, USASAM, ATTN: MCCS-HA, Fort Rucker, AL 36362-5377, http://usasam.amedd.army.mil.

CONTINUATION TRAINING

1-10.   The requirement for continuation training applies to all Army crewmembers in operational flying positions. The POI must be conducted once a year. The following subjects provide the minimum training necessary for the unit to reach adequate safety and efficiency in the aviation environment:

- Altitude physiology.
- Spatial disorientation (SD).
- Aviation protective equipment.
- Stress, fatigue, and exogenous factors.

MISSION CONSIDERATIONS

1-11.   The unit commander must evaluate the unit's missions to incorporate mission considerations into the aeromedical training POI. This analysis should include—

- Combat missions.
- Installation support missions.
- Contingency missions.
- Geographic and climatic considerations.
- Programmed training activities.

1-12. The supporting flight surgeon will help identify the aeromedical factors present during various flight conditions and their effects on aircrew performance. The flight surgeon and the unit commander will then develop a POI that meets the unit's specific needs. For example, a unit stationed in the Northwest may have a war-trace mission in Southeast Asia. The unit commander and flight surgeon would evaluate the environmental concerns of that region and incorporate those factors into the aeromedical training program.

1-13. The commander must include all crewmembers in the unit aeromedical training program. Individual crewmembers will be evaluated on their aeromedical knowledge during the Annual Proficiency and Readiness Test (APART) period in accordance with the appropriate aircrew training manual (ATM). Lesson materials can be obtained at http://usasam.amedd.army.mil.

RESPONSIBILITIES

U.S. ARMY SCHOOL OF AVIATION MEDICINE

1-14. USASAM is responsible for planning, supervising, and conducting all formal aeromedical Army aviation training programs. USASAM also advises and assists unit commanders and flight surgeons in developing local unit aeromedical training programs.

UNIT COMMANDER

1-15. The unit commander, assisted by the flight surgeon, will develop a local unit aeromedical training program. The program should be designed to meet the unit's mission requirements.

FLIGHT SURGEON

1-16. The flight surgeon provides medical support. He or she also assists the unit commander in developing, presenting, and monitoring a unit aeromedical training program.

REVALIDATION AND WAIVER

REVALIDATION

1-17. Crewmembers are required to stay current in aeromedical training and hypobaric (low pressure/high altitude) chamber training per Army Regulation (AR) 95-1, TC 1-210, and the appropriate ATM. If a crewmember's aeromedical training currency lapses, that individual must meet the requirements of paragraph 1-3 or 1-10 as appropriate.

WAIVERS AND EXTENSIONS

1-18. AR 95-1 contains waiver procedures. An extension to hypobaric training may be granted prior to the expiration period on a case-by-case basis for those individuals who will exceed the 5-year currency requirement. The waiver request will be forwarded with the local flight surgeon's recommendation to the commander with aircrew training plan (ATP) authority. The commander has approval authority for DA Form 4186 (Medical Recommendation for Flying Duty) to grant the extension. The extension period will not exceed 30 days. Individuals who do not have a current altitude chamber exposure or valid extension will be administratively restricted from flying duties and processed according to AR 600-105 and AR 600-106.

TRAINING RECORD DOCUMENTATION

1-19. Upon completion of prescribed qualifications, training will be documented in the crewmember's health record and Individual Flight Records Folder (IFRF) and retained by the individual.

INITIAL AEROMEDICAL TRAINING

1-20. After the crewmember has completed training, the following entry will be made in the REMARKS section of DA Form 759: "Individual has completed initial physiological training prescribed in TC 3-04.93, including hypobaric (low pressure/high altitude) chamber qualification and/or rapid decompression, on (date)."

CONTINUATION AEROMEDICAL TRAINING

1-21. After the crewmember has completed training, the remarks section of DA Form 759 should contain the following entry: "Individual has completed refresher physiological training prescribed in TC 3-04.93, including hypobaric (low pressure/high altitude) chamber or ROBD and/or rapid decompression qualification, on (date)." The following entry is required for individuals who meet paragraph 1-4 requirements: "Individual has 240 TOFDC as of (date) and four successful chamber runs (dates) and has completed refresher flight physiology academic training on (date)." The unit is responsible for verifying official documentation and requirements for paragraph 1-4. Assistance is available through the Chief, Warrior Track, USASAM.

SPECIAL TRAINING BY OTHER SERVICES

1-22. When aeromedical training is conducted by the U.S. Air Force or U.S. Navy and the forms listed in paragraph 1-18 are not available, the forms listed below may be used to document the training qualification. Appropriate entries will be made in the REMARKS section of the applicable form when the crewmember completes training. The forms other services may use are—

- AF1274 (Physiological Training).
- AF702 (Individual Physiological Training Record).
- NAVMED 6150/2 (Special Duty Medical Abstract).
- NAVMED 6410/7 (Completion of Physiological Training).

1-23. Appropriate entries will be made on Standard Form 600 (Health Record-Chronological Record of Medical Care), which is filed with DA Form 3444 (Inpatient Treatment Records and Dental Records [Orange]). This information will document any medical difficulties the individual might have encountered during altitude chamber qualification.

Chapter 2

Altitude Physiology

Humans are not physiologically equipped for high altitudes. To cope, humans rely on preventive measures and, in some cases, life-support equipment. Although Army aviators primarily fly rotary-wing aircraft at relatively low altitudes, aircrews may still encounter altitude-associated problems that cause hypoxia, hyperventilation, and trapped- and evolved-gas disorders. By understanding the characteristics of the atmosphere, aircrews are better prepared for the physiological changes that occur with increasing altitudes.

SECTION I – THE ATMOSPHERE

PHYSICAL CHARACTERISTICS

2-1. The Earth's atmosphere is a mixture of water and gases. The atmosphere extends from the surface of the Earth to approximately 1,200 miles (1,931 kilometers) in space. Gravity holds the atmosphere in place. The atmosphere exhibits few physical characteristics; however, it shields the Earth from ultraviolet radiation and other hazards in space. Without the atmosphere, the Earth would be as barren as the moon.

Contents

STRUCTURE

2-2. The atmosphere consists of several concentric layers, also known as spheres, each displaying its own unique characteristics. Thermal variances within the atmosphere help define these spheres, offering aviation personnel an insight into atmospheric conditions within each area. Between each sphere is an imaginary boundary known as a pause. Figure 2-1 (page 2-2) provides an illustration of the Earth's atmospheric structure.

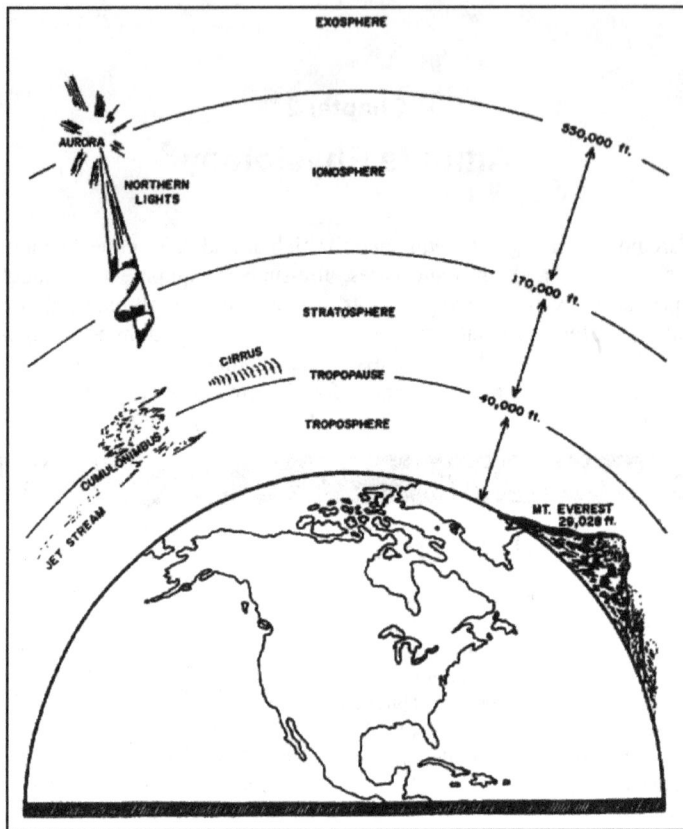

Figure 2-1. Earth's atmospheric structure

TROPOSPHERE

2-3. The troposphere extends from sea level to about 26,405 feet (8 kilometers) over the poles to nearly 52,810 feet (16 kilometers) above the equator. It is distinguished by a relatively uniform decrease in temperature and the presence of water vapor, along with extensive weather phenomena.

> ## Mean Temperature Lapse Rate
>
> -1.98 degrees Celsius per 1,000 feet

2-4. Temperature changes in the troposphere can be accurately predicted using a mean temperature lapse rate of −1.98 degrees Celsius per 1,000 feet. Temperatures continue to decrease until the rising air mass achieves an altitude where temperature is in equilibrium with the surrounding atmosphere. Table 2-1 (page 2-3) illustrates the mean lapse rate and the pressure decrease associated with ascending altitude.

Table 2-1. Standard pressure and temperature values at 40 degrees latitude for specific altitudes

Altitude (ft)	Pressure (in/Hg)	Pressure (mm/Hg)	Pressure (psi)	Temperature (°C)	Temperature (°F)
Sea level	29.92	760.0	14.69	15.0	59.0
10,000	20.58	522.6	10.11	−4.8	23.3
18,000	14.95	379.4	7.34	−20.7	−5.3
20,000	13.76	349.1	6.75	−24.6	−12.3
25,000	10.51	281.8	5.45	−34.5	−30.1
30,000	8.90	225.6	4.36	−44.4	−48.0
34,000	7.40	187.4	3.62	−52.4	−62.3
35,332	6.80	175.9	3.41	−55.0	−67.0
40,000	5.56	140.7	2.72	−55.0	−67.0
43,000	4.43	119.0	2.30	−55.0	−67.0
50,000	3.44	87.3	1.69	−55.0	−67.0

STRATOSPHERE

2-5. The stratosphere extends from the tropopause to about 158,430 feet (30 miles or 48 kilometers). The stratosphere is subdivided into two regions based on thermal characteristics. Although these regions differ thermally, the water-vapor content of both regions is virtually nonexistent.

2-6. The first region of the stratosphere is the isothermal layer. In this layer, temperature is constant at −55 degrees Celsius (−67 degrees Fahrenheit). Turbulence is a common occurrence in the stratosphere and can be attributed to the presence of fast-moving jet streams.

2-7. The stratosphere's second region is the ozonosphere. It is characterized by rising temperatures. The ozonosphere serves as a double-sided barrier that absorbs harmful solar ultraviolet radiation while allowing solar heat to pass through to the Earth's surface unaffected. In addition, the ozonosphere reflects heat from rising air masses back toward the Earth's surface, keeping the lower regions of the atmosphere warm even at night, when there is an absence of significant solar activity.

MESOSPHERE

2-8. The mesosphere extends from the stratopause to an altitude of 264,050 feet (50 miles or 80 kilometers). Temperatures decline from a high of −3 degrees Celsius at the stratopause to nearly −113 degrees Celsius at the mesopause. Noctilucent clouds are a characteristic of this atmospheric layer. Made of water ice vapor, these cloud formations are visible only at night when illuminated by sunlight from below the horizon while the ground and lower layers of the atmosphere are in the Earth's shadow.

THERMOSPHERE

2-9. The uppermost atmospheric region, the thermosphere extends from the mesopause to approximately 435 miles (700 kilometers) above the Earth. Thermosphere temperatures increase with altitude and are in direct relation to solar activity. Temperatures in the thermosphere range from −113 degrees Celsius at the mesopause to 2,000 degrees Celsius during periods of extreme solar activity.

2-10. The presence of ionic particles is a characteristic of the thermosphere. These particles are the result of high-speed subatomic particles emanating from the sun that collide with gas atoms and are split apart.

COMPOSITION

2-11. The Earth's atmosphere contains many gases; however, few are essential to human survival. Those gases required for human life are nitrogen, oxygen, and carbon dioxide. Table 2-2 indicates the percentage concentrations of gases commonly found in the atmosphere.

Table 2-2. Percentages of atmospheric gases

Gas	Symbol	Volume (%)
Nitrogen	N_2	78.0840
Oxygen	O_2	20.9480
Argon	Ar	0.9340
Carbon dioxide	CO_2	0.0314
Neon	Ne	0.0018
Helium	He	0.0005
Hydrogen	H_2	<0.0001

NITROGEN

2-12. The Earth's atmosphere consists mainly of nitrogen. Although a vital ingredient in the chain of life, nitrogen is not readily used by the human body. However, nitrogen saturates body fluids and tissues as a result of respiration. Aircrews must be aware of possible evolved-gas disorders due to the decreased solubility of nitrogen at higher altitudes.

OXYGEN

2-13. Oxygen is the second most plentiful gas in the atmosphere. Oxygen and sugars are combined through the process of respiration to meet the human body's energy requirements. A lack of oxygen in the body at altitude can cause drastic physiological changes resulting in death.

CARBON DIOXIDE

2-14. Carbon dioxide is the product of cellular respiration in most life forms. Although not present in large amounts, carbon dioxide in the atmosphere plays a vital role in maintaining Earth's oxygen supply. Through photosynthesis, plants use carbon dioxide to create energy and release oxygen as a byproduct. Due to animal metabolism and photosynthesis, carbon dioxide and oxygen supplies in the atmosphere remain constant.

OTHER GASES

2-15. Other gases such as argon, xenon, and helium are present in trace amounts in the atmosphere. They are not as critical to human survival as nitrogen, oxygen, and carbon dioxide.

ATMOSPHERIC (BAROMETRIC) PRESSURE

2-16. Standard atmospheric (barometric) pressure is the force (or weight) exerted by the atmosphere at any given point. Atmospheric pressure is an observable characteristic and can be expressed in different forms such as psi, millimeter/mercury (mm/Hg), inches of Hg, or in feet as indicated by an altimeter. Atmospheric pressure decreases with increasing altitude, which causes difficulties with the body's ability to circulate oxygen. This decrease in pressure is the cause of most physiological problems in flight. Figure 2-2 (page 2-5) illustrates standard atmospheric pressure measurements at 59 degrees Fahrenheit (15 degrees Celsius) at sea level.

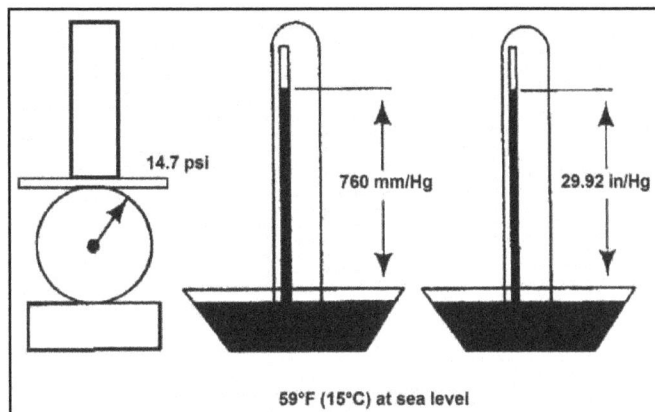

Figure 2-2. Standard atmospheric pressure measurements

DALTON'S LAW OF PARTIAL PRESSURES

2-17. A close relationship exists between atmospheric pressure and the amount of various gases present in the atmosphere. This relationship is referred to as Dalton's Law of Partial Pressures. Dalton's Law states that the pressure exerted by a mixture of ideal (nonreacting) gases is equal to the sum of the partial pressures of each gas in the mixture. The independent pressure of each gas is termed the partial pressure of that gas. Figure 2-3 (page 2-6) represents the concept of Dalton's Law as related to the Earth's atmosphere. Mathematically, Dalton's Law can be expressed as follows:

Dalton's Law

$$PT = PN_2 + PO_2 + PCO_2 + ... \text{ (at constant V and T)}$$

PT = total pressure of the mixture

PN_2 = partial pressure of nitrogen

PO_2 = partial pressure of oxygen

PCO_2 = partial pressure of carbon dioxide

$PN_2 + PO_2 + PCO_2$ = partial pressures of each individual gas

V = volume

T = temperature

2-18. To determine the partial pressure of gases in the atmosphere (or any gaseous mixture whose concentrations are known), the following mathematical formula can be used:

Partial Pressure of Gases in the Atmosphere

Percentage of atmospheric concentration of the individual gas x

Total atmospheric pressure at a given altitude =

100

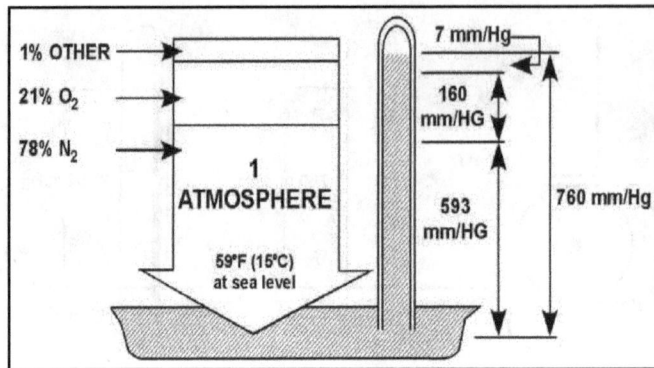

Figure 2-3. Dalton's Law and the Earth's atmosphere

2-19. Dalton's law illustrates that as altitude increases, there is a proportional decrease in partial pressures of gases in the atmosphere. Although the percentage concentration of gases remains stable with increasing altitude, each partial pressure decreases in direct proportion to the total barometric pressure. Table 2-3 shows the relationship between barometric pressure and partial pressure.

Table 2-3. Partial pressures of oxygen at various altitudes

Altitude (ft)	Atmospheric Pressure (mm/Hg)	PAO_2 (mm/Hg)	PVO_2 (mm/Hg)	Pressure Differential (mm/Hg)	Blood Saturation (%)
Sea level	760	100	40	60	98
10,000	523	60	31	29	87
18,000	380	38	26	12	72
22,000	321	30	22	8	60
25,000	282	7	4	3	9
35,000	179	0	0	0	0

2-20. Any change in the partial pressure of oxygen dramatically affects respiratory function. A decrease in the partial pressure of oxygen quickly results in physiological impairment. Although this impairment might not initially be noticed at lower altitudes, the effects are cumulative and grow progressively worse as altitude increases.

2-21. A decrease in the partial pressure of nitrogen, especially at high altitude, can lead to a decrease in the solubility of nitrogen in the body and possibly result in decompression sickness (DCS).

PHYSIOLOGICAL ZONES OF THE ATMOSPHERE

2-22. Humans are unable to adapt physiologically to all the physical changes that occur in the different regions of the atmosphere. Humans are especially susceptible to the dramatic temperature and pressure changes that take place during ascent and sustained aerial flight. For these reasons, the atmosphere is further divided (by altitude) into three distinct physiological zones. These zones are based on pressure changes and the resultant effects on human physiology.

THE EFFICIENT ZONE

2-23. Extending upward from sea level to 10,000 feet, the efficient zone provides aircrews with a near-ideal physiological environment. Although barometric pressure drops from 760 mm/Hg at sea level to 523 mm/Hg at 10,000 feet, partial pressure of oxygen (PO_2) levels within this range permit humans to operate without protective equipment. However, sustained flight in the upper portions of this area might require acclimatization. Some minor problems associated with the efficient zone are ear and sinus blockages and gas expansion in the digestive tract. Without use of supplemental oxygen, a decrease in night vision capabilities occurs above 4,000 feet.

THE DEFICIENT ZONE

2-24. The deficient zone ranges from 10,000 feet at its base to 50,000 feet at its highest point. Because atmospheric pressure at 10,000 feet is only 523 mm/Hg, missions in the deficient zone carry a high degree of risk unless supplemental oxygen/cabin pressurization systems are used. As flights approach the upper limit of the deficient zone, decreasing barometric pressure (down to 87 mm/Hg) increases the frequency of trapped-gas disorders.

THE SPACE EQUIVALENT ZONE

2-25. Extending from 50,000 feet and continuing to the atmosphere's outer fringes, the space equivalent zone is deadly to humans. Therefore, flight in the space equivalent zone requires an artificial atmospheric environment. Unprotected exposure to the extremely low temperatures and pressures found at these high altitudes can quickly result in death. For example, at 63,000 feet (Armstrong's line), the barometric pressure is only 47 mm/Hg, equal to the partial pressure of water in the body at 37 degrees Celsius. At this pressure, water begins to boil within the body as it changes into a gaseous vapor.

SECTION II – CIRCULATORY SYSTEM

STRUCTURE AND FUNCTION OF THE CIRCULATORY SYSTEM

2-26. The circulatory system (figure 2-4) constitutes the physiologic framework required to transport blood throughout the body. A fundamental function of the circulatory system (along with the lymphatic system) is fluid transport. Other important functions of this system include meeting body cell nutrition and excretion demands, along with body heat and electrochemical equilibrium requirements. Circulatory components include arteries, capillaries, and veins.

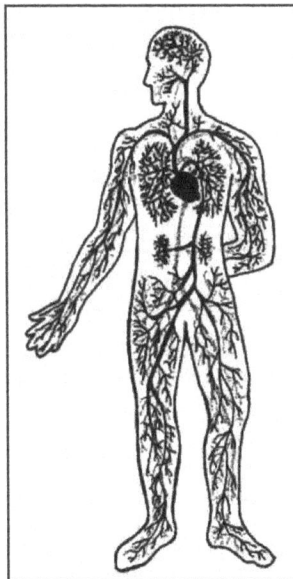

Figure 2-4. The circulatory system

ARTERIES

2-27. Arteries are strong, elastic vessels that transport blood away from the ventricles of the heart. Arterial vessels generally carry oxygen-rich blood to the capillaries for use by the tissues. Arteries can withstand relatively high pressures.

CAPILLARIES

2-28. Capillaries are the body's smallest blood vessels and form the junction between the smallest arteries (arterioles) and the smallest veins (venules). Capillaries are actually semipermeable extensions of the inner linings of the arterioles and venules and provide body tissues with access to the bloodstream. Capillaries are found virtually everywhere in the body, providing needed gas and nutrient exchange capabilities to nearly every cell.

VEINS

2-29. Veins transport blood from the capillaries back to the atria of the heart. A low-pressure pathway, veins possess flap-like valves to ensure blood flows only in the direction of the heart. In addition, veins can constrict or dilate based on body requirements. This unique ability allows blood flow and pressure to be modified based on factors such as body heat or trauma.

COMPONENTS AND FUNCTIONS OF BLOOD

2-30. Although blood volume varies with body size, the average adult has a blood volume approaching 5 liters. Blood accounts for approximately 5 percent of total body weight and is a form of connective tissue whose cells are suspended in a liquid, intercellular material. The cellular portions of blood compose roughly 45 percent of blood volume and consist mainly of red blood cells (RBCs), white blood cells (WBCs), and blood platelets. Plasma makes up the remaining 55 percent of blood. Each component performs unique functions (figure 2-5).

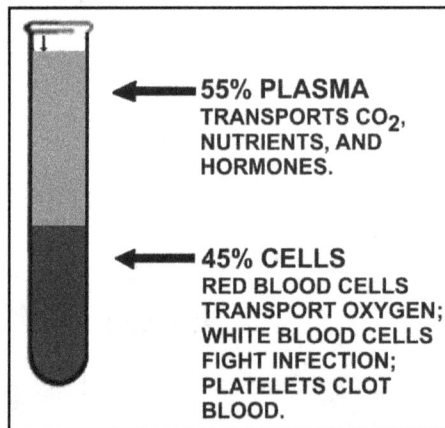

55% PLASMA
TRANSPORTS CO_2,
NUTRIENTS, AND
HORMONES.

45% CELLS
RED BLOOD CELLS
TRANSPORT OXYGEN;
WHITE BLOOD CELLS
FIGHT INFECTION;
PLATELETS CLOT
BLOOD.

Figure 2-5. Functions of blood components

RED BLOOD CELLS

2-31. RBCs, or erythrocytes, are produced in red bone marrow. They transport most of the body's supply of oxygen and transfer carbon dioxide from the tissues to the lungs. The red blood count is a count of the number of RBCs per cubic millimeter of blood. The number of RBCs in circulating blood is relatively stable; however, environmental factors play a large role in determining actual red blood count. Smoking, an inadequate diet, and the altitude where one lives all contribute to fluctuations in red blood count. In fact, people residing above 10,000 feet sea level could have up to 30 percent more erythrocytes than those living at sea level.

2-32. Because oxygenation of RBCs depends on the PO_2 in the atmosphere, aircrews could suffer from hypoxia (oxygen deficiency; see section IV) even at low altitudes. RBC structure, appearance, and production are among the factors affected when a crewmember experiences hypoxia.

2-33. Hemoglobin makes up about one-third of every RBC. Composed of several polypeptide chains and iron-containing heme groups, hemoglobin attracts oxygen molecules through an electrochemical magnetic process. Just as opposing poles on a magnet attract, so does the iron content within hemoglobin (Fe^{2+}) attract oxygen (O_2^{2-}).

2-34. When the blood supply is fully saturated with oxygen (in the case of arterial blood), blood takes on a bright red color as oxyhemoglobin forms. As blood passes through the capillaries, it releases oxygen to the surrounding tissues. As a result, deoxyhemoglobin forms and gives venous blood a dark red color.

WHITE BLOOD CELLS

2-35. The principal role of WBCs, or leukocytes, is to fight and control various disease conditions, especially those caused by invading microorganisms. Although WBCs are typically larger than RBCs, they can squeeze between the cells of blood vessels to reach diseased tissues. WBCs also help form natural immunities against numerous disease processes.

PLATELETS

2-36. Although not complete cells, platelets, or thrombocytes, arise from small, fragmented portions of much larger cells produced in red bone marrow. About half the size of RBCs, platelets react to any breach in the circulatory system by initializing blood coagulation and blood vessel contraction.

PLASMA

2-37. The liquid portion of blood is a translucent, straw-colored fluid known as plasma. All cellular structures in the bloodstream are suspended in this liquid. Composed mainly of water, plasma also contains proteins and inorganic salts. One important function of plasma is the transport of nutrients (such as glucose) and waste products (such as carbon dioxide).

SECTION III – RESPIRATORY SYSTEM

BREATHING AND RESPIRATION

2-38. All living organisms exchange gases with their environment. This gas exchange is known as respiration. The processes of respiration are breathing, external respiration, and internal respiration.

BREATHING

2-39. Breathing can be described as a spontaneous and rhythmic mechanical process. Contraction and relaxation of the respiratory muscles cause gases to move in and out of the lungs, thereby providing the body a gaseous media for exchange purposes.

EXTERNAL RESPIRATION

2-40. External respiration takes place in the alveoli of the lungs. Air moves to the alveoli by the mechanical process of breathing. Once in the alveolar sacs, oxygen diffuses from incoming air into the bloodstream. At the same time, carbon dioxide diffuses from venous blood into the alveolar sacs.

INTERNAL RESPIRATION

2-41. Internal respiration includes the use of blood oxygen and carbon dioxide production by tissue cells and gas exchange between cells and the surrounding fluid medium. Together these mechanisms, known as the metabolic process, produce the energy needed for life.

FUNCTIONS OF RESPIRATION

2-42. Respiration has several functions. It brings oxygen into the body, removes carbon dioxide from the body, and helps maintain body temperature and acid-base balance.

OXYGEN INTAKE

2-43. The primary function of respiration is the intake of oxygen. Oxygen enters the body through the respiratory system and is transported within the body through the circulatory system. All body cells require oxygen to metabolize food material.

CARBON DIOXIDE REMOVAL

2-44. Carbon dioxide is one byproduct of the metabolic process and dissolves in blood plasma. The plasma transports it from the tissues to the lungs for release.

BODY HEAT BALANCE

2-45. Body temperature is usually maintained within a narrow range (from 97 to 100 degrees Fahrenheit). Evaporation of perspiration produces heat loss and helps maintain body heat balance. During exhalation, the release of warm, moist air also aids in this process.

BODY CHEMICAL BALANCE

2-46. A delicate balance exists between the amounts of oxygen and carbon dioxide in the body. The uptake of oxygen and carbon dioxide takes place through extensive chemical changes in hemoglobin and plasma. Disrupting these pathways changes the body's chemical balance.

2-47. The measure of a solution's hydrogen ion concentration is its pH level. The higher the pH level, the more alkaline and oxygen rich blood is; the lower the pH level, the more acidic and oxygen deprived blood is. Level pH 7 is considered neutral because it is the accepted pH of water at 25 degrees Celsius. Under normal conditions, the body's relative acidity or alkalinity (pH level) measures in a very narrow pH range (between 7.35 to 7.45).

2-48. During respiration, the partial pressure of carbon dioxide (PCO_2) elevates, the acidity level increases, and the pH value lowers to less than 7.3. Conversely, too little carbon dioxide causes blood to become more alkaline and the pH value to rise. Figure 2-6 (page 2-11) shows how the amount of carbon dioxide in the body affects the pH level of blood.

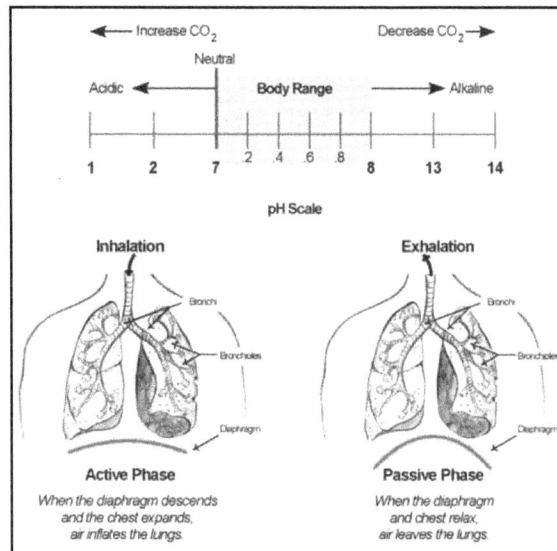

Figure 2-6. Respiratory cycle

2-49. Because the human body maintains equilibrium within narrow limits, the brain's respiratory centers sense any shift in blood pH and PCO_2 levels. When unusual levels occur, chemical receptors trigger the respiratory process to help return PCO_2 and pH levels to normal limits. Without proper pH balance, the body does not function correctly. Normal pH levels of 7.2 to 7.6 are critical for the necessary uptake of oxygen by blood and release of oxygen to tissues.

PHASES OF EXTERNAL RESPIRATION

2-50. The respiratory cycle is an involuntary process that continues unless a conscious effort is made to control it. External respiration occurs in two phases—active (inhalation) and passive (exhalation). Figure 2-6 (page 2-10) illustrates these phases.

ACTIVE PHASE (INHALATION)

2-51. Inhalation (the movement of air into the lungs) is the active phase of external respiration. It is caused by the expansion of the chest wall and downward motion of the diaphragm. Inhalation creates an area of low pressure due to increased volume in the lungs. Because of the greater outside pressure, air will rush into the lungs to inflate them.

PASSIVE PHASE (EXHALATION)

2-52. During exhalation (the passive phase of external respiration), the diaphragm relaxes and the chest wall contracts downward to create increased pressure in the lungs. Once the epiglottis (the lid-like flap of cartilage attached to the root of the tongue) opens, this pressure causes air to rush out, which releases carbon dioxide into the atmosphere.

COMPONENTS OF THE RESPIRATORY SYSTEM

2-53. The respiratory system consists of passages and organs that bring atmospheric air into the body. The components of the respiratory system, shown in figure 2-7 (page 2-12), include the oral-nasal passage, pharynx, larynx, trachea, bronchi, bronchioles, alveolar ducts, and alveoli.

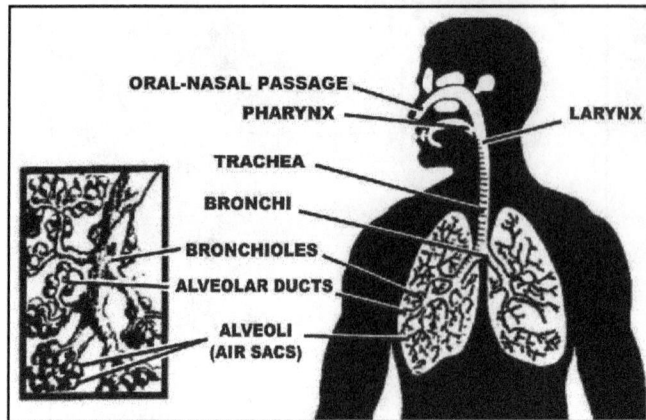

Figure 2-7. Components of the respiratory system

ORAL-NASAL PASSAGE

2-54. The oral-nasal passage includes the mouth and nasal cavity. The nasal passages are lined with a mucous membrane that contains many fine, ciliated hair cells. The membrane's primary purpose is to filter air as it enters the nasal cavity. The hairs continually clean the membrane by sweeping filtered material to the back of the throat, where it is either swallowed or expelled through the mouth. Therefore, air that enters through the nasal cavity is better filtered than air that enters through the mouth.

PHARYNX

2-55. The pharynx is a fibromuscular, cone-shaped tube found in the back of the throat. It is connected to the nasal and oral cavities. It primarily humidifies and warms air entering the respiratory system.

TRACHEA

2-56. The trachea (windpipe) is a tube through which air moves down into the bronchi. From there, air continues to move down increasingly smaller passages, or ducts, until it reaches the small alveoli within the lung tissue.

ALVEOLI

2-57. Each tiny alveolus is surrounded by a network of capillaries that joins veins and arteries. The microscopic capillaries, each having a wall only one cell in thickness, are so narrow that RBCs move through them in single file. The actual gaseous exchange between carbon dioxide and oxygen occurs in the alveoli.

2-58. Carbon dioxide and oxygen move in and out of the alveoli due to pressure differentials between gas levels in surrounding capillaries. This movement is based on the law of gaseous diffusion: gas always moves from an area of high pressure to an area of lower pressure. Figure 2-8 (page 2-13) illustrates the exchange of carbon dioxide and oxygen between an alveolus and a capillary.

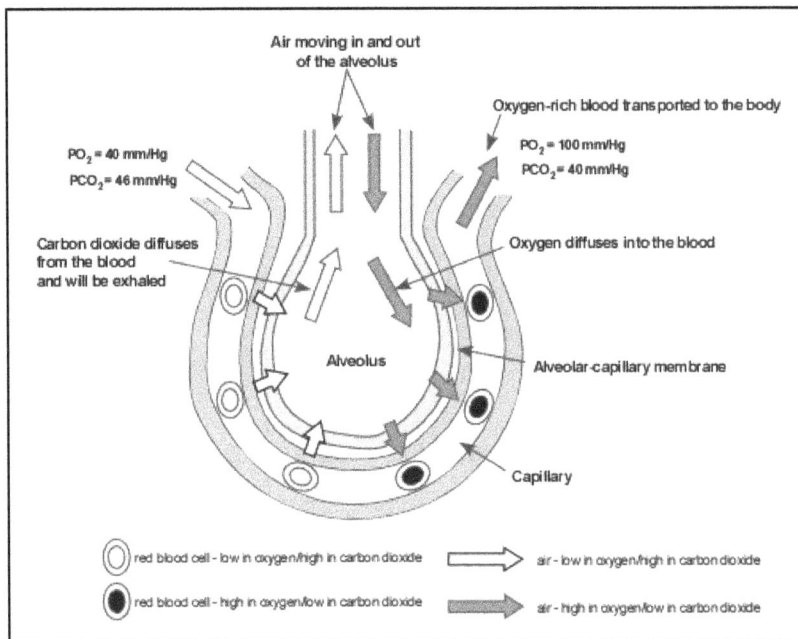

Figure 2-8. Exchange of carbon dioxide and oxygen between an alveolus and a capillary

2-59. When oxygen reaches the alveoli, it crosses a thin cellular barrier and moves into the capillary bed to reach the oxygen-carrying RBCs. As oxygen enters the alveoli, it has a PO_2 of approximately 100 mm/Hg. Within blood, the PO_2 of venous return blood is approximately 40 mm/Hg. As blood traverses the capillary networks of the alveoli, oxygen flows from the area of high pressure within the alveoli to the area of low pressure within the blood. Thus, oxygen saturation takes place.

2-60. Carbon dioxide diffuses from blood to the alveoli in the same manner. The PCO_2 in the venous return blood of the capillaries is roughly 46 mm/Hg, as compared to 40 mm/Hg in the alveoli. As blood moves through the capillaries, carbon dioxide moves from the high PCO_2 in the capillaries to an area of lower PCO_2 in the alveoli. Carbon dioxide is then released during exhalation, the next passive phase of respiration.

2-61. The exchange of oxygen and carbon dioxide between tissue and capillaries occurs in the same manner as between alveoli and capillaries. Figure 2-9 (page 2-14) shows this exchange between tissue and a capillary.

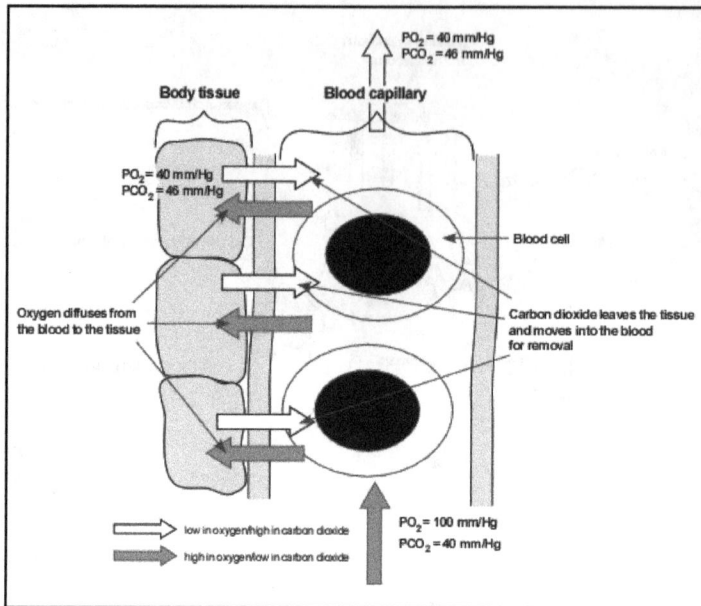

Figure 2-9. Oxygen and carbon dioxide exchange between tissue and a capillary

2-62. The amount of oxygen and carbon dioxide transferred across the alveolar-capillary membrane into the blood depends primarily on the difference between the alveolar pressure of oxygen (PAO_2) in relation to the venous pressure of oxygen (PVO_2). This pressure differential is critical; blood oxygen saturation decreases as altitude increases, which can cause hypoxia. Table 2-4 shows the relationship between altitude and oxygen saturation.

Table 2-4. Correlation of altitude and blood oxygen saturation

Altitude (ft)	Atmospheric Pressure (mm/Hg)	PAO_2 (mm/Hg)	PVO_2 (mm/Hg)	Pressure Differential (mm/Hg)	Blood Saturation (%)
Sea level	760	100	40	60	98
10,000	523	60	31	29	87
18,000	380	38	26	12	72
22,000	321	30	22	8	60
25,000	282	7	4	3	9
35,000	179	0	0	0	0

SECTION IV – HYPOXIA

CHARACTERISTICS OF HYPOXIA

2-63. Hypoxia results when the body lacks oxygen. It generally is associated with flights at high altitude. However, other factors such as alcohol abuse, heavy smoking, and various medications can interfere with blood's ability to carry and absorb oxygen, thereby reducing the body's tolerance to hypoxia.

TYPES OF HYPOXIA

2-64. There are four major types of hypoxia: hypoxic, hypemic, stagnant, and histotoxic. Each type is classified according to cause.

HYPOXIC HYPOXIA

2-65. Hypoxic hypoxia occurs when there is not enough oxygen in the air or when decreasing atmospheric pressure prevents diffusion of oxygen from the lungs to the bloodstream. Aviation personnel are most likely to encounter this type of hypoxia at high altitudes due to the reduction of PO_2 in the atmosphere (figure 2-10).

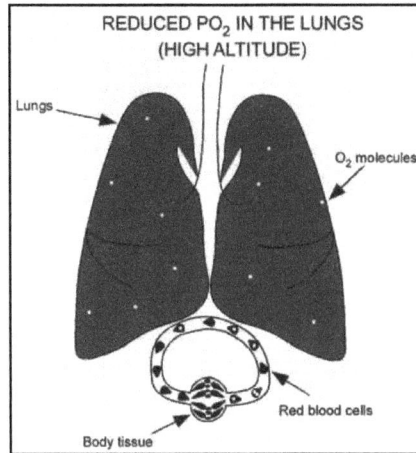

Figure 2-10. Hypoxic hypoxia

HYPEMIC HYPOXIA

2-66. Hypemic, or anemic, hypoxia is caused by a reduction in blood's oxygen-carrying capacity (figure 2-11). Anemia and blood loss are the most common causes of this type of hypoxia. Other possible causes include exposure to carbon monoxide, nitrites, and sulfa drugs, which form compounds with and reduce the amount of hemoglobin available to combine with oxygen.

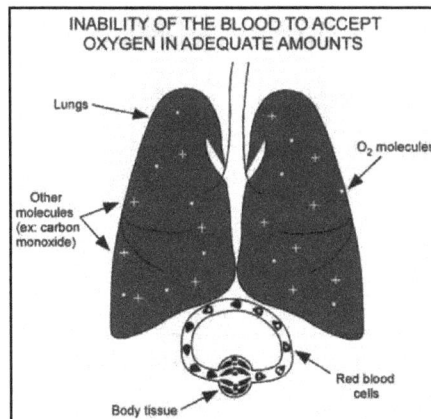

Figure 2-11. Hypemic hypoxia

STAGNANT HYPOXIA

2-67. With stagnant hypoxia, blood's oxygen-carrying capacity is adequate but circulation is inadequate (figure 2-12). Conditions such as heart failure, arterial spasm, and blood vessel occlusion predispose affected individuals to stagnant hypoxia. This type of hypoxia often occurs when a crewmember experiences extreme gravitational forces and blood flow is disrupted, causing blood to stagnate.

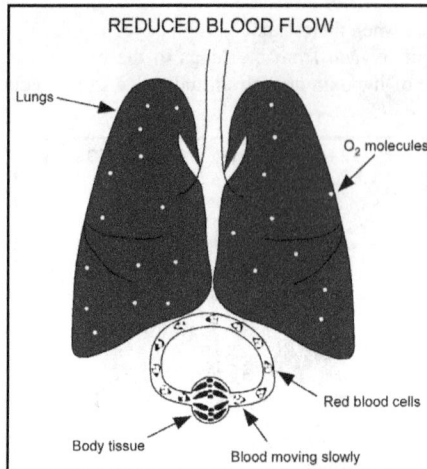

Figure 2-12. Stagnant hypoxia

HISTOTOXIC HYPOXIA

2-68. Histotoxic hypoxia results from an interference with the use of oxygen by body tissues (figure 2-13). Alcohol, narcotics, and certain poisons such as cyanide interfere with a cell's ability to use an adequate supply of oxygen.

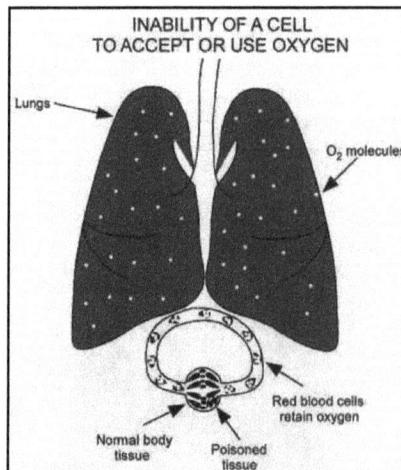

Figure 2-13. Histotoxic hypoxia

SIGNS, SYMPTOMS, AND SUSCEPTIBILITY TO HYPOXIA

SIGNS AND SYMPTOMS OF HYPOXIA

2-69. Signs of hypoxia can be observed by other crewmembers and are therefore considered objective. However, individual crewmembers can observe or feel their own symptoms. Since symptoms can vary from person to person, they are considered subjective.

2-70. Aviation personnel commonly experience mild hypoxia at altitudes at or above 10,000 feet (3 kilometers). Personnel must be able to recognize possible signs and symptoms of hypoxia, as its onset is subtle and produces a false sense of wellbeing. Crewmembers engrossed in flight activities often do not readily notice such symptoms. However, most individuals experience two or three unmistakable symptoms or signs that cannot be overlooked. Table 2-5 lists possible signs and symptoms of hypoxia.

Table 2-5. Possible signs and symptoms of hypoxia

Symptoms (Subjective)		Signs (Objective)
Increased breathing rate	Euphoria	Hyperventilation
Apprehension	Belligerence	Cyanosis
Fatigue	Blurred vision	Mental confusion
Headache	Tunnel vision	Poor judgment
Dizziness	Numbness	Lack of muscle coordination
Hot and cold flashes	Tingling	
= UNCONSCIOUSNESS		

SUSCEPTIBILITY TO HYPOXIA

2-71. An individual's susceptibility to hypoxia varies widely. Several factors determine individual susceptibility. These factors include—

- **Onset Time and Severity.** The onset time and severity of hypoxia varies with the amount of oxygen deficiency. The primary concern is to recognize and immediately determine the cause of hypoxia.
- **Physiological Altitude.** An individual's physiological altitude, or the body's perceived altitude, is as important as true altitude. Self-imposed stressors such as tobacco and alcohol increase physiological altitude.
  - **Tobacco.** The hemoglobin molecules of RBCs have a 200- to 300-times greater affinity for carbon monoxide than for oxygen. Cigarette smoking significantly increases the amount of carbon monoxide bound with hemoglobin, a combination known as carboxyhemoglobin (CoHb). Thus, carbon monoxide reduces the capacity of blood to combine with oxygen. Smoking 3 cigarettes in rapid succession or 20 to 30 cigarettes within 24 hours before a flight can saturate 8 to 10 percent of blood's hemoglobin. Physiological effects of this condition include loss of about 20 percent of a smoker's night vision at sea level and a physiological altitude of 5,000 feet at sea level (figure 2-14, page 2-18).

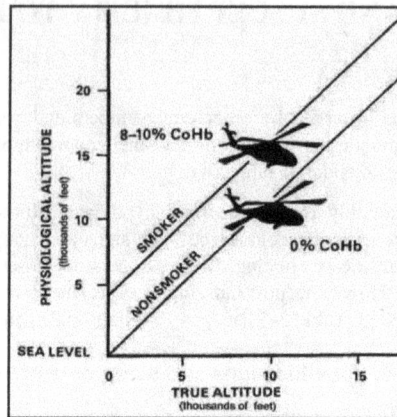

Figure 2-14. Physiological altitude limitations of a smoker

- **Alcohol.** Alcohol creates conditions in the body for histotoxic hypoxia. For example, an individual who has consumed 1 ounce of alcohol can have a physiological altitude of 2,000 feet sea level.
- **Individual Factors.** Metabolic rate, diet and nutrition, and emotions greatly influence an individual's susceptibility to hypoxia. Some areas to consider include—
  - **Physical Activity.** When physical activity increases, the body demands a greater amount of oxygen. This increased oxygen demand causes a more rapid onset of hypoxia.
  - **Physical Fitness.** An individual who is physically conditioned normally has a higher tolerance to altitude problems than one who is not. Physical fitness raises an individual's tolerance ceiling.
  - **Diet and Nutrition.** Some preprocessed foods can increase the occurrence of an oxygen-depleting agent similar to carbon monoxide, which lowers blood's ability to absorb and deliver oxygen and thereby decreases altitude tolerance. Many crewmembers have noticed a positive difference when they eat a balanced diet.
- **Ascent Rate.** Rapid ascent rates affect an individual's susceptibility to hypoxia. High altitudes can occur before a crewmember notices serious symptoms.
- **Exposure Duration.** The effects of exposure to altitude relate directly to an individual's length of exposure. The longer the exposure, the more detrimental the effects; however, the higher the altitude, the shorter the exposure time required before symptoms of hypoxia occur.
- **Ambient Temperature.** Extremes in temperature generally increase the body's metabolic rate. A rise in temperature increases an individual's oxygen requirements while decreasing the body's tolerance to hypoxia. These conditions can cause hypoxia to develop at lower altitudes than usual.

EFFECTS OF HYPOXIA

2-72. The most important effects of hypoxia are those directly or indirectly related to the nervous system. Nerve tissue has a heavy requirement for oxygen. Brain tissue is one of the first areas affected by oxygen deficiency, and a prolonged or severe lack of oxygen destroys brain cells. Hypoxia demonstrations conducted in an altitude chamber do not produce any known brain damage since the severity and duration of hypoxia are minimized.

2-73. The time of useful consciousness (TUC) is the period of time between interruption of the oxygen supply and when an individual loses the ability to take corrective action. Table 2-6 (page 2-19) shows the TUC varies with the altitude at which an individual is flying. In a pressurized aircraft that loses cabin pressurization—as in rapid decompression—an individual has only one-half the TUC shown in table 2-6.

Table 2-6. Relationship between time of useful consciousness and altitude

Altitude (ft)	TUC
>50,000	9–12 seconds
43,000	9–12 seconds
35,000	30–60 seconds
25,000	4–6 minutes
22,000	8–10 minutes
18,000	20–30 minutes

STAGES OF HYPOXIC HYPOXIA

2-74. There are four stages of hypoxic hypoxia: indifferent, compensatory, disturbance, and critical. Table 2-7 shows the variance of stages according to altitude and severity of symptoms.

Table 2-7. Stages of hypoxic hypoxia

Stages	Altitude (thousands of ft)	Symptoms
Indifferent (98%–90% oxygen saturation)	0–10	Decreased night vision
Compensatory (89%–80% oxygen saturation)	10–15	Drowsiness; poor judgment; impaired coordination and efficiency
Disturbance (79%–70% oxygen saturation)	15–20	Impaired flight control, handwriting, speech, vision, intellectual function, and judgment; decreased coordination, memory, and sensation to pain
Critical (69%–60% oxygen saturation)	20–25	Circulatory and central nervous system failure; convulsions; cardiovascular collapse; death

INDIFFERENT STAGE

2-75. Mild hypoxia in the indifferent stage causes night vision to deteriorate at about 4,000 feet (1,219 meters). Crewmembers who fly above 4,000 feet at night should be aware that visual acuity decreases significantly in this stage due to dark conditions and the development of mild hypoxia.

COMPENSATORY STAGE

2-76. The circulatory system and, to a lesser degree, the respiratory system provide some defense against hypoxia at the compensatory stage. Pulse rate, systolic blood pressure, circulation rate, and cardiac output increase. Respiration increases in depth and sometimes in rate. At 12,000 feet (3,658 meters) to 15,000 feet (4,572 meters), the effects of hypoxia on the nervous system become increasingly apparent. After 10 to 15 minutes, impaired efficiency is obvious. Crewmembers might become drowsy and make frequent errors in judgment. They might also find it difficult to perform even simple tasks requiring alertness or moderate muscular coordination. Crewmembers preoccupied with duties can easily overlook hypoxia at this stage.

DISTURBANCE STAGE

2-77. In the disturbance stage, physiological responses can no longer compensate for oxygen deficiency. Occasionally, crewmembers can become unconscious from hypoxia without undergoing the subjective symptoms described in table 2-7. Fatigue, sleepiness, dizziness, headache, breathlessness, and euphoria are the symptoms most often reported at this stage. Other symptoms include—

- **Loss of Senses.** Peripheral vision and central vision are impaired, and visual acuity is diminished. Weakness and loss of muscular coordination are experienced. The sensations of touch and pain are diminished or lost. Hearing is one of the last senses to be lost.
- **Reduced Mental Processes.** Intellectual impairment is an early sign that often prevents an individual from recognizing disabilities. Thinking is slowed, and calculations are unreliable. Short-term memory is poor, and judgment—as well as reaction time—is affected.
- **Unusual Personality Traits.** There might be a display of basic personality traits and emotions much the same as with alcoholic intoxication. Euphoria, aggressiveness, overconfidence, or depression can occur.
- **Reduced Psychomotor Functions.** Muscular coordination is decreased, and delicate or fine muscular movements might be impossible to complete. Stammering and illegible handwriting are typical of hypoxic impairment.
- **Cyanosis.** When cyanosis occurs, the skin becomes bluish in color. This effect is caused by oxygen molecules failing to attach to hemoglobin molecules.

CRITICAL STAGE

2-78. Within 3 to 5 minutes without oxygen, judgment and coordination usually deteriorate. Mental confusion, dizziness, incapacitation, and unconsciousness subsequently occur.

PREVENTION OF HYPOXIC HYPOXIA

2-79. Understanding the causes and types of hypoxia assists in its prevention. Hypoxic hypoxia is the type most often encountered in aviation. It can be prevented by ensuring sufficient oxygen is available to maintain PAO_2 between 60 and 100 mm/Hg. Prevention methods include limiting time at altitude, using supplemental oxygen, and pressurizing the cabin.

LIMITING TIME AT ALTITUDE

2-80. The amount or percentage of oxygen required to maintain normal saturation levels varies with altitude. At sea level, a 21-percent concentration of ambient air oxygen is necessary to maintain the normal blood oxygen saturation of 96 to 98 percent. At 20,000 feet (6,096 meters), however, a 49-percent concentration of oxygen is required to maintain the same saturation.

2-81. The upper limit of continuous-flow oxygen is reached at about 34,000 feet. Above 34,000 feet, positive pressure is necessary to maintain an adequate oxygen saturation level. Positive pressure, however, cannot exceed 30 mm/Hg because—

- Most oxygen masks cannot hold positive pressures of more than 25 mm/Hg without leaking.
- Excess pressure might enter the middle ear through the Eustachian tubes, causing a painful condition where the eardrum bulges outward.
- Crewmembers can encounter difficulty when exhaling against the pressure, resulting in hyperventilation.

USING SUPPLEMENTAL OXYGEN

2-82. During night flights above 4,000 feet (1,219 meters), crewmembers should use supplemental oxygen when available. Supplemental oxygen is necessary because of the risks of mild hypoxia and loss of visual acuity.

PRESSURIZING THE CABIN

2-83. Pressurization such as that found in C-12 aircraft can prevent hypoxia. Supplemental oxygen should be available in the aircraft in case of pressurization loss.

TREATMENT OF HYPOXIA

2-84. Individuals who exhibit signs and symptoms of hypoxia must be treated immediately. Treatment consists of giving the individual 100-percent oxygen. If oxygen is not available, descent to an altitude below 10,000 feet is mandatory. When hypoxia symptoms persist, the type and cause must be determined and treatment administered accordingly.

SECTION V – HYPERVENTILATION

CHARACTERISTICS

2-85. Hyperventilation is an excessive rate and depth of respiration that leads to an abnormal loss of carbon dioxide from blood. This condition occurs more often among aviators than is generally recognized. Hyperventilation seldom incapacitates an individual completely, but it causes disturbing symptoms that can alarm an uninformed aviator. In such cases, an increased breathing rate and heightened anxiety further aggravate the problem.

CAUSES

2-86. The human body reacts automatically under conditions of stress and anxiety regardless of whether a problem is real or imaginary. A marked increase in breathing rate often occurs, which then leads to a significant decrease in the body's carbon dioxide content and a change in the acid-base balance. Among the factors that can initiate this cycle are emotions, pressure breathing, and hypoxia.

EMOTIONS

2-87. An individual might attempt to consciously control breathing when fear, anxiety, or stress alters his or her normal breathing pattern. The respiration rate is then likely to increase without an elevation in carbon dioxide production, causing hyperventilation.

POSITIVE-PRESSURE BREATHING

2-88. Positive-pressure breathing is used to prevent hypoxia at altitude. It reverses the normal respiratory cycle of inhalation and exhalation.

Inhalation

2-89. Under positive-pressure conditions, an aviator is not actively involved in inhalation as in the normal respiratory cycle. Oxygen is not inhaled into the lungs; instead, it is forced into the lungs under positive pressure.

Exhalation

2-90. Under positive-pressure conditions, an aviator is forced to breathe out against the pressure. The force the individual must exert when exhaling results in an increased rate and depth of breathing. At this point, too much carbon dioxide is lost and alkalosis, or increased pH, occurs. Pauses between exhaling and inhaling can reverse this condition and maintain a near-normal level of carbon dioxide during pressure breathing.

HYPOXIA

2-91. With the onset of hypoxia and the resultant decreased blood oxygen saturation level, the respiratory center triggers an increase in breathing rate to gain more oxygen. Although rapid breathing is beneficial for oxygen uptake, it can cause an excessive loss of carbon dioxide if continued too long.

SIGNS AND SYMPTOMS OF HYPERVENTILATION

2-92. The signs and symptoms of hyperventilation are caused by chemical imbalance and an excessive loss of carbon dioxide. Signs and symptoms include—

- Dizziness.
- Muscle spasms.
- Unconsciousness.
- Visual impairment.
- Tingling sensations.
- Hot and cold sensations.

2-93. The signs and symptoms of hyperventilation and hypoxia are similar, making them difficult to differentiate. The following indications help distinguish the two conditions.

HYPERVENTILATION

2-94. Hyperventilation results in nerve and muscle irritability and muscle spasms. Symptoms appear gradually.

FAINTING

2-95. Fainting produces loose muscles but no muscle spasms. Symptoms appear rapidly.

TREATMENT

2-96. The most effective treatment for hyperventilation is voluntary reduction in the affected individual's rate of respiration. However, an extremely apprehensive person might not respond to directions to breathe more slowly.

2-97. Although it is difficult, the affected individual should try to control their respiration rate (the normal rate is 12 to 16 breaths per minute). If conscious control of respiration is not possible and symptoms continue, the individual should talk or read a checklist aloud. It is physiologically impossible to talk and hyperventilate at the same time. Talking or singing elevates the body's carbon dioxide level and helps regulate breathing.

2-98. When hypoxia and hyperventilation occur concurrently, a decrease in the respiratory rate and intake of 100-percent oxygen will correct the condition. If hypoxia is severe, the affected individual must return to ground level before becoming incapacitated.

SECTION VI – PRESSURE-CHANGE EFFECTS

2-99. The human body can withstand enormous changes in barometric pressure as long as air pressure in the body cavities equals ambient air pressure. Difficulties occur when expanding gas cannot escape the body, allowing ambient and body pressures to equalize. The discussion in this section applies to nonpressurized flight and direct exposure of aircrews to potentially harmful altitudes.

DYSBARISM

2-100. Dysbarism refers to the various manifestations of gas expansion induced by decreased barometric pressure. These manifestations can be just as dangerous, if not more so, than hypoxia or hyperventilation.

The direct effects of decreased barometric pressure can be divided into two groups: trapped-gas disorders and evolved-gas disorders.

TRAPPED-GAS DISORDERS

2-101.   During ascent, the free gas normally present in various body cavities expands. If escape of this expanded volume is impeded, pressure builds within the cavity and causes pain. The expansion of trapped gas accounts for abdominal pain, ear pain, sinus pain, and toothache.

BOYLE'S LAW

2-102.   Trapped-gas problems are explained by the physical laws governing the behavior of gases under conditions of changing pressure. Boyle's Law (figure 2-15) states that, at constant temperature, the volume of a gas is inversely proportional to the pressure exerted upon it. Differences in gas expansion are found under dry- and wet-gas conditions.

- **Dry-Gas Conditions.** Under dry-gas conditions, the atmosphere is not saturated with moisture. With constant temperature and increased altitude, gas volume expands as pressure decreases.
- **Wet-Gas Conditions.** Gases within the body are saturated with water vapor. Under constant temperature and at the same altitude and barometric pressure, the volume of wet gas is greater than dry gas.

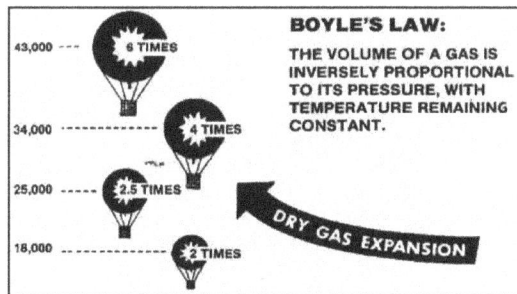

Figure 2-15. Boyle's Law

TRAPPED-GAS DISORDERS OF THE GASTROINTESTINAL TRACT

2-103.   With a rapid decrease in atmospheric pressure, aircrews frequently experience discomfort from gas expansion within the digestive tract. At low or intermediate altitudes, symptoms are not serious in most individuals. Above 25,000 feet (7,620 meters), however, enough distension might occur to produce severe pain. Figure 2-16 shows the dramatic expansion of trapped gas as altitude increases.

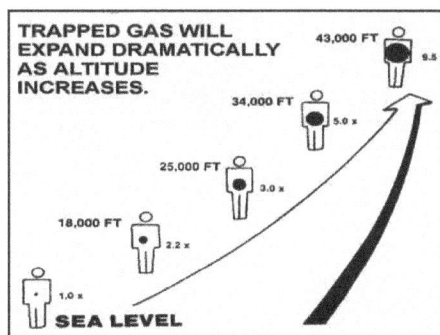

Figure 2-16. Expansion of trapped gas

Cause

2-104. The stomach and small and large intestines normally contain a variable amount of gas at a pressure roughly equal to the surrounding atmospheric pressure. The stomach and large intestine contain considerably more gas than the small intestine. The primary sources of this gas are swallowed air and, to a lesser degree, gas formed by digestive processes, fermentation, bacterial decomposition, and decomposition of food undergoing digestion. The gases normally present in the gastrointestinal tract are oxygen, carbon dioxide, nitrogen, hydrogen, methane, and hydrogen sulfide. The proportions vary, but the highest percentage of the gas mixture is always nitrogen.

Effects

2-105. The absolute volume or location of gas can cause gastrointestinal pain at high altitude. Sensitivity or irritability of the intestine, however, is a more important cause of gastrointestinal pain. Therefore, an individual's response to high altitude varies depending on factors such as fatigue, apprehension, emotion, and general physical condition. Gas pains of even moderate severity can produce a marked lowering of blood pressure and loss of consciousness if distension is not relieved. For this reason, any individual experiencing gas pains at altitude should be watched for pallor or other signs of fainting. If these signs are noted, an immediate descent should be made.

Prevention

2-106. Aircrews should maintain good eating habits to prevent gas pains at high altitudes. Some foods that commonly produce gas are onions, cabbages, raw apples, radishes, dried beans, cucumbers, and melons. Crewmembers who participate regularly in high-altitude flights should avoid foods that disagree with them. Chewing food well is also important. When people drink liquids or chew gum, they unavoidably swallow air. Therefore, crewmembers should avoid drinking large quantities of liquids, particularly carbonated beverages, before high-altitude missions and chewing gum during ascent. Eating irregularly, hastily, or while working makes individuals more susceptible to gas pains. Crewmembers who fly frequent, long, and difficult high-altitude missions should be given special consideration in diet and in the environment in which they eat. They should watch their diet, chew food well, and keep regular bowel habits.

Relief

2-107. If trapped-gas problems exist in the gastrointestinal tract at high altitude, belching or passing flatus ordinarily will relieve gas pains. If pain persists, descent to a lower altitude is necessary.

TRAPPED-GAS DISORDERS OF THE EARS

2-108. The ear is not only an organ of hearing but also one of regulating equilibrium. When ascending to altitude, crewmembers often experience physiological discomfort as atmospheric pressure changes. As barometric pressure decreases during ascent, expanding air in the middle ear (figure 2-17, page 2-25) is intermittently released through the Eustachian tube (a slender tube between the middle ear and pharynx) into the nasal passages. As inside pressure increases, the eardrum bulges until an excess pressure of approximately 12 to 15 mm/Hg is reached. At this time, air trapped in the middle ear is forced out into the Eustachian tube, producing a sensation of fullness in the ear and often a click or pop as the eardrum resumes its normal position.

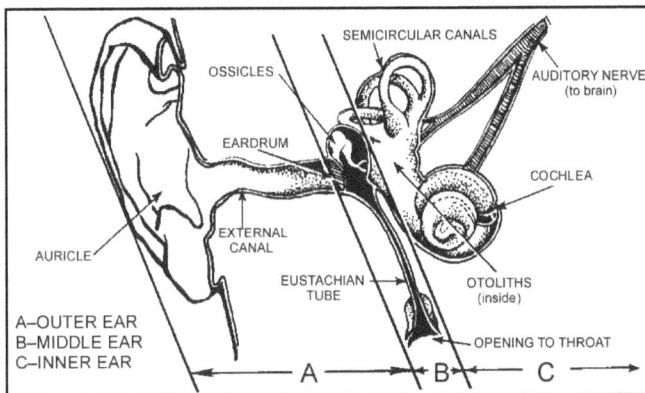

Figure 2-17. Expanding air in the middle ear

Cause

During Flight

2-109. During descent, pressure changes within the ear might not occur automatically. Equalizing pressure in the middle ear with that of outside air can be difficult. The Eustachian tube allows air to pass easily outward but resists passage in the opposite direction. With the increase in barometric pressure during descent, the pressure of external air is higher than that in the middle ear. As a result, the eardrum is pushed inward (figure 2-18). If the pressure differential increases appreciably, it might be impossible for the Eustachian tube to open. This painful condition could cause the eardrum to rupture because the Eustachian tube cannot equalize the pressure. Marked pain will ensue if the ears cannot be cleared. When pain increases with further descent, the only option for relief is ascending to a level at which pressure can be equalized. A slow descent is then recommended.

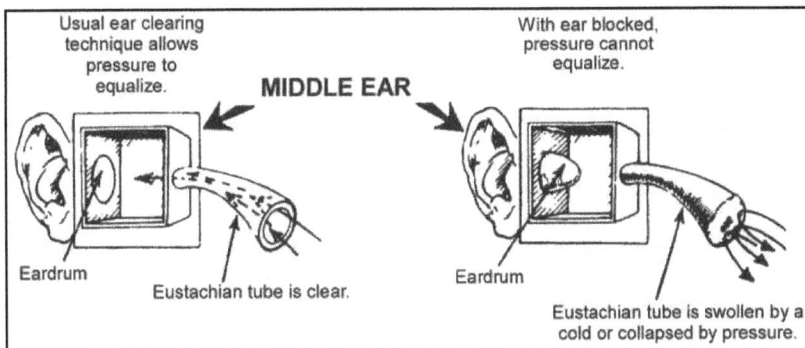

Figure 2-18. Middle ear and eardrum pressure during descent

2-110. Descending rapidly from 30,000 feet (9,144 meters) to 20,000 feet (6,096 meters) often causes no discomfort for crewmembers. A rapid descent from 15,000 feet (4,572 meters) to 5,000 feet (1,524 meters), however, causes great distress. The change in barometric pressure is much greater in the latter situation. For this reason, special care is necessary during rapid descents at low altitudes.

After Flight

2-111. Crewmembers who have breathed pure oxygen during an entire flight sometimes develop delayed ear blocks several hours after landing, even though they adequately cleared their ears during descent.

Delayed ear blocks are caused by oxygen saturation of the middle ear. After crewmembers return to breathing ambient air, their tissue gradually reabsorbs oxygen present in the middle ear. When a sufficient amount of oxygen is absorbed, pressure in the ear becomes less than that outside the eardrum. Ear pain might awaken crewmembers after they have gone to sleep, or they might notice it when they awake the following morning. This condition usually is mild and can be relieved by performing the Valsalva maneuver explained in paragraph 2-114 below.

Complications from Preexisting Physical Conditions

Respiratory Infections

2-112. Crewmembers often complain of discomfort in the ears caused by an inability to ventilate the middle ear adequately. Such inability occurs most frequently when the Eustachian tube or its opening is swollen shut as the result of inflammation or infection coinciding with a head cold, sore throat, middle ear infection, sinusitis, or tonsillitis. In such cases, forceful opening of the tube might cause disease-carrying infection to enter the middle ear along with the air. Therefore, crewmembers who have colds and sore throats should not fly. If flight is essential, slow descents will equalize pressure more easily.

Temporal Bone and Jaw Problems

2-113. Upper respiratory infections are the primary culprits in narrowing of the Eustachian tubes, but there can be other causes. Crewmembers with abnormal positioning of the temporomandibular joint (temporal bone and jaw) can experience ear pain and difficulty in both hearing and ventilating the middle ear. In these cases, jaw movement (or yawning) relaxes the surrounding soft tissues and clears the Eustachian tube opening.

Prevention and Treatment

During Flight

2-114. Crewmembers can equalize pressure during descent by swallowing, yawning, or tensing the throat muscles. If these methods do not work, personnel can perform the Valsalva maneuver. To do this, close the mouth, pinch the nose shut, and blow sharply. This maneuver forces air through the previously closed Eustachian tube into the middle ear cavity and equalizes pressure. With repeated practice in rapidly clearing the ears, crewmembers can more easily tolerate increased rates of descent.

> *Note.* To avoid over-pressurization of the middle ear, crewmembers should never attempt a Valsalva maneuver during ascent.

After Flight

2-115. If middle ear and ambient pressures do not equalize after landing and the condition persists, aviation personnel should consult a flight surgeon to prevent barotitis media. This disorder is an acute or chronic traumatic inflammation of the middle ear caused by a difference in pressure on opposite sides of the eardrum. It is characterized by congestion, inflammation, discomfort, and pain in the middle ear and might be followed by temporarily or permanently impaired hearing (usually the former).

TRAPPED-GAS DISORDERS OF THE SINUSES

2-116. Like the middle ear, sinuses can trap gas during flight. The sinuses (figure 2-19, page 2-27) are air-filled, relatively rigid, bony cavities lined with mucous membranes. They connect to the nose by means of one or more small openings. The two frontal sinuses are located within the bones of the forehead; the two maxillary sinuses are found within the cheekbones; and the two ethmoid sinuses are located within the bones of the nose.

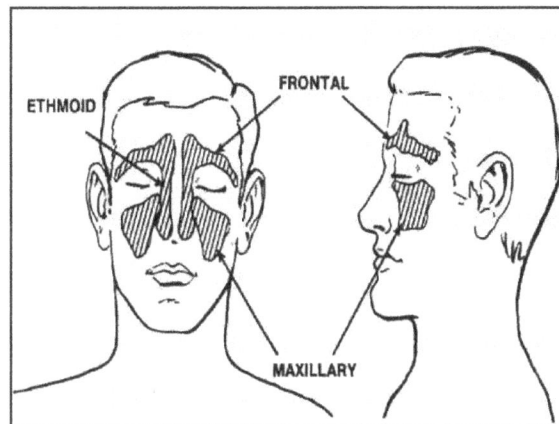

Figure 2-19. Sinus cavities

Cause

2-117. If the sinus openings work properly, air passes into and out of these cavities without difficulty and pressure equalizes during ascent or descent. However, swelling of the mucous membrane lining, caused by an infection or allergic condition, can obstruct the sinus openings. Viscous secretions that coat tissues also might cover the openings. These conditions can make it impossible to equalize pressure. A change in altitude produces a pressure differential between the inside and outside of the cavity, sometimes causing severe pain. Unlike the ears, ascent and descent affect the sinuses almost equally. If the frontal sinuses are involved, pain extends over the forehead and above the bridge of the nose. If the maxillary sinuses and/or ethmoid sinuses are affected, pain is felt on either side of the nose in the cheekbone regions. Maxillary sinusitis or inflammation of the sinuses and nasal passages can cause pain in the teeth of the upper jaw, which could be mistaken for toothache.

Prevention

2-118. Like middle ear problems, sinus problems during flight are usually preventable. Crewmembers should avoid flying when they have a cold or congestion. During descent, they can perform the Valsalva maneuver often. The openings to the sinus cavities are quite small as compared to the Eustachian tubes and unless pressure is equalized, extreme pain will result. If crewmembers notice sinus pain on ascent, they should avoid any further increase in altitude.

Treatment

2-119. If a crewmember experiences sinus blockage during descent, the aircrew should avoid further descent. The crewmember should attempt a forceful Valsalva maneuver; if this does not clear the blockage, the aircrew should ascend to a higher altitude to ventilate the sinuses. The crewmember also can perform the normal Valsalva maneuver during slow descent to the ground. If the aircraft is equipped with pressure-breathing equipment, the crewmember can use oxygen under positive pressure to ventilate the sinuses. The crewmember should consult the local flight surgeon if pressure does not equalize after landing.

TRAPPED-GAS DISORDERS OF THE TEETH

2-120. Changes in barometric pressure can cause toothache, or barodontalgia. This indisposition is significant but correctable. Toothache usually results from an existing dental problem. The onset of toothache generally occurs from 5,000 feet (1,524 meters) to 15,000 feet (4,572 meters). In a given individual, the altitude at which pain occurs shows remarkable constancy. The pain might or might not become more severe as altitude increases. Descent almost invariably brings relief, and the toothache often disappears at the same altitude at which it first occurred.

EVOLVED-GAS DISORDERS

2-121.   Evolved-gas disorders occur in flight when atmospheric pressure is reduced because of an increase in altitude. Gases dissolved in body fluids at sea-level pressure are released and enter the gaseous state as bubbles as ambient pressure decreases. These disorders cause various skin and muscle symptoms, which are sometimes followed by neurological symptoms. Evolved-gas disorders are also known as DCS.

HENRY'S LAW

2-122.   Henry's Law states the amount of gas dissolved in a solution is directly proportional to the pressure of the gas over the solution. Henry's Law is similar to the example of gases being held under pressure in a soda bottle (figure 2-20). When the cap is removed, the liquid inside the bottle is subject to pressure less than that required to hold the gases in the solution; therefore, the gases escape in the form of bubbles. Nitrogen in blood is affected by pressure changes in this same manner.

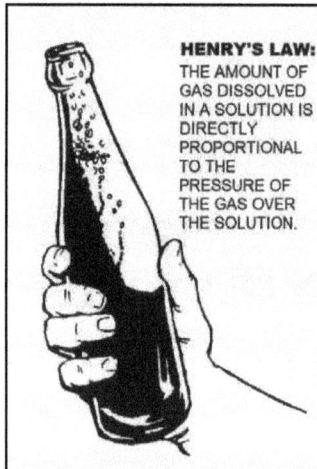

Figure 2-20. Henry's Law

2-123.   Inert gases in body tissues (principally nitrogen) are in equilibrium with the partial pressures of the same gases in the atmosphere. When barometric pressure decreases, the partial pressures of atmospheric gases decrease proportionally. This decrease in pressure leaves the tissues temporarily supersaturated. The body responds by attempting to establish a new equilibrium by transporting the excess gas volume in venous blood to the lungs.

CAUSE

2-124.   DCS can be attributed to nitrogen saturation of the body. This condition is related in turn to inefficient removal and transport of expanded nitrogen gas volume from the tissues to the lungs. Nitrogen diffusion to the outside atmosphere normally would take place at this point.

2-125.   Body tissues and fluid contain 1 to 1.5 liters of dissolved nitrogen, depending on the pressure of nitrogen in the surrounding air. As altitude increases, the partial pressure of atmospheric nitrogen decreases, and nitrogen leaves the body to reestablish equilibrium. If change is rapid, recovery of equilibrium lags, leaving the body supersaturated. Excess nitrogen diffuses into the capillaries and is carried by venous blood for elimination. With rapid ascent to altitudes of 30,000 feet (9,144 meters) or above, nitrogen tends to form bubbles in the tissues and blood. In addition to nitrogen, these bubbles contain small quantities of carbon dioxide, oxygen, and water vapor. Additionally, fat dissolves five or six times more nitrogen than blood. Thus, tissues having the highest fat content are more likely to form bubbles.

INFLUENTIAL FACTORS

2-126. Evolved-gas disorders do not affect everyone who flies. The following factors tend to increase the likelihood of evolved-gas problems.

Rate of Ascent, Level of Altitude, and Duration of Exposure

2-127. In general, the more rapid the ascent, the greater the chance evolved-gas disorders will occur. The body does not have time to adapt to rapid pressure changes. At altitudes below 25,000 feet (7,620 meters), symptoms are less likely to occur; above 25,000 feet, they are more likely to occur. The longer the exposure—especially above 20,000 feet (6,096 meters)—the more likely evolved-gas disorders will occur.

Age and Body Fat

2-128. The incidence of DCS increases with age, with a three-fold rise in incidence between the 19- to 25-year-old and 40- to 45-year-old age groups. The reason for this increase is not understood but could result from changes in circulation caused by aging. No scientific validation exists to support any link between obesity and the incidence of DCS.

Physical Activity

2-129. Physical exertion during flight significantly lowers the altitude at which evolved-gas disorders occur. Exercise also shortens the amount of time that normally passes before symptoms occur.

Frequency of Exposure

Types of Evolved-Gas Disorders

2-130. Frequency of exposure tends to increase the risk of evolved-gas disorders. The more often individuals are exposed to altitudes above 18,000 feet (5,486 meters) without pressurization, the more they are predisposed to evolved-gas disorders. There are two major types of DCS: Type I and Type II. Type I DCS is considered less serious than Type II DCS. However, it is important to remember both types are medical emergencies. Table 2-8 provides a listing of symptoms for Type I and Type II DCS.

Table 2-8. Decompression sickness symptoms

Type I DCS:
(a) Bends. At the onset of bends, pain in the joints and related tissues might be mild but can become deep, gnawing, penetrating, and eventually intolerable. Pain tends to be progressive and becomes worse if ascent is continued. Severe pain can cause loss of muscular power in the involved extremity and, if sustained, could result in bodily collapse. Pain sensations might diffuse from the joint over the entire area of the arm or leg. In some instances, pain will arise initially in muscle or bone rather than a joint. Larger joints such as the knees and shoulders are most frequently affected. The hands, wrists, and ankles also are commonly involved. In successive exposures, pain tends to recur in the same location. It also might occur in several joints at the same time and worsen with movement and weight bearing. Coarse tremors of the fingers often are noted when bends occur in joints of the arm.
(b) Skin manifestations. Tingling, itching, and cold and warm sensations known as paresthesias are believed to be caused by bubbles formed either locally or in the central nervous system, where they involve nerve tracts leading to affected areas in the skin. Cold and warm sensations of the eyes and eyelids, as well as occasional itching and gritty sensations, are sometimes noted. A mottled red rash might appear on the skin. More rarely a welt might appear and be accompanied by a burning sensation. Bubbles might develop just under the skin and cause localized swelling. In affected regions with excess fat beneath the skin, soreness and abnormal fluid accumulation might be present for 1 or 2 days.

Table 2-8. Decompression sickness symptoms

Type II DCS:
(a) Chokes. Symptoms occurring in the thorax probably are caused in part by innumerable small bubbles that block smaller pulmonary vessels. At first, a burning sensation is noted under the sternum. As the condition progresses, a stabbing pain is felt and inhalation becomes markedly deeper. The sensation in the chest is similar to one an individual experiences after completing a 100-yard dash. Short breaths are necessary to avoid distress. There is an almost uncontrollable desire to cough, but the cough is ineffective and nonproductive. Finally, there is a sensation of suffocation; breathing becomes shallower and the skin turns bluish. When symptoms of chokes occur, immediate descent is imperative. If allowed to progress, the condition leads to collapse and unconsciousness. Fatigue, weakness, and soreness in the chest might persist several hours after the aircraft lands.
(b) Central nervous system disorders. In rare cases when aircrews are exposed to high altitude, symptoms might indicate the brain or spinal cord is affected by nitrogen bubble formation. The most common symptom is visual disturbance (for example, the perception lights are flashing or flickering when they are actually steady). Other symptoms include a dull to severe headache, partial paralysis, inability to hear or speak, and loss of orientation. Paresthesia or one-sided numbness and tingling also might occur. Hypoxia and hyperventilation can cause similar numbness and tingling; however, these symptoms are bilateral—they occur in arms, legs, or sides on both sides of the body. Central nervous system disorders are a medical emergency; if they occur at high altitude, immediate descent and hospitalization are required.

PREVENTION

2-131.   During high-altitude flight and hypobaric chamber operations, aircrews can be protected against DCS. Protective measures include—

- Denitrogenation.
- Cabin pressurization.
- Limitation of time at high altitude.
- Aircrew restrictions.

Denitrogenation

2-132.   Aircrews are required to breathe 100-percent oxygen for 30 minutes before takeoff for flights above 18,000 feet (5,486 meters). Denitrogenation rids the body of excess nitrogen. This dumping of nitrogen takes place because the oxygen mask provides only 100-percent oxygen. The amount of nitrogen lost depends strictly on time. Within the first 30 minutes of denitrogenation (figure 2-21), the body loses about 30 percent of its nitrogen.

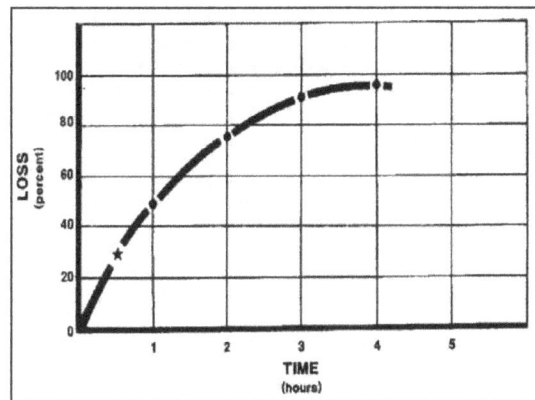

Figure 2-21. Denitrogenation

Cabin Pressurization

2-133. Aircraft cabin pressurization usually is maintained at a pressure equivalent to an altitude of 10,000 feet (3,048 meters) or below. This pressure decreases the possibility of nitrogen bubble formation.

Limitation of Time at High Altitude

2-134. The longer an individual stays at high altitude, the more nitrogen bubbles will form. Extended, unpressurized flight above 20,000 feet (6,096 meters) should be minimized.

Aircrew Restrictions

2-135. AR 40-8 restricts crewmembers from flying for 24 hours after self-contained underwater breathing apparatus (scuba) diving. During scuba diving, an individual experiences excessive nitrogen uptake while using compressed air. Flying at 8,000 feet (2,438 meters) within 24 hours after scuba diving at 30 feet (9 meters) subjects an individual to the same factors a nondiver faces when flying unpressurized at 40,000 feet (12,192 meters) and causes nitrogen bubbles to form.

TREATMENT

2-136. When signs or symptoms of evolved-gas disorders appear, crewmembers should take the following corrective actions:

- Descend to ground level immediately.
- Place the affected individual on 100-percent oxygen to eliminate any additional nitrogen uptake and remove excess nitrogen from the system.
- Immobilize the affected area to prevent further movement of nitrogen bubbles in the circulatory system.
- Report to a flight surgeon or the best medical assistance available.
- Undergo compression therapy in a hyperbaric chamber if symptoms persist and when prescribed by a flight surgeon.

DELAYED ONSET OF DECOMPRESSION SICKNESS

2-137. The onset of DCS can occur as long as 48 hours after exposure to altitudes above 18,000 feet (5,486 meters). Delayed onset can occur even if no signs or symptoms were evident during flight.

This page intentionally left blank.

Chapter 3

Stress and Fatigue in Flying Operations

Stress and fatigue in flying operations adversely affect mission execution and aviation safety. Consequently, crewmembers must be familiar with the effects of stress and fatigue on the body and how their behavior and lifestyle might reduce or, alternatively, increase the amount of stress and fatigue they experience. This chapter reviews aviation stressors and their effects on crewmember performance, presents several strategies for coping with stress, and concludes with a discussion of fatigue and its prevention and treatment.

STRESS DEFINED

3-1. In 1926, Hans Selye, an Austrian endocrinologist, identified what he believed was a consistent pattern of mind-body reactions he called "the nonspecific response of the body to any demand." He later referred to this pattern as the "rate of wear and tear on the body." In search of a term that best described these concepts, he turned to the physical sciences and borrowed the term "stress."

3-2. Selye's definition is necessarily broad because the notion of stress involves a wide range of human experiences. However, it incorporates two very important basic points: stress is a physiological phenomenon involving actual changes in the body's chemistry and function, and it involves some perceived or actual demand for action. This definition does not qualify these demands as either positive or negative; both types of demands can be

Contents

stressful. For example, coming into the zone for promotion to a higher rank generally is considered a positive, potentially rewarding event; however, the ambiguity and uncertainty of the process are stressful.

IDENTIFYING STRESSORS

3-3. A stressor is any stimulus or event that requires an individual to adjust or adapt in some way—emotionally, physiologically, or behaviorally. Stressors can be psychosocial, environmental, physiological (self-imposed), and cognitive (mental). The first step an individual must take in devising an effective stress-management plan is identifying the significant stressors in his or her life. This section reviews stressors aviation crewmembers typically encounter.

PSYCHOSOCIAL STRESSORS

3-4. Psychosocial stressors are life events. These stressors can trigger adaptation or change in one's lifestyle, career, and/or interaction with others.

Job Stress

3-5. Work responsibilities can be a significant source of stress for crewmembers. Regardless of job assignment, carrying out assigned duties often produces stress. Conflict in the workplace, low morale and unit cohesion, boredom, fatigue, overtasking, and poorly defined responsibilities all are potential debilitating job stressors.

3-6. Crewmembers who lack confidence in their abilities or have problems communicating and cooperating with others experience considerable stress.

3-7. Poor coworker performance also can impose stress on an aviator. For example, flight crews might not trust those who service their aircraft to perform proper maintenance. As a result, crewmembers could experience anxiety during flight that adversely affects the unit's cohesion and morale.

Illness

3-8. Although the aviation population undergoes frequent and thorough medical examination, organic disease can occur and should be considered a source of stress. In addition, fatigue is a common symptom of many diseases.

Family Issues

3-9. Although family can be a source of emotional strength for crewmembers, it also can cause stress. Family commitments might adversely affect performance, particularly when duty assignments separate crewmembers from their families. Concern for family might become a distraction during flight operations or increase fatigue or irritability. The potential dangers of flight operations also act as a stressor on families and could cause tension in spousal relationships.

ENVIRONMENTAL STRESSORS

Altitude

3-10. Stress caused by altitude is most evident at altitudes below 5,000 feet (1,524 meters). This is where the greatest atmospheric changes occur and crewmembers are subject to problems resulting from trapped gas. Even a common cold can cause ear and sinus problems during descent. Because flights seldom exceed an altitude of 18,000 feet (5,486 meters), hypoxia and evolved-gas problems such as the bends are not significant sources of stress for most Army aviators. Chapter 2 covers the effects of evolved gas, trapped gas, and hypoxia in more detail.

Speed

3-11. Flight usually is associated with speeds greater than those experienced in an everyday, earthbound environment. These speeds are stressful because they require a high degree of alertness and concentration over prolonged periods.

Hot or Cold Environments

3-12. Extreme heat or cold causes stress in the aviation environment. Heat problems might be due to hot, tropic-like climates or direct sunlight entering through large canopies. Cold problems might be due to altitude or arctic climates. To reduce temperature stress, crewmembers should gradually adapt to extremes and use proper clothing and equipment.

Aircraft Design

3-13. Human factors engineering items such as cockpit illumination, instrument location, accessibility of switches and controls, and seat comfort significantly affect aviator performance. Other influential human factors include visibility, noise level, and the adequacy of heating and ventilating systems. When such items are inadequate or uncomfortable, crewmembers will experience increased stress, which might divert their attention from performing operational duties.

Airframe Characteristics

3-14. Airframe handling and flight characteristics are potential stress factors. For example, fixed-wing aircraft have innate stability so that, when trimmed, they can be flown relatively well with minimal pilot attention. Rotary-wing aircraft, however, require constant pilot attention to maintain stability.

Instrument Flight Conditions

3-15. Poor weather resulting in instrument flight conditions imposes significant stress on aircrews and increases fatigue. Awareness of a greater potential for physical danger and the need for increased vigilance and accuracy in reading, following, and monitoring flight instruments are very stressful. A high correlation exists between adverse weather and accident rates.

3-16. The stress of night flying is similar to the stress of flying in poor weather. Aviators lose their usual visual references and must rely on flight instruments.

PHYSIOLOGICAL (SELF-IMPOSED) STRESSORS

3-17. Although crewmembers often have limited control over many aspects of aviation-related stress, they can exert significant control over self-imposed stress. Many crewmembers engage in maladaptive behaviors that are potentially debilitating and threaten aviation safety. This category can be remembered using the acronym DEATH, which stands for drugs, exhaustion, alcohol, tobacco, and hypoglycemia (discussed further in chapter 8).

Drugs

Self Medication

3-18. Commercial advertising continually encourages the purchase of nonprescription, over-the-counter medications for a range of minor ailments. The primary purposes of such medications are to cure or control symptoms of a medical problem. According to AR 40-8, crewmembers must keep their flight surgeon informed of any significant changes in their physical health. Furthermore, most drugs, whether prescribed or over-the-counter, have unwanted side effects that can vary from person to person. In general, no crewmember taking medication is fit to fly unless cleared to do so by a flight surgeon.

Predictable Side Effects

3-19. Side effects accompany the use of a drug and are incidental to its desired effect. Table 3-1 (page 3-4) includes examples of common over-the-counter drugs and their known side effects. These side effects highlight the need for crewmembers to be aware of known potential problems with drugs. Although crewmembers might not experience all the listed side effects, they should know these might occur.

Overdose Problems

3-20. Drugs are to be taken in a given amount over a specified time. Taking more than the recommended dosage of a medication does not reduce recovery time and can be dangerous.

Table 3-1. Possible side effects of commonly used drugs

Substance (Generic or Brand Name)	Possible Side Effects
Alcohol (beer, liquor, wine)	• Impaired judgment, perception, coordination, motor control, and sensory perception • Reduced reaction time, intellectual functions, and tolerance to G-forces • Inner-ear disturbance and spatial disorientation (up to 48 hours) • Central nervous system depression
Nicotine (cigars, cigarettes, pipe and chewing tobacco, snuff)	• Sinus and respiratory system infection and irritation • Impaired night vision • Hypertension • Carbon monoxide poisoning (from smoking)
Amphetamines (Ritalin®, Obetrol®, Eskatrol®)	Used to treat obesity and tiredness • Prolonged wakefulness or sleep disturbance • Nervousness, shakiness, and rapid heart rate • Impaired vision • Suppressed appetite • Excessive sweating • Seriously impaired judgment
Caffeine (coffee, tea, chocolate, No-Doz®, energy drinks)	• Impaired judgment • Reduced reaction time • Sleep disturbance • Increased motor activity, tremors, and rapid heart rate • Hypertension • Irregular heart rate • Body dehydration (through increased urine output) • Headaches
Antacid (Alka-2®, Di-Gel®, Maalox®)	Used to treat stomach acid • Liberation of carbon dioxide at altitude (distension can cause acute abdominal pain and mask other medical problems)
Antihistamines (Coricidin®, Contac®, Dristan®, Dimetapp®, Chlor-Trimeton®)	Used to treat allergies and colds • Drowsiness and dizziness (sometimes recurring) • Visual disturbances (when medications also contain antispasmodic drugs)
Aspirin (Bayer®, Bufferin®, Alka-Seltzer®)	Used to treat headaches, fever, aches, and pains • Irregular body temperature • Variation in rate and depth of respiration • Hypoxia and hyperventilation
Aspirin can contribute to nausea, ringing in the ears, deafness, diarrhea, and hallucinations when taken in excessive dosages; corrosion of the stomach lining; gastrointestinal problems; and decreased clotting ability of blood (clotting ability could be the difference between life and death in a survival situation).	

Allergic Reactions

3-21. Some individuals might experience an exaggerated or pathological reaction to a given medication. An example is an allergic reaction to penicillin.

Synergistic Effects

3-22. This term refers to undesired effects resulting from the combination of two or more drugs or from a stressful situation experienced while taking a prescribed drug.

Caffeine

3-23. Many people commonly ingest caffeine. However, it is a drug with potentially negative effects on flight operations if not used properly and in moderation. Many beverages and foods such as tea, chocolate, and most cola-type drinks contain caffeine. Table 3-2 shows the varying amounts of caffeine in these products.

Table 3-2. Caffeine content of common beverages, foods, and over-the-counter drugs

Product	Amount	Caffeine Content (mg)
Coffee		
Brewed	8 oz	107.5
Instant	8 oz	57
Decaffeinated (brewed)	8 oz	6
Espresso	1.5 oz	77
Tea		
Leaf or bag	8 oz	50
Snapple®, all varieties	16 oz	42
Cola-Type and Energy Drinks		
Coca-Cola Classic®	12 oz	34
Diet Coke®	12 oz	45
Red Bull®	8 oz	80
Mountain Dew®	12 oz	55
Dr. Pepper®	12 oz	41
Chocolate		
Hershey's® Chocolate Bar	1 bar	9
Hershey's® Special Dark	1 bar	31
Over-the-Counter Drugs		
No Doz®/Vivarin® (maximum strength)	1 tablet	200
Dexatrim®	1 tablet	200
Excedrin®	1 tablet	65
Midol® (maximum strength)	1 tablet	60
Anacin®	1 tablet	32
Dristan®	1 tablet	16

3-24. Caffeine is a central nervous system stimulant that counteracts and delays drowsiness and fatigue. Although it increases alertness, the side effects of caffeine might degrade crewmember performance. Caffeine can elevate blood pressure, impair hand-eye coordination and timing, and cause nervousness or irritability. Some people can experience adverse effects when ingesting only 150 to 200 milligrams of caffeine (the equivalent of one or two cups of coffee or several cups of tea). Caffeine also is addictive, and continued use builds tolerance. Over time, people must ingest increasing amounts of caffeine to obtain the same physiological and behavioral effects.

Exhaustion

Lack of Rest and Sleep

3-25. Crewmembers require adequate rest to ensure optimal flight performance. Sleep problems are common during deployments, when the sleep environment might be hot, cold, or noisy. Changes in time zones also can affect sleeping patterns. Crewmembers should discuss sleeping difficulties with their flight surgeon, as inadequate sleep is a potential flight-safety hazard. Changing the work routine or improving the environment can promote sleep and increase operational efficiency.

Physical Conditioning

3-26. Exercise stimulates the various body systems and has well-documented positive effects on mental health. Lack of exercise impairs circulatory efficiency, reduces endurance, and increases the likelihood of illness. General toning of the muscles, heart, and lungs is essential in preparing aircrews for field exercises and survival situations. Sports that require agility, balance, and endurance are an excellent means of keeping the body and mind in top form.

Alcohol

3-27. Ethyl alcohol acts as a depressant and adversely affects normal body functions. Even a small amount has detrimental effects on judgment, perception, reaction time, impulse control, and coordination. Alcohol reduces the ability of brain cells to use oxygen. Each ounce of alcohol consumed increases physiological altitude by 2,000 feet.

3-28. The effects of alcohol on the body and brain depend on the following three factors:
- The amount of alcohol consumed.
- The rate of absorption from the stomach and small intestine.
- The body's rate of metabolism, which is relatively constant at about 1 ounce every 3 hours.

3-29. After drinking alcohol, an aviator should wait at least 12 hours before beginning flying duties. Alcohol's side effects are dangerous. If side effects (hangover symptoms) are present, the nonflying period should be extended beyond 12 hours. Taking cold showers, drinking coffee, or breathing 100-percent oxygen does not increase the body's metabolism of alcohol. Only time dissipates alcohol's effects.

3-30. Crewmembers should recognize alcohol as a potential safety hazard and assess their own risk for developing an alcohol-abuse problem. This assessment involves examining the frequency and amount of one's consumption as well as the reasons for consumption. Alcohol should not be a stress-coping strategy.

3-31. Some individuals are more prone to develop an alcohol-abuse problem. For example, people with a family history of alcoholism are at greater risk for developing an alcohol problem than those without such a history. The following four questions will help crewmembers determine if they are misusing or have misused alcohol:
- Have you ever tried to cut back on your alcohol consumption?
- Are you annoyed by comments people make about your drinking?
- Have you ever felt guilty about your drinking?
- Have you ever had a drink first thing in the morning to get you started?

3-32. Answering "yes" to two or more of these questions might indicate inappropriate alcohol use. Crewmembers should more closely examine how frequently, how much, and why they drink alcohol.

Tobacco

3-33. The detrimental effects of tobacco on the body are well known. Apart from the long-term association with lung cancer and coronary heart disease, there are other important, but less dramatic, effects. For example, chronic irritation of the lining of the nose and lungs caused by tobacco increases the likelihood of infection in those areas. This is a significant problem for aviators because it affects their ability to cope with the effects of pressure changes in the ears and sinuses. In addition, even a mildly irritating cough causes distress when oxygen equipment is used.

3-34. Although smoking has many long-term effects including emphysema and lung cancer, aviators should be just as concerned about the acute effects of carbon monoxide produced by smoking tobacco. Carbon monoxide combines with hemoglobin to form carboxyhemoglobin (CoHb). Carbon monoxide attaches to hemoglobin molecules 200 to 300 times more readily than oxygen. The net effect is a degree of hypoxia. Average cigarette smokers have about 8 to 10 percent CoHb in their blood, which adds about 5,000 feet of physiological altitude. Cigarette smoking also decreases night vision. A pilot who does not smoke begins to experience decreased night vision at 4,000 to 5,000 feet because of hypoxia, but a pilot who does smoke begins flight at sea level with a physiological night-vision deficit of 5,000 feet.

Hypoglycemia

3-35. Aviation medicine experts recognize the importance of a nutritious, well-balanced diet. The body requires periodic refueling to function. Normal, regular eating habits are important, but nutrition depends largely on individual behavior. Crewmembers should consume meals at regular intervals whenever possible. Because mission requirements can disrupt regular eating habits, crewmembers often skip meals. Missing meals or substituting a quick snack and coffee for a balanced meal can induce fatigue and inefficiency.

3-36. The liver stores energy in the form of glycogen, a blood sugar. The liver readily converts glycogen to glucose, which maintains the body's blood-sugar level. Unless food is consumed at regular intervals, stored glycogen depletes and results in a low blood-sugar condition called hypoglycemia. When the blood-sugar level falls, weakness or fainting occurs and the body's efficiency decreases.

3-37. Insulin lowers the blood-sugar level, but at the same time, blood sugar also decreases through its normal function of fueling the body. These two factors can result in hypoglycemia. It is important to maintain a balanced diet of proper foods that include proteins, fats, and carbohydrates.

3-38. Aviators must guard against obesity because of its detrimental effects on general health and performance. Inactivity and boredom during standby duty and long flights easily can lead to overeating. Therefore, it is wise to weigh oneself regularly and adjust diet to maintain desired weight. This habit is easier and safer than repeated dieting. In addition, crewmembers should consult a flight surgeon before beginning a weight-loss regimen. Herbal or dietary supplements need to be discussed with and approved by a flight surgeon prior to use.

COGNITIVE (MENTAL) STRESSORS

3-39. How one perceives a given situation or problem is a potentially significant and frequently overlooked source of stress. Pessimism, obsession, failure to focus on the present, and/or low self-confidence can create a self-fulfilling prophecy that will ensure a negative outcome. Below are some typical thought problems crewmembers might encounter that can increase overall stress.

"Musts" and "Shoulds"

3-40. Albert Ellis, a renowned clinical psychologist, observed that stress results when individuals believe things must go their way or should conform to their own needs and desires or they cannot function. This lack of flexibility in thinking causes problems when reality does not accommodate one's wishes. Failure to accept the possibility things might happen contrary to one's wishes leaves one unprepared, frustrated, and dysfunctional.

Responsbility of Choice

3-41. Life is full of choices; depending on the situation, some choices are adaptive and others maladaptive. However, not all adaptive choices are favorable, and while certain consequences might make some choices unpalatable, they are choices nonetheless. Some individuals actively make choices, increasing their sense of personal control and decreasing stress in their life. Others tend to believe in "fate" or "destiny" and see the world as the cause of their problems, which can lead to unhappiness and increased stress.

Failure to Focus on the Here and Now

3-42. Living in the past or future and overemphasizing what should have been or could be can increase one's overall stress. Although there is utility in both learning from the past and planning for the future, over engaging in either of these activities can cause people to fail at tasks and miss opportunities in the present.

STRESS RESPONSES

3-43. Stress affects individuals in a variety of ways. These effects can include emotional, behavioral, cognitive (thought), and physical responses.

EMOTIONAL RESPONSES

3-44. Emotional responses to stress range from increased anxiety, irritability, or hostility to depressed mood, loss of self-esteem, hopelessness, and an inability to enjoy life. Crewmembers should consult a flight surgeon if emotional responses are severe and interfere significantly with social or occupational functioning. Aviation personnel often are reluctant to seek help for emotional problems, but it is important to recognize stress can become overwhelming at times and present a serious threat to aviation safety.

BEHAVIORAL RESPONSES

3-45. High stress can adversely affect one's work performance, decrease motivation, and increase the likelihood of conflict, insubordination, and violence in the workplace. Some individuals might become socially isolated. Others might abuse drugs or alcohol as an ineffective stress-coping strategy.

Suicide Risk

3-46. Suicidal thoughts and intent can occur in individuals under high stress. The following are danger signs of suicide risk:
- Talking or hinting about suicide.
- Having a specific plan to commit suicide and the means to accomplish it.
- Obsession with death.
- Giving away possessions or making a will.
- A history of prior suicide attempts.
- Multiple, recent life stressors.
- Alcohol consumption, which increases the risk of following through on suicidal thoughts.

3-47. Crewmembers should always take these danger signs seriously. Individuals exhibiting some or all of these signs should be approached supportively and referred to a mental health provider for evaluation. The local flight surgeon should be contacted to make an appropriate referral to a mental health provider.

COGNITIVE RESPONSES

3-48. Stress can significantly affect one's thought processes. It can decrease attention and concentration, interfere with judgment and problem solving, and impair memory. Stress can cause aviators to commit errors in thought and take mental shortcuts that could be potentially fatal.

The Simplification Heuristic

3-49. Under high-stress conditions, people tend to oversimplify problem solving, ignore important relevant information, and take the easy way out. For example, an aviator experiencing high stress before going into combat might think "I just have to get in and start up," an oversimplification of the steps involved in preparing the aircraft that results in failure to follow all preflight inspection steps.

Stress-Related Regression

3-50. Many individuals under high-stress conditions forget learned procedures and skills and revert to previously learned and often bad habits. For example, a student aviator preparing for takeoff might forget to turn on the fuel switch and then, realizing the problem and feeling stressed and embarrassed, turn the switch on and risk overheating the engine. This action is clearly contrary to training and represents a kind of regression or failure to use prior learning.

Perceptual Tunneling

3-51. Perceptual tunneling is a phenomenon in which an individual or entire crew under high stress becomes focused on one stimulus such as a flashing warning signal and neglects to attend to other important tasks or information involved in flying the aircraft. A similar situation might occur when an aviator realizes during flight that he or she overlooked some aspect of flight such as missing a radio communication. The stressed aviator might then over attend to rectifying this problem, become emotionally and mentally fixated on the error, and fall "behind the aircraft," missing new information and further compromising the mission.

PHYSICAL RESPONSES

3-52. The immediate physical response to a stressful situation involves overall heightened arousal of the body, including increased heart rate and blood pressure, rapid breathing, muscle tension, and the release of sugars and fats into circulation to provide fuel for "fight or flight."

3-53. Prolonged stress and its continuous effects on the body can produce longer-term physical symptoms such as muscle tension and pain, headaches, high blood pressure, gastrointestinal problems, and decreased immunity to infectious diseases.

STRESS UNDERLOAD

3-54. Having too little stress in one's life can be as dysfunctional as having too much stress. A lack of challenges can lead to complacency, boredom, and impulsive risk taking. Individuals should strive to balance stress so they are optimally challenged without overwhelming their coping resources. The effects of stress underload are of particular concern in peacekeeping operations. In such operations, Soldiers often have a considerable amount of unstructured time, and work tasks can become routine and monotonous. Thus, leaders need to minimize unstructured time as much as possible, using it instead as an opportunity for skills training, cross-training, physical training, and other activities that challenge and develop subordinates.

STRESS AND PERFORMANCE

3-55. The relationship between stress and performance depends on a variety of factors.

MENTAL SKILLS REQUIRED BY THE TASK OR SITUATION

3-56. The degree to which a given task or situation requires specific cognitive skills (including attention, concentration, memory, problem solving, or visual-spatial orientation) influences the extent to which stress degrades performance. Performance in situations involving simple mental tasks tends to be less affected by stress than performance in situations that require more complex cognitive skills. For example, writing a letter under high stress would probably result in fewer errors than taking a written exam under high stress.

STRESS CHARACTERISTICS OF THE SITUATION

3-57. The degree to which stress affects performance also depends on the environment and conditions under which a given task is performed. For example, taking a stressful, timed problem-solving test in a quiet, comfortable room is much easier and results in fewer errors than taking the same test in a hot, noisy room.

PHYSICAL CHARACTERISTICS OF THE INDIVIDUAL

3-58. Individual differences in strength, endurance, and physical health greatly influence the extent to which stress affects performance. This is especially true in aviation operations, where crewmembers must be in top physical condition to perform in the physically challenging environments of continuous operations and combat.

PSYCHOLOGICAL MAKEUP OF THE INDIVIDUAL

3-59. Mental health, much like physical health, serves to moderate the effects of stress on performance. Individuals with good coping, problem solving, and social skills perform much better under stress than those who are weaker in these areas.

STRESS MANAGEMENT

3-60. Stress-coping mechanisms are psychological and behavioral strategies for managing the external and internal demands imposed by stressors. Coping mechanisms can be characterized according to the following categories.

AVOIDING STRESSORS

3-61. This is the most powerful coping mechanism. Crewmembers can avoid stressors with good planning, foresight, realistic training, good time management, and effective problem solving. Staying physically fit and eating right also are effective strategies for avoiding fatigue, illness, and related stressors. Good crew coordination and communication (including asking questions, using three-way confirm responses, and briefing lost communication) also help mitigate flight stress.

CHANGING THINKING

3-62. As indicated in the earlier discussion on cognitive stressors, how individuals perceive their environment and choose to think about themselves and others greatly affects their stress level and performance. Crewmembers can greatly enhance stress management and personal effectiveness by—
- Practicing positive self-talk.
- Taking responsibility for their actions.
- Recognizing the choices they make.
- Avoiding perfectionism and inflexibility in thinking.
- Focusing on the here and now rather than the past or future.

LEARNING TO RELAX

3-63. Relaxation is incompatible with stress. It is impossible to be relaxed and anxious at the same time. Learning and regularly practicing relaxation techniques, breathing exercises, or meditation or regularly engaging in a quiet hobby greatly reduce stress. Although this recommendation might sound simple, few people actually practice relaxation regularly. Making time to relax during a busy schedule is perhaps the biggest obstacle to this coping strategy.

VENTILATING STRESS

3-64. This strategy involves "blowing off steam" in some manner, either through talking or vigorous exercise. Talking out problems can be accomplished informally with friends or family, or professionally with a mental-health practitioner or chaplain. Exercise should be a regular part of everyone's lifestyle; it is effective in both preventing and coping with stress. Volumes of research have documented the positive benefits of exercise for both physical and mental health.

FATIGUE

3-65. Fatigue is the state of feeling tired, weary, or sleepy that results from prolonged mental or physical work, extended periods of anxiety, exposure to harsh environments, or loss of sleep. Boring or monotonous tasks can increase fatigue.

3-66. As with many other physiological problems, crewmembers might not be aware of fatigue until they make serious errors. Sleep deprivation, disrupted diurnal (circadian) cycles, or life-event stress can produce fatigue and concurrent performance reduction. The three types of fatigue are acute, chronic, and motivational exhaustion (burnout).

ACUTE FATIGUE

3-67. Acute fatigue is associated with physical or mental activity between two regular sleep periods. Loss of coordination and lack of error awareness are the first signs of fatigue to develop. Crewmembers might experience these symptoms, for example, at night after being awake 12 to 15 hours. With adequate rest or sleep, typically after one regular sleep period, crewmembers will overcome this fatigue. These and other mental deficits (listed below) are apparent to others before the individual notices any physical signs of fatigue. Acute fatigue is characterized by—

- Inattention.
- Distractibility.
- Errors in timing.
- Neglect of secondary tasks.
- Loss of accuracy and control.
- Lack of awareness of error accumulation.
- Irritability.

CHRONIC FATIGUE

3-68. This type of fatigue is much more serious than acute fatigue, occurs over a longer period, and is typically the result of inadequate recovery from successive periods of acute fatigue. Mental tiredness develops in addition to physical tiredness. It might take several weeks of rest to eliminate chronic fatigue. There also might be underlying social causes such as family or financial difficulties that must be addressed before any amount of rest will help the individual recover. The crewmember or unit commander must identify chronic fatigue early and initiate a referral to the flight surgeon for evaluation and treatment. Chronic fatigue is characterized by some or all of the following characteristics:

- Insomnia.
- Depressed mood.
- Irritability.
- Weight loss.
- Poor judgment.
- Loss of appetite.
- Slowed reaction time.
- Poor motivation and performance on the job.

MOTIVATIONAL EXHAUSTION (BURNOUT)

3-69. If chronic fatigue remains untreated for too long, the individual will eventually "shut down" and cease functioning occupationally and socially. Motivational exhaustion is also known as burnout.

EFFECTS OF FATIGUE ON PERFORMANCE

REACTION-TIME CHANGES

3-70. Fatigue can result in either increases or decreases in reaction time. Decreased reaction times occur because of the general decrease in motivation and sluggishness that often accompany fatigue. Increased reaction times occur when individuals become impulsive and react quickly and poorly. When fatigued, both increased and decreased reaction times can lead to inaccurate results.

REDUCED ATTENTION

3-71. Crewmembers might exhibit the following signs and symptoms of reduced attention:
- Tendency to overlook or misplace sequential task elements (for example, forgetting items on preflight checklists).
- Preoccupation with single tasks or elements (for example, paying too much attention to a bird and forgetting to fly the aircraft, the cause of many accidents).
- Reduction of audiovisual scan both inside and outside the cockpit.
- Lack of awareness of poor performance.

DIMINISHED MEMORY

3-72. Crewmembers might be experiencing diminished memory when they display the following characteristics:
- Short-term memory and processing capacity decrease, although long-term memory tends to be well preserved despite fatigue.
- Integrating new information and making decisions becomes more challenging, as does adaptability to change in general.
- Inaccurate recall of operational events (for example, forgetting the objective rally point location).
- Neglect of peripheral tasks (for example, forgetting to check if the landing gear is down).
- Tendency to revert to bad habits.
- Decreased ability to integrate new information and analyze and solve problems.

CHANGES IN MOOD AND SOCIAL INTERACTION

3-73. Fatigued individuals can become irritable and combative. They also might experience mild depression and withdraw socially.

IMPAIRED COMMUNICATION

3-74. Fatigue impairs a person's abilities to communicate and receive information. Crewmembers might leave out important details in the messages they send to others. They might neglect or misinterpret information they receive. Fatigue also can affect a crewmember's pronunciation, rate of speech, tone, or volume.

DIURNAL (CIRCADIAN) RHYTHMS AND FATIGUE

3-75. Humans have an intrinsic biological clock with a cycle of roughly 24 to 25 hours. Many important body functions such as core body temperature, alertness, heart rate, and sleep cycle occur along these diurnal rhythms. In the typical circadian cycle, performance, alertness, and body temperature—

- Peak between 0800 and 1200.
- Drop off slightly between 1300 and 1500.
- Begin to increase again from 1500 to 2100.
- Drop off again and fall to a minimum circadian trough between 0300 and 0600.

3-76. While the body clock can monitor the passage of time, it differs from most clocks in that it is flexible and must be set, or synchronized, before it can accurately predict the timing of events. External synchronizers or "zeitgebers" (a German word that means "time givers") are—

- Sunrise and sunset.
- Ambient temperature.
- Meals and other social cues.

CIRCADIAN DESYNCHRONIZATION (JET LAG)

3-77. Rapid travel between time zones causes the body to resynchronize its diurnal or daytime rhythms to the local geophysical and social time cues. Until intrinsic rhythms are reset, sleep disorders and fatigue will prevail. Traveling eastward shortens the day; westward travel lengthens the day. Consequently, resynchronization occurs much more rapidly when traveling west. Shift work can have effects similar to crossing time zones because of the changes in light exposure and activity times.

THE SLEEP CYCLE

3-78. Sleep is not simply being unconscious—it is an active process essential to life. The sleeping brain cycles between rapid eye movement (REM) and non-REM sleep through five stages. This cycling occurs every 90 minutes. In 8 hours of sleep, an individual normally attains five to six REM stages.

3-79. The duration and quality of sleep depend on body temperature. People sleep longer and report a better night's sleep when they retire near the temperature trough (the lowest average temperature in a given climate).

3-80. As indicated in the section above on diurnal rhythms, it is the timing of sleep, not necessarily the amount of sleep, that is most significant. A sleep schedule inconsistent with one's circadian rhythm and environmental light and social cues ultimately will result in fatigue, as will frequent changes in one's sleep schedule.

3-81. Sleep efficiency deteriorates with age. Older individuals spend less time in deep non-REM sleep. Nighttime awakenings and daytime sleepiness result.

SLEEP REQUIREMENTS

3-82. Individuals cannot accurately determine their own impairment from sleep loss. During operations in which sleep loss is expected, crewmembers should closely monitor each other's behavior for indicators of fatigue such as those identified in paragraphs 3-73 through 3-77.

3-83. The average person sleeps 7 to 9 hours per day. Sleep length can be reduced 1 to 2 hours without performance reduction over an extended period. Once the period ends, however, the individual must return to his or her normal sleep length.

3-84. As a rule, 5 hours of sleep per night is the minimum for continuous operations. However, some individuals can tolerate as little as 4 hours of sleep per night for short periods.

3-85. AR 385-10 provides guidance on crew endurance planning. The following factors regarding fatigue and sleep restriction decisions should be considered during crew endurance planning:

- Complexity of the job tasks to be performed under conditions of fatigue.
- Potential for loss from errors committed because of fatigue.
- The individual's tolerance for sleep loss.

PREVENTION OF FATIGUE

3-86. Total prevention of fatigue is impossible, but its effects can be moderated significantly. The following recommendations should be considered in any individual or crew endurance plan.

CONTROL THE SLEEP ENVIRONMENT

3-87. The sleep environment should be cool, dark, and quiet. It is best to avoid working or reading in bed, which could contribute to problems with falling asleep. The bed should be associated only with sleeping and sexual activity. If an individual wants to read before going to bed, they should do so in a chair, preferably in a room other than the bedroom, and then go to bed.

ADJUST TO SHIFT WORK

3-88. Crewmembers should adhere to the following measures to better adjust to shift work and prevent circadian desynchronization:

- Maintain a consistent sleep-wake schedule, even on days off.
- When on the night shift, avoid exposure to daylight from dawn to 1000. Wear sunglasses if necessary before the sun rises (as long as doing so does not pose a safety hazard). Consider wearing a sleep mask to avoid exposure to light.
- Do not go to sleep too full or too hungry, although a light snack may be eaten before bedtime.
- Avoid caffeine consumption for 6 hours before going to sleep.

MAINTAIN GOOD HEALTH AND PHYSICAL FITNESS

3-89. Crewmembers can maintain good physical fitness with regular strenuous exercise, which also promotes healthy sleep. However, strenuous exercise should be avoided within a few hours of bedtime because it can increase core body temperature and delay sleep. Elimination of tobacco use also promotes good health and sleep.

PRACTICE GOOD EATING HABITS

3-90. It is important to maintain a balanced diet that includes proteins, fats, and carbohydrates. Failing to give the body the quality fuel it needs contributes to crewmember fatigue and poor work performance.

PRACTICE MODERATE, CONTROLLED USE OF ALCOHOL AND CAFFEINE

3-91. Use of alcohol as a sleep aid can interfere with REM sleep and disrupt sleep patterns. Frequent use of caffeine often contributes to insomnia.

PLAN AND PRACTICE GOOD TIME MANAGEMENT

3-92. Planning and practicing good time management help avoid last-minute crises. A reasonable, realistic work schedule also assists greatly in preventing fatigue.

PRACTICE REALISTIC PLANNING

3-93. Practice realistic planning for total duty and flying hours as outlined in AR 95-1. Studies have shown the relative fatigue factor of a flight hour varies with the flight environment. For example, chemical mission-oriented protective posture (MOPP) flight is more fatiguing than day nap-of-the-earth (NOE) flight.

Maintain Optimal Working Conditions

3-94. Particular attention should be devoted to addressing problems associated with the following factors:

- Glare.
- Vibration.
- Noise levels.
- Poor ventilation.
- Temperature extremes.
- Uncomfortable seating.
- Inadequate oxygen supply.
- Instrument and control location.
- Anthropometry (body measurements).

Take Naps

3-95. Naps are a viable alternative when sleep is not possible or is shortened by operational concerns. In general, longer naps (greater than 1 hour) are more beneficial than shorter naps, but even naps as short as 10 minutes can increase one's energy level. Longer naps can result in sluggishness (sleep inertia) for 5 to 20 minutes after awakening. Therefore, when deciding how long to nap, the crewmember should consider what work requirements will be following the nap. The best time to nap is when body temperature is low (around 0300 and 1300).

Note. Anyone having problems sleeping during their normal sleep period should not take naps during the rest of the day. Napping can delay sleep onset during the regular sleep period.

TREATMENT OF FATIGUE

3-96. The most important actions for treating fatigue are resting and getting natural (not drug-induced) sleep. Alcohol is the number-one sleep aid in the United States, but it suppresses REM sleep. Correcting bad sleep habits is one treatment for fatigue.

3-97. After lying awake in bed for more than 30 minutes, the individual should get up and read a boring book or listen to relaxing music until he or she is ready to fall asleep. Lying awake in bed could produce a mental association between being in bed and anxiety and wakefulness, which might promote insomnia. If the individual returns to bed and remains awake for more than 30 minutes, he or she should get up again and continue to do so as often as needed. Fatigue eventually will take over and the individual will fall asleep.

3-98. When attempting to recover from 24 to 48 hours of sleep deprivation, the individual should not sleep longer than 10 hours. Sleeping too long could further disrupt the sleep-wake schedule and cause sluggishness during the day.

3-99. Other measures that can be taken to prevent or treat fatigue are—

- Modifying the workplace to promote rest and prevent further fatigue.
- Rotating or changing duties to avoid boredom.
- Pacing and avoiding heavily task-loaded activities, those requiring short-term memory, or those demanding prolonged or intense mental activity.
- Limiting work periods and delegating responsibility.
- If possible, suspending activity during periods when fatigue is higher and efficiency is lower (for example, between 1300 and 1500 hours).
- Using brief periods of physical exercise immediately before task performance, particularly administrative work. However, individuals should not exercise within 1 hour before bedtime, as exercising might delay sleep onset.
- Removing a crewmember from flying duties when fatigue affects flight safety.

This page intentionally left blank.

Chapter 4

Gravitational Forces

Army aviation crewmembers must understand gravitational forces and the body's physiological responses to them in the aviation environment. This chapter discusses the physics of motion and acceleration and covers the types and directions of accelerative forces and their influences and effects. It also discusses deceleration and, more importantly, crash sequence and how aircraft design offers protection from crash forces. Crewmembers must have a fundamental but thorough understanding of the accelerative forces encountered during flight and their relationship to the human body.

TERMS OF ACCELERATION

4-1.   Acceleration is the rate of change in velocity and is measured in units of acceleration, or Gs. Several terms are used in discussing acceleration; these include speed, velocity, inertial force, centrifugal force, and centripetal force.

4-2.   Speed is an object's magnitude of motion and rate of change. It is expressed as distance covered in a unit of time such as miles per hour.

4-3.   Velocity is an object's speed in a given direction. It describes magnitude and direction of motion. Velocity is measured in distance per unit of time such as feet per second.

4-4.   Inertial force is an object's resistance to change in a state of rest or motion. A body at rest tends to remain at rest, while a body in motion tends to remain in motion.

4-5.   Centrifugal force is the force exerted on an object moving in a circular pattern. It causes the object to break away and move outward in a straight line.

4-6.   Centripetal (radial) force is the force acting on an object moving in a circular pattern that holds the object on its circular path.

TYPES OF ACCELERATION

4-7.   Flight imposes its greatest effects on the body through the accelerative forces applied during aerial maneuvering. In constant speed and straight-and-level flight, crewmembers encounter no human limitations. With changes in velocity, however, they can experience severe physiological effects. Crewmembers must understand where and how accelerative forces—linear, centripetal (radial), and angular—develop in flight.

LINEAR ACCELERATION

4-8.   Linear acceleration occurs when there is a change in an object's speed without a change in direction. It occurs during takeoffs and changes in forward airspeed. Linear acceleration also is encountered when speed is decreased. Figure 4-1 illustrates the concept of linear acceleration.

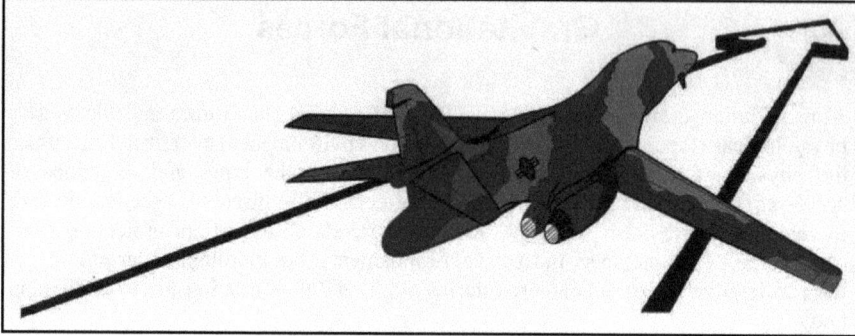

Figure 4-1. Linear acceleration

CENTRIPETAL (RADIAL) ACCELERATION

4-9.   Centripetal (radial) acceleration can occur during any change of direction without a change in speed. Crewmembers might encounter this type of acceleration during banks, turns, loops, or rolls (figure 4-2).

Figure 4-2. Centripetal (radial) acceleration

ANGULAR ACCELERATION

4-10. Angular acceleration is complex and involves a simultaneous change in both speed and direction. A good example of this is an aircraft put into a tight spin. For practical purposes, angular acceleration does not pose a problem in understanding the physiological effects of accelerative forces. Its principal effects are important, however, because they produce many of the disorientation problems encountered in flight (figure 4-3, page 4-3).

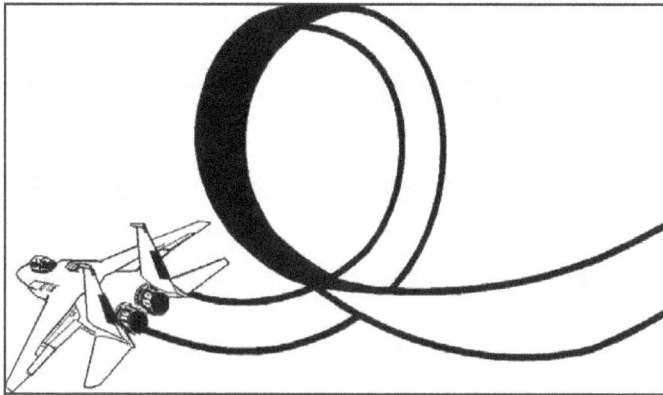

Figure 4-3. Angular acceleration

GRAVITATIONAL FORCES

4-11. Newton's three laws of motion describe the forces of acceleration. The first law states a body remains at rest or in motion unless acted upon by a force, which describes inertia. Newton's second law states that to overcome inertia, a force (F) is required, the result of which is proportionate to the acceleration (a) applied and its mass (m), so F = ma. Newton's third law states that for every action, there is an equal and opposite reaction. For example, when an aircraft is in a bank (a change in direction without a change in speed), the centripetal force is directed toward the center of the aircraft's circular path. Crewmembers, however, experience the opposite force acting on their bodies. This force, called inertial centrifugal force, is directed away from the center of the aircraft's circular path.

4-12. Gravitational force (G-force) and the direction in which the body receives that force are important physiological factors that affect the body during acceleration. G-force can affect the body in three axes: G_x, G_y, and G_z. G_x pushes the body forward or backward. G_y pushes the body left or right. G_z pushes the body up or down.

4-13. The physiological effects of prolonged acceleration depend on the direction of accelerative (centripetal) force and, consequently, how inertial (centrifugal) force acts upon the body. Inertial force is always equal to but opposite of the accelerative force; however, in terms of the physiological effects of sustained acceleration, inertial force is of greater significance. The various G-forces are explained below and illustrated in figure 4-4 (page 4-4):

- Positive G, or $+G_z$, acceleration occurs when the body is accelerated headward. Inertial force acts in the opposite direction toward the feet, and the body is forced down into the cockpit seat.
- Negative G, or $-G_z$, acceleration occurs when the body is accelerated footward. Inertial force is directed toward the head, and the body is lifted out of the cockpit seat.
- Forward transverse G, or $+G_x$, acceleration occurs when accelerative force acts across the body in a chest-to-back direction. This acceleration is experienced during acceleration.
- Backward transverse G, or $-G_x$, acceleration occurs when accelerative force acts across the body in a back-to-chest direction. This acceleration is experienced during deceleration.
- Right- or left-lateral G, or $+/-G_y$, acceleration occurs when accelerative force acts across the body in a shoulder-to-shoulder direction. This acceleration is experienced primarily during sideward flight in rotary-wing aircraft.

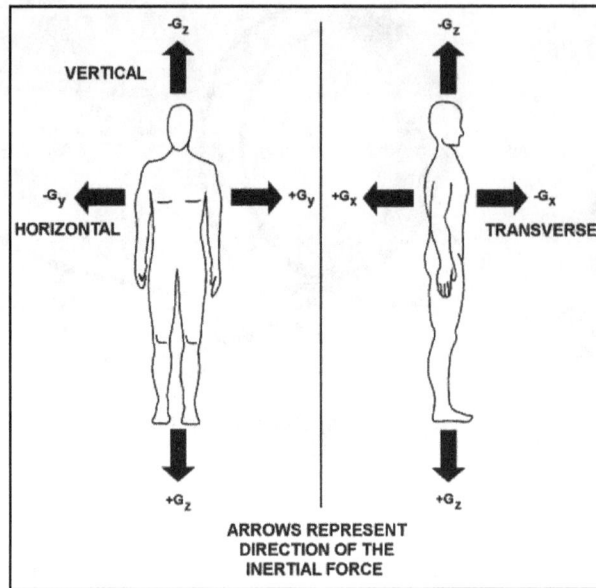

Figure 4-4. Effects of G-force on the body

FACTORS AFFECTING ACCELERATIVE FORCES

4-14. Crewmembers must consider several factors to determine the effects of accelerative forces on the human body. These factors include intensity, duration, rate of onset, body area and site, and impact direction.

INTENSITY

4-15. In general, the greater the intensity, the more severe the effects of accelerative force. Intensity, however, is not the only factor that determines the effects.

DURATION

4-16. The longer force is applied, the more severe the effects. The body can absorb high G-forces applied for extremely short durations without harm, while low G-forces can be tolerated for longer periods. A force of 5 Gs applied for 2 to 3 seconds is usually harmless, but the same force applied for 5 to 6 seconds can cause blackout or unconsciousness. In ejection seats, pilots can tolerate a headward acceleration of 15 Gs for approximately 0.2 second without harm but will become unconscious when the same force is applied for 2 seconds. A force of 40 Gs received intermittently for fractions of a second during a crash landing is tolerable, but the same force is fatal if applied steadily for 2 to 3 seconds.

RATE OF ONSET

4-17. The rate of onset of accelerative or decelerative forces is another factor that determines effects. When an aircraft decelerates gradually, such as in a wheels-up landing, decelerative forces are exerted at a rather slow rate. Generally, when the rate of application is higher, such as when an aircraft decelerates suddenly during an accident, the effects are more severe. When an aircraft impacts vertically, the stopping distance is considerably shorter, and the rate of accelerative force application is many times greater. The application rate is often slowed in helicopter crashes by spreading of the skids and crumpling of the fuselage, giving the body 3 or 4 extra feet in which to decelerate. Therefore, both distance and time are important factors in acceleration or deceleration. The shorter the stopping distance, the greater the G-force.

BODY AREA AND SITE

4-18. The size of the body area over which a given force is applied is important; the greater the body area, the less harmful the effects. The body site to which a force is applied is also important. The accelerative effect of a given force, such as a blow to the head, is much more serious than the same force applied to another body part such as the leg.

IMPACT DIRECTION

4-19. The direction from which a prolonged accelerative force acts on the body also determines the physiological effects that occur. The body tolerates a force applied to the G_x axis better than to the G_z, or long, axis (figure 4-5).

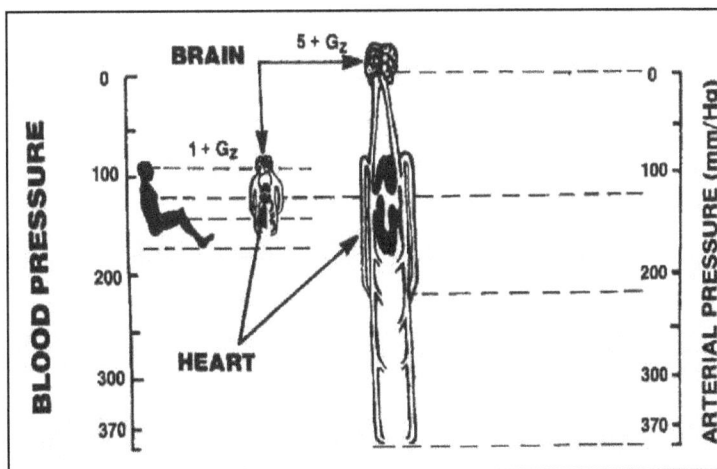

Figure 4-5. Impact direction

PHYSIOLOGICAL EFFECTS OF LOW-MAGNITUDE ACCELERATION

4-20. The physiological effects of low-magnitude acceleration are the result of inertial centrifugal force and increased weight of the body and its components. Low-magnitude acceleration is described as Gs in the range of 1 to 10 with prolonged time of application lasting for at least several seconds. During aircraft maneuvers, the main body part affected by excessive force is the cardiovascular system. The skeleton and soft tissues can withstand such stress without harm. The circulatory system, however, consists of elastic blood vessels and needs well-defined blood pressure and volume to perform properly. Excessive gravitational forces such as those experienced in prolonged acceleration can disrupt normal circulatory function.

PHYSIOLOGICAL EFFECTS OF +G_Z ACCELERATION

4-21. Positive G_z is acceleration in a headward direction, such as the centripetal force experienced in a turn. However, individuals are more aware of centrifugal (inertial) force, which acts in the opposite direction toward the feet. Crewmembers experience $+G_z$ during pullout from a dive or execution of a high, banking turn.

4-22. During a maneuver that produces $+G_z$, body weight increases in direct proportion to the magnitude of the force. For example, a 200-pound person weighs 800 pounds during a 4-G maneuver. Normal activities are greatly curtailed, and the person is pushed downward into the seat. The arms and legs feel heavy, the cheeks sag, and the body becomes incapable of free movement. In fact, a pilot cannot escape unassisted from a spinning aircraft if the magnitude of the force exceeds 2 to 3 $+G_z$. This is the primary reason for the implementation of ejection seats in tactical jet aircraft.

4-23. Internal organs are pulled downward during $+G_z$ maneuvers. The increased weight of the internal organs pulls the diaphragm downward, increases relaxed thoracic volume, and disturbs the mechanics of respiration.

4-24. Comparing the body to a long cylinder helps explain the effects of a $+G_z$ maneuver on arterial blood pressure. In a seated individual, the heart lies approximately at the junction of the upper and middle thirds of the cylinder. The head and brain (the structures most sensitive to decreased blood pressure) are at the upper end of this vertical cylinder, about 30 centimeters from the heart. When a force of 5 $+G_z$ is exerted on the body, a standing blood column of 30 centimeters exerts a pressure of 120 mm/Hg upon its base. Because this pressure is equal to the normal arterial systolic blood pressure, it exactly balances out the arterial pressure and causes the brain's blood perfusion to cease. Unconsciousness can result when a force of 5 $+G_z$ is applied to the body. Figure 4-6 shows the effects of 1 $+G_z$ to 5 $+G_z$ conditions.

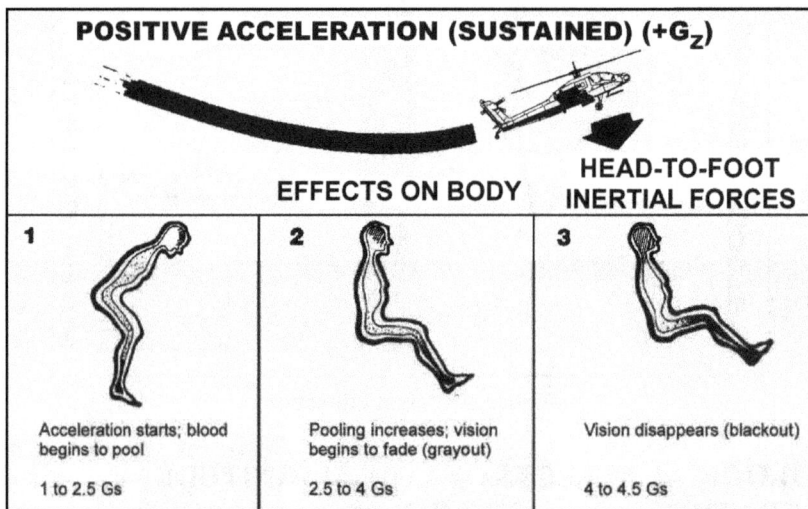

Figure 4-6. Physiological effects of $+G_z$ acceleration

4-25. At about 4 $+G_z$—the point at which vision is completely lost before a loss of consciousness—blackout occurs. Static intraocular pressure is about 20 mm/Hg. When a positive G-force is sufficient to reduce systolic arterial blood pressure in the head to 20 mm/Hg, intraocular pressure causes the collapse of retinal arteries. The retinas cease to function as the blood supply fails, and vision narrows from the periphery. At about 4 to 4.5 G_z, vision disappears and blackout occurs. When the force reaches about 5 $+G_z$, cerebral blood flow stops and unconsciousness ensues. Therefore, the sequence of events following exposure to $+G_z$ is the dimming of vision, blackout, and then unconsciousness.

4-26. The effects described above are usually progressive, as shown in figure 4-6. In relaxed subjects in the human centrifuge, for example, the first symptoms from increased $+G_z$ forces occur at 2.5 to 4 $+G_z$ and involve a graying or dimming of visual fields. At slightly higher accelerations (4 to 4.5 $+G_z$), blackout occurs and individuals can no longer see although they remain conscious. The retinal arteries have collapsed, but some blood still flows through the brain's blood vessels. At 4.5 to 5 $+G_z$, unconsciousness occurs.

4-27. Blood pools in the lower extremities, and there is a relative loss of blood volume and blood pressure to the brain. Stagnant hypoxia and hypoxic hypoxia, caused by unoxygenated blood from impaired respiration, also occur. Blood oxygen saturation can fall from the normal 98 percent to 85 percent during an exposure of 7 $+G_z$ for 45 seconds.

4-28. With the loss of blood pressure and induced hypoxic state combined, it can take up to 1 minute following the end of acceleration for an individual to recover. After regaining consciousness, the crewmember might still experience a period of disorientation and memory loss for some time.

INDIVIDUAL TOLERANCE FACTORS

4-29. Although G-force tolerance limits are relatively constant from one person to another, certain factors decrease or increase an individual's tolerance to $+G_z$. These factors are classified as decremental and incremental.

Decremental Factors

4-30. Any factor that reduces the body's overall efficiency, especially that of the circulatory system, causes a marked reduction in an individual's tolerance to $+G_z$. Loss of blood volume, varicose veins, and decreased blood pressure (chronic hypotension) can affect the circulatory system. Self-imposed stress such as that caused by alcohol abuse also affects an individual's tolerance to $+G_z$.

Incremental Factors

4-31. The L-1 maneuver is an anti-G straining maneuver (AGSM) that increases a crewmember's G tolerance and offers protection that does not overstress the larynx. In this maneuver, crewmembers maintain a normal upright sitting position, tense the skeletal muscles, and simultaneously attempt to exhale against a closed glottis at 2- to 3-second intervals. Although the L-1 maneuver was developed by the U.S. Air Force for its fighter pilots, rotary-wing crewmembers experiencing grayout conditions also will benefit from this maneuver.

PHYSIOLOGICAL EFFECTS OF $-G_Z$ ACCELERATION

4-32. When accelerative force acts on the body in a direction toward the feet (as would be experienced in a rapid descent), $-G_z$ occurs. In this case, the accelerative, or centripetal, force acts toward the axis of the turn. Actually, $-G_z$ does not present a great problem in military flying. Because it is an uncomfortable experience, pilots tend to avoid it.

4-33. Negative acceleration, or the inertial force applied from foot to head, causes a sharp rise in arterial and venous pressures at the head level. Increased pressure within the veins outside the cranial cavity could be sufficient to rupture the thin-walled venues, or small veins. Intracranial venous pressure also rises, but it is counterbalanced by an accompanying rise in intracranial cerebral spinal fluid pressure. Therefore, there is little actual danger of intracranial hemorrhage or cerebral vascular damage as long as the skull remains intact. Hemorrhages within the eye present the primary source of damage from $-G_z$. Distension of the jugular and sinus veins and conjunctiva is caused by $-G_z$.

4-34. Sudden acceleration producing a force of 3 $-G_z$ reaches the limit of human tolerance. When such a force is applied, venous pressure of 100 mm/Hg develops and causes small conjunctival bleeding and marked discomfort in the head region.

4-35. Redout might be experienced during a $-G_z$ maneuver (figure 4-7, page 4-8). This phenomenon occurs when gravitational pull acts on a lower eyelid, causing it to cover the cornea. The constant pull of gravity tends to weaken the lower eyelid muscles.

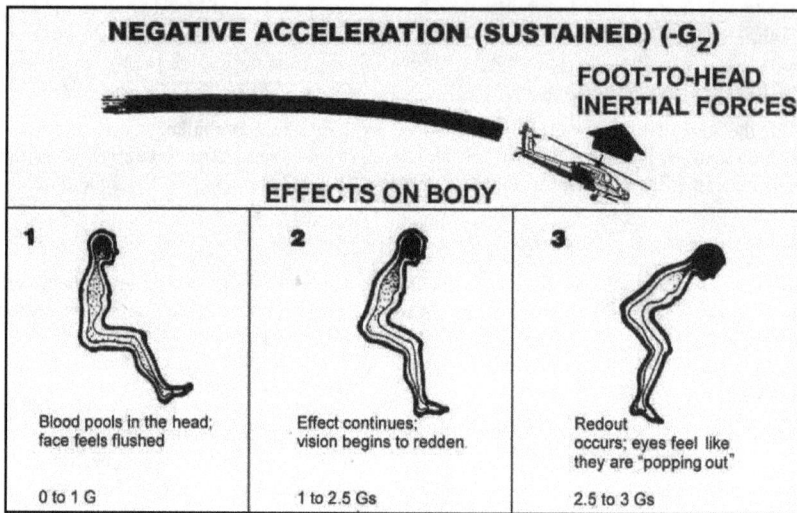

Figure 4-7. Physiological effects of –G$_z$ acceleration

4-36. If sufficiently prolonged, gravitational pull in the foot-to-head direction leads to eventual circulatory distress. Blood pools in the head and neck regions, which results in the passage of fluid from the blood to the head and neck tissues. In addition, the return of blood to the heart becomes inadequate due to the loss of effective blood volume. Therefore, blood stagnates in the head and neck. The cerebral-arterial and venous pressure differential is inadequate to sustain consciousness.

PHYSIOLOGICAL EFFECTS OF +/–G$_X$ ACCELERATION

4-37. Transverse G occurs when accelerative force impacts across the body at right angles to the long axis. Inertial (centrifugal) force crosses the body in the opposite direction. Crewmembers undergo mild transverse acceleration during takeoffs and landings. The physiological effects of transverse acceleration are important in manned space missions because they are experienced during initial lift-off and reentry.

4-38. Individuals are more tolerant of forces received in the positive or +/–G$_x$ axis than those received in the other axes because transverse G interferes very little with blood flow. Extreme values of transverse G (12 to 15 +/–G) acting for 5 seconds or more can displace organs or shift the heart's position and interfere with respiration.

4-39. At levels above 7 +G$_x$, breathing becomes more difficult because of the effect on chest movement. Some individuals, however, have withstood levels of 20 +G for several seconds with no severe difficulty.

PHYSIOLOGICAL EFFECTS OF +/–G$_Y$ ACCELERATION

4-40. The human body has minimal tolerance to G$_y$ (right- or left-lateral) acceleration. In general, most aircraft do not apply significant lateral accelerative forces; therefore, this type of G-force is of little significance during low-magnitude acceleration.

PHYSIOLOGICAL EFFECTS OF HIGH-MAGNITUDE ACCELERATION AND DECELERATION

4-41. High-magnitude acceleration and deceleration affect aircraft accident survivability. High-magnitude acceleration occurs when acceleration exceeds 10 Gs and lasts for less than 1 second. The effects of high-magnitude acceleration usually are the result of linear acceleration. The terms acceleration and deceleration (negative acceleration) are synonymous when used to describe the forces encountered in aircraft crashes, ejection-seat operations, and parachute-opening shock.

HIGH-MAGNITUDE ACCELERATION

4-42. Adverse effects and injury result from the abruptness and magnitude of forces. Other factors include the body area to which the force is applied and the extent of distortion in shearing, compressing, or stretching body structures. The severity of effects progresses from discomfort, incapacitation, minor injury, and irreversible injury to lethal injury. A thorough examination of the causes of injury and effects on the body is essential to determining survival limits and devising protective and preventive measures.

HIGH-MAGNITUDE DECELERATION

4-43. Several factors cause the adverse effects of high-magnitude decelerative forces. These factors include—

- Degree of acceleration intensity, known as the "peak G."
- Peak G duration and total deceleration time.
- Rate of acceleration application or onset, known as the "jolt." The jolt, expressed in feet per second or Gs per second, is the rate of change of acceleration or the rate of onset of accelerative forces.
- Direction or axis of force application, which determines whether acceleration or deceleration occurs.

CRASH SEQUENCE

4-44. Occupant survival during the crash sequence depends on three criteria. These criteria are crash forces transmitted to the occupants, occupiable living space, and aircraft design features.

Crash Forces

4-45. The intensity of the decelerative force to which the body is subjected is not a single decelerative G. Instead, crash forces produce a series of decelerations at various G loads until all motion is stopped (figure 4-8, page 4-10). These crash forces occur in all three axes (G_x, G_y, and G_z) at the same time (figure 4-9, page 4-10). Tolerance limits to high-magnitude deceleration vary with force duration and direction. The human body is far more vulnerable to injury when exposed to a series of high-G shocks in all three axes and can withstand these forces for only an extremely short time (less than 0.1 second). If this time is exceeded, injury or death occurs.

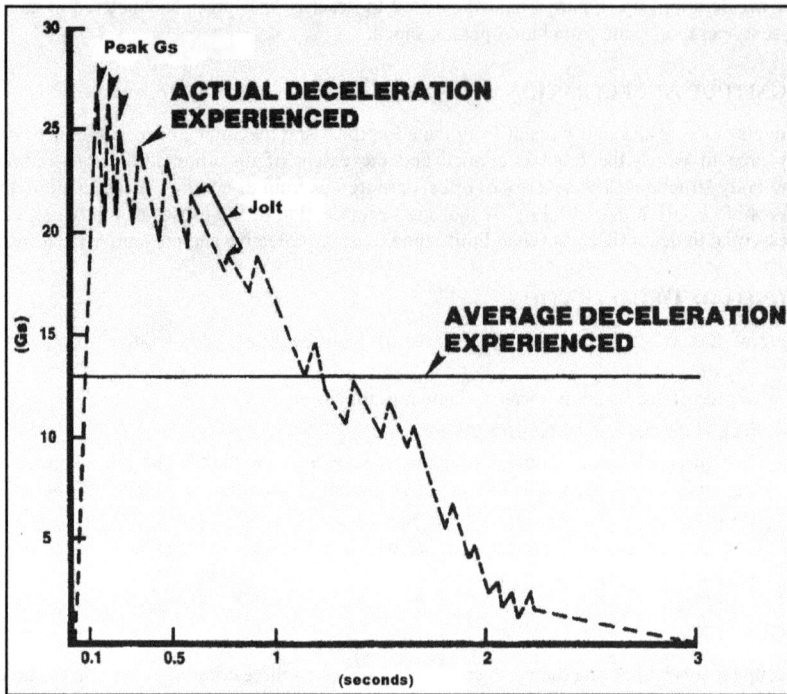

Figure 4-8. Crash force decelerations

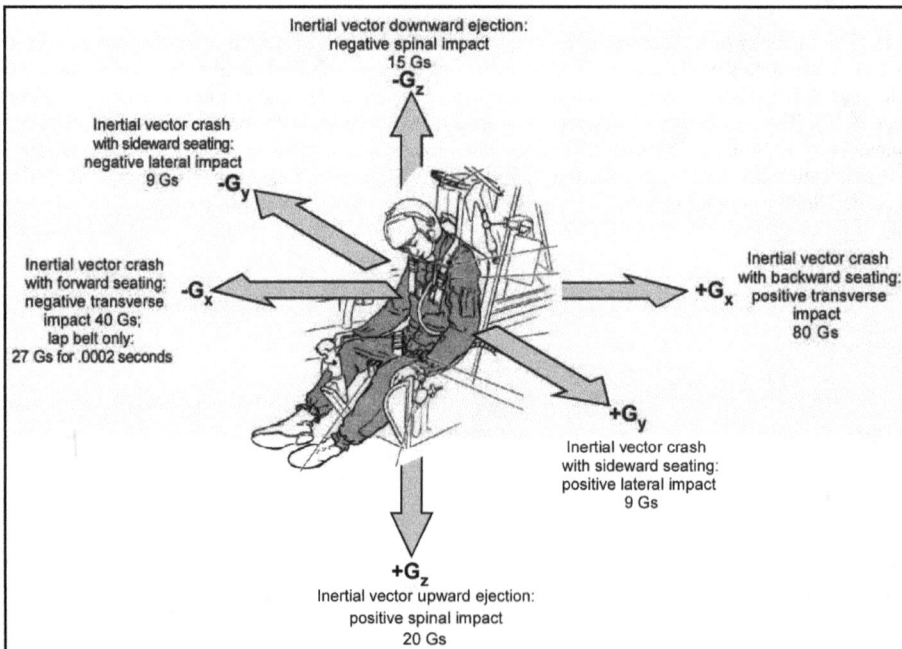

Figure 4-9. Crash forces in G_x, G_y, and G_z axes

Occupiable Living Space

4-46. Occupiable living space influences survivability and must not be compromised by either airframe failure or possible penetration of the cabin area by outside objects. If human tolerance limits to decelerative forces are exceeded or living space is lost, accident survivability decreases significantly. Certain design features can be built into aircraft to absorb crash forces and provide maximum protection to crewmembers during an accident. The UH-60 Black Hawk provides a good example of crashworthy design (figure 4-10).

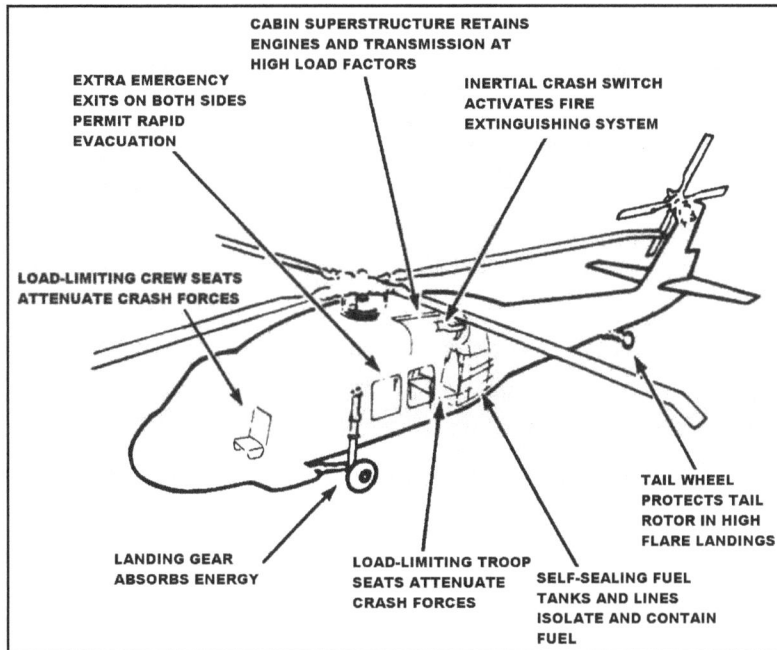

Figure 4-10. UH-60 Black Hawk crashworthy design

Aircraft Design Features

4-47. Design features that promote crash survival are commonly referred to as CREEP factors. These factors include—

- **C—Container.** An aircraft must be designed with an effective protective shell around the occupants. Its maximum structural and component weight should be below the occupants to reduce cabin crushing by inertial loading. The airframe should contain crushable material to attenuate crash forces before they are transmitted to crewmembers. Fuel cells (tanks) should be of crashworthy design and protected by the airframe to prevent outside objects from penetrating them.
- **R—Restraint Systems.** Restraint systems should attenuate crash forces and protect the occupants in all flight conditions. These systems should be comfortable to wear and not interfere with cockpit duties. The head is the most likely point of injury in a crash sequence; therefore, occupants should use shoulder harnesses to minimize upper-body motion. A failure in any part of the restraint system—seat, seat belt, or anchor points—results in a higher degree of exposure to injury.
- **E—Environment.** The cockpit and cabin area must be made less lethal to the occupants, to include adequate equipment restraints for withstanding crash forces.
- **E—Energy Absorption.** With their energy-absorbing features, aircraft are designed to withstand disruptive forces. Some of these features include the aircraft undercarriage, landing

gear, and seats that deform during a crash sequence. These features modify high peak G loads of short duration into more survivable G loads of longer duration.

- **P—Postcrash Protection.** Two major postcrash factors must be considered in aircraft design: fire and evacuation. The crashworthy fuel system has drastically reduced the fire hazard in Army aircraft accidents. However, timely evacuation is still desirable. Timeliness in evacuating aircraft occupants who survive an impact is often governed by the adequacy of emergency exits. Other factors that enhance timely evacuation are convenience of location, ease of operation (the UH-1 cargo door window is a prime example), and adequacy of markings.

PREVENTIVE MEASURES

INCREASE THE AREA TO WHICH FORCE IS APPLIED

4-48. This measure is accomplished through a variety of methods. The HGU-56/P protective helmet distributes pinpoint pressure over a larger area and reduces the chance of head injury. Seat belts with shoulder harnesses distribute decelerative forces over a larger area of the body and help prevent hazardous contact with the cabin environment. Backward seating arrangements also distribute decelerative forces normally found in a crash sequence.

INCREASE THE DISTANCE OVER WHICH DECELERATION OCCURS

4-49. The aircraft's built-in design features can absorb and dissipate much kinetic energy during a crash. These features increase the distance over which deceleration occurs.

ALIGN THE BODY TO TAKE ADVANTAGE OF THE MUSCULOSKELETAL SYSTEM'S STRUCTURAL STRENGTH

4-50. Correct alignment of the body is a preventive measure that can be taken during a crash. Crewmembers can align their bodies to take advantage of the musculoskeletal system's structural strength by properly using seat belts, shoulder harnesses, and the crash position (with the body bent forward) ensures the strongest body parts absorb crash forces.

Chapter 5

Toxic Hazards in Aviation

The effects of toxic chemicals in the aviation environment could lead to human error, which is the leading cause of aviation accidents. The exposure of crewmembers to toxins during flight can range from a sudden, incapacitating event after acute (short-term) exposure to long-term health effects secondary to chronic (long-term) exposure. Aviation personnel must understand the dangers and recognize the often near-imperceptible effects of toxic hazards. The flight surgeon or aeromedical physician assistant educates aircrews in the prevention of toxic exposure and treatment of flight personnel exposed to known toxic substances.

SECTION I – AVIATION TOXICOLOGY PRINCIPLES

5-1. In aviation, the unique toxicological environment is limited primarily to an enclosed environment. Thus, this chapter's focus is on aircraft cockpit exposures. Included, however, are some important issues facing Class III (petroleum, oil, and lubricant) supply personnel.

Contents

ACUTE TOXICITY

5-2. The greatest toxicological risk during flight is an acute, high-dose exposure to a toxic agent. Cabin air quality can change rapidly or insidiously. Air quality changes might be due to the generation of toxic substances from fluid leaks, fire, and/or variations in altitude and ventilation rates.

5-3. Exposure to chemical fumes from burning wire insulation or engine exhaust can degrade a pilot's ability to function. Two types of acute inflight exposure are—

- Sudden, incapacitating exposure.
- Subtle, performance decrement exposure.

5-4. Exposure to toxic chemicals has contributed to some accidents that were erroneously attributed to pilot error. During the most demanding flight modes, the balance between critical flight tasks and human abilities is sometimes delicate and fragile even for well-trained crews. Therefore, any performance decrement caused by toxic substances is a cause for concern.

CHRONIC TOXICITY

5-5. Chronic (long-term) exposure to potentially toxic agents can occur during ground support and aviation operations. Chronic exposure over time can lead to adverse health outcomes many years later. This type of exposure does not cause immediate health effects. The handling of munitions and propellants and storage of fuels and fluids pose special problems.

TIME AND DOSE RELATIONSHIP

5-6. With most substances, the medical effects of exposure depend on chemical concentration and the duration and method of exposure. As concentration increases, the interval between initial exposure and onset of symptoms decreases. The adverse physical effects of many chemicals change as concentration increases. At high concentrations, gases such as nitrogen dioxide, numerous petrochemicals, and other mechanical fluids are highly irritating to the upper respiratory tract, nasal passages, and mucous membranes. At lower concentrations, these chemicals might have little to no effect.

PHYSIOCHEMICAL FACTORS

5-7.   The kidneys and liver are the principal organs that detoxify chemicals within the body. The body attempts to break down toxic and foreign substances into less toxic material it can use, but in some cases a more toxic substance is produced with adverse effects. For example, when ethylene glycol is ingested, the body produces oxalic acid crystals it cannot excrete, causing kidney damage and/or death. Specific organs or tissues selectively absorb chemical substances as they enter the bloodstream. For example, fat-soluble compounds such as carbon tetrachloride and most aviation fuels tend to accumulate in nervous system tissues. Heavy metals from lead-acid batteries tend to produce kidney damage, as these organs are the point of exit from the bloodstream.

ENTRY POINTS

5-8.   Toxic agents enter the body through inhalation into the lungs, ingestion into the stomach, or absorption through the skin. The most common route of entry in the aviation environment is inhalation. Crewmembers often are in close contact with volatile fuels and other potentially hazardous petroleum products, oils, lubricants, and hydraulic fluids. For example, a well-intentioned crew chief might choose to eat while working on the engine deck without realizing the potential danger of ingesting toxins through contaminated food or water. A crewmember, hurried after aircraft refueling, might not wash his or her hands and then smoke a cigarette and inhale hazardous petroleum vapors. Acute toxic exposures are characteristically related to inhalation or ingestion, whereas toxin exposure through skin absorption usually produces symptoms only after chronic, repeated exposures. Contact dermatitis is the most common health effect from skin contact.

PREEXISTING CONDITIONS

5-9.   People with organ impairment (such as liver or lung damage), sickle cell disease, or an active disease process are generally more susceptible to toxic agents.

INDIVIDUAL VARIABILITY

5-10.   Due to individual variability, not everyone responds the same way to toxic exposure. Metabolic rate, fat content, and physical fitness level varies greatly among individuals. In addition, some people have genetic conditions that predispose them to adverse health effects at lower concentrations of toxic substance exposure. Therefore, physical responses to exposure vary considerably. For example, in an environment in which several people are in daily contact with a specific chemical at a low concentration, only one person might exhibit signs or symptoms because of his or her unique genetic characteristics (metabolic rate, retention and excretion rates, and physical fitness level).

ALLOWABLE DEGREE OF BODILY IMPAIRMENT

5-11.   Even a slight degree of inflight impairment is hazardous to crewmember performance of required tasks. The flight surgeon, working with the industrial hygienist, should be aware of chemicals within the flight line area and ensure personnel exposure remains within safe limits.

THRESHOLD LIMIT VALUES

5-12.   Threshold limit values (TLVs) are chemical concentration limits. These values are time-weighted, average concentrations that should produce no apparent adverse effects for the average worker who is routinely exposed 8 hours a day and 40 hours a week for a working lifetime of 40 years. TLVs usually are measured in parts per million for gases and vapors and milligrams per cubic meter for fumes and dusts.

SHORT-TERM EXPOSURE LIMITS

5-13. Short-term exposure limits (STELs) are maximum time-weighted average concentrations of specific chemicals that are allowed for only 15 minutes during the workday. These limits were developed to protect against acute toxicity. STELs should not be reported more than four times daily per person.

CEILING CONCENTRATION

5-14. Ceiling concentration is the maximum allowable concentration of a specific chemical that must never be exceeded during any part of the workday. Even an instantaneous value in excess of the TLV ceiling is prohibited.

BODY DETOXIFICATION

5-15. The human body has varied and intricate chemical defense mechanisms. Upon entry of a toxic substance, the body immediately begins to reduce the substance's concentration through multiple processes. These processes include metabolism (the chemical breakdown of a substance), detoxification, and excretion. The flight surgeon must be familiar with the metabolic pathways of well-known poisons and understand the physical and psychological symptoms of subtle chemical intoxication. For example, the amount of carbon monoxide eliminated by the body during a single exposure decreases by 50 percent every 4 hours.

SECTION II – AIRCRAFT ATMOSPHERE CONTAMINATION

CONTAMINATION OVERVIEW

5-16. Depending on the mission and other circumstances, an aircraft's interior might contain various contaminants that could pose risks to crewmembers. Aircrews and ground crews transporting hazardous cargo should refer to AR 50-5, AR 50-6, AR 95-1, AR 95-27, and TM 38-250. Information concerning chemical, biological, radiological, and nuclear (CBRN) environments is beyond the scope of this field manual but can be found in FM 3-11.5 and TM 3-4240-280-10 (Air Force Joint Manual 44-151 contains more detailed medical information on CBRN environments). Aircraft atmosphere contamination can include—

- Exhaust gases.
- Tetraethyl lead.
- Carbon monoxide.
- Jet propulsion fuels.
- Hydraulic fluid vapors.
- Coolant fluid vapors.
- Engine lubricants.
- Solvents and degreasers.
- Composite materials.
- Fire extinguishing agents (including halogenated hydrocarbons).
- Fluorocarbon plastics and polyurethane.
- Oxygen contamination.

EXHAUST GASES

5-17. The physical relationship of engine positioning to the cockpit is important. Depending on aircraft age and the power plant used (jet or reciprocating), there are a wide range of potential cockpit air contaminants caused by exhaust gases. Single-engine, piston-type aircraft with the engine located directly in front of the fuselage are subject to greater contamination than multiengine aircraft with lateral engines. Reciprocating engines uniformly produce much more carbon monoxide than modern jet engines. Liquid-cooled, single-engine airplanes are less likely to be contaminated by exhaust gases than air-cooled, radial-engine airplanes.

CARBON MONOXIDE

5-18. The effects of carbon monoxide are subtle but deadly. Carbon monoxide, a product of incomplete fuel combustion, is the most common gaseous poison found in the aviation environment. An engine that yields complete combustion produces only carbon dioxide. As the fuel-to-air ratio decreases and complete combustion increases, the percentage of carbon dioxide in exhaust gas rises while the percentage of carbon monoxide declines. Conversely, as the mixture becomes richer (increasing the fuel-to-air ratio), the percentage of carbon monoxide in exhaust gas increases. Carbon monoxide is a colorless, odorless gas slightly lighter than air and should be suspected whenever exhaust odors are detected.

5-19. Carbon monoxide is the most common cause of both intentional and unintentional poisoning in the United States. More deaths have been attributed to carbon monoxide than any other toxic gas. Carbon monoxide acts as a tissue asphyxiant that produces hypoxia at both sea level and altitude. It preferentially combines with hemoglobin to the partial exclusion of oxygen and thus interferes with blood's oxygen uptake. Carbon monoxide greatly reduces hemoglobin's oxygen-carrying capacity; it combines with hemoglobin to produce CoHb, creating a bind 256 times stronger than that of oxygen. The carbon monoxide concentration in blood is based on a variety of factors, including gas concentration, respiratory rate, hemoglobin-carbon monoxide saturation, and exposure duration. Table 5-1 shows the body's physiological responses to various concentrations of carbon monoxide.

Table 5-1. Physiological responses to various carbon monoxide concentrations

Carbon monoxide concentration in air (ppm*)	CoHb saturation in blood (%)	Exposure time	Symptoms
0-50			No appreciable effect
0-100	0-17		No significant effects except possible headache and flushing of skin
200-300	23-30	5-6 hours	Weakness, headache, dizziness, loss of visual acuity, nausea, and vomiting
400-600	36-44	4-5 hours	Same as above, with lack of muscular coordination
700-1,000	47-53	3-4 hours	Same as above, with increased pulse and respiration
1,100-1,500	55-60	1.5-3 hours	Coma
1,600-2,000	61-64	0.5-1 hour	Depressed heart rate and respiration
5,000-10,000	73-76	2-15 minutes	Death
*ppm = parts per million			

5-20. A relatively low concentration of carbon monoxide in the air can, in time, produce high blood concentrations of carbon monoxide. For example, a resting person who inhales air with a 0.5-percent carbon monoxide concentration for 30 minutes will have a 45-percent blood saturation. As noted in Table 5-1, this saturation is sufficient to produce a near-coma condition.

5-21. Reduced oxygen concentration in the air and increased temperature or humidity can increase the concentration of carbon monoxide-bound hemoglobin. Any of these changes or an increase in physical activity can accelerate carbon monoxide's toxic effects.

5-22. The effects of carbon monoxide on the human body vary. Symptoms of carbon monoxide intoxication include—

- Tremors.
- Headache.
- Weakness.
- Joint pain.
- Hoarseness.
- Nervousness.
- Muscular cramps.
- Muscular twitching.
- Loss of visual acuity.
- Speech and hearing impairment.
- Mental confusion and disorientation.

5-23. The symptoms of carbon monoxide poisoning are the same as those of hypemic hypoxia. Of particular importance to aviators is the loss of visual acuity. Peripheral vision and, more importantly, night vision is significantly decreased, even with blood carbon monoxide saturation as low as 10 percent.

5-24. The dangers of carbon monoxide rise sharply with increasing altitude. When experienced separately, a mild degree of hypoxic hypoxia (caused by increased altitude and decreased partial pressures of oxygen) or exposure to small amounts of carbon monoxide can be harmless. When experienced simultaneously, however, their effects become additive. These cumulative effects can cause serious pilot impairment and result in loss of aircraft control.

5-25. For practical purposes, the elimination rate of carbon monoxide depends on respiratory volume and the percentage of oxygen in inspired (inhaled) air. Smoking one to three cigarettes in rapid succession or one and one-half packs per day can raise an individual's carbon monoxide hemoglobin saturation to 10 percent. At sea level, it can take a full day to eliminate that small percentage of carbon monoxide because carbon monoxide gas is reduced by a factor of only 50 percent about every 4 hours.

5-26. When flight personnel suspect the presence of carbon monoxide in their aircraft, they should turn off all exhaust heaters, inhale 100-percent oxygen if available, and land as soon as practical. After landing, they can investigate the source and evaluate their own possible symptoms of carbon monoxide intoxication.

AVIATION GASOLINE

5-27. Aviation gasoline, a mixture of hydrocarbons and additives such as tetraethyl lead and xylene, is used only as an emergency fuel. A gallon of evaporated aviation gasoline will form about 30 cubic feet of vapors at sea level. Personnel exposed to these vapors might suffer adverse physical or psychological reactions.

5-28. Aviation gasoline vapors, which are heavier than air, are readily absorbed in the respiratory system and can produce symptoms in exposed personnel after only a few minutes. Unconsciousness can occur if vapors equal to one-tenth of the concentration that could cause combustion or explosion are inhaled for more than a short time. The maximum safe concentration for exposure to ordinary fuel vapors is about 500 ppm, or 0.05 percent. However, aviation gasoline vapors are at least twice as toxic as ordinary fuel vapors. Symptoms of exposure to aviation gasoline vapors include—

- Burning and tearing of the eyes.
- Restlessness.
- Excitement.
- Disorientation.
- Speech, vision, or hearing disorders.
- Convulsions.
- Coma.
- Death.

TETRAETHYL LEAD IN AVIATION GASOLINE

5-29. Tetraethyl lead, an antiknock substance, is highly toxic. Poisoning can occur through both skin absorption and vapor inhalation. Tetraethyl lead poisoning primarily affects the central nervous system. Symptoms include insomnia, mental irritability, and instability. In less dramatic cases, sleep interruption with restlessness and terrifying dreams can occur. Other symptoms include nausea, vomiting, muscle pain and weakness, tremors, and visual difficulty. The amount of tetraethyl lead in aviation gasoline is so small (only about 4.6 cubic centimeters per gallon, or about one teaspoon) that encountering a lead hazard through normal handling is remote. However, poisoning has resulted from personnel entering fuel storage tanks containing concentrated amounts of tetraethyl lead within accumulated sludge. Maintenance personnel who work (welding, buffing, or grinding) on engines that have burned leaded gasoline are at risk of significant exposure to lead compounds.

JET PROPULSION FUELS

5-30. Jet propulsion fuel, type 4 (JP-4); jet propulsion fuel, type 5 (JP-5); and jet propulsion fuel, type 8 (JP-8) are mixtures of hydrocarbons that produce different grades of kerosene. Each JP fuel has a specific vapor pressure and flashpoint. JP fuels do not contain tetraethyl lead. The recommended threshold limit for JP fuel vapors is 500 parts per million. However, toxic symptoms can occur below explosive levels, so JP fuel intoxication is possible even in the absence of a fire hazard. Excessive inhalation of JP fuels degrades central nervous system function and poses an irritant hazard to skin and mucous membranes. JP fuels can produce narcotic effects in high enough concentrations.

HYDRAULIC FLUID

5-31. Hydraulic fluid can be based in petroleum, castor oil, silicon, or phosphate ester. A leak from a hydraulic hose or gauge under pressure up to 1,200 pounds per square inch can produce a finely divided aerosol that diffuses quickly throughout the cockpit. Large leaks can cause liquid to accumulate on the floor. In either case, a high level of aerosolized hydraulic fluid can develop quickly in cockpit air. Like other hydrocarbons, hydraulic fluid can be toxic when inhaled. For example, phosphate ester-based hydraulic fluid has effects identical to military nerve agents known as organ ophosphoesterase inhibitors. Increasing temperature or altitude can aggravate the toxic effects of inhaled aerosolized hydraulic fluid. These effects include—

- Irritation of the eyes and respiratory tract.
- Headache.
- Vertigo.
- Nerve dysfunction in the limbs.
- Impairment of judgment and vision.

COOLANT FLUID

5-32. The coolant fluid used in liquid-cooled engines consists of ethylene glycol diluted with water. Ethylene glycol is toxic when ingested. Although volatile, its vapors rarely exert any significant acute toxic effects when inhaled. Respiratory passages can become moderately irritated, however, with continued exposure to ethylene glycol vapors.

5-33. Ruptured coolant lines frequently produce smoke in the cockpit resulting from either engine overheating or leaking fluid. Cockpit smoke is always a concern for pilots—some have abandoned their aircraft because of coolant line leaks. Pure ethylene glycol has a flash point of 177 degrees Fahrenheit; however, the fire hazard from leaking coolant is not especially great because its ethylene glycol content has been diluted with water.

ENGINE LUBRICANTS

5-34. Oil hose connections in aircraft consist of various types of adjustable clamps rather than the pressure-type connections used in the hydraulic system. Hose clamps occasionally break or loosen. When oil escapes onto hot engine parts, smoke often forms and enters the cockpit. Inhaling hot oil fumes causes symptoms similar to those of carbon monoxide poisoning:

- Headache.
- Nausea.
- Vomiting.
- Irritation of the eyes and upper respiratory passages.

SOLVENTS AND DEGREASERS

5-35. Solvents and degreasers are organic bases used to dissolve other petroleum products. Organic solvents irritate the skin (causing contact dermatitis), and they all produce nervous system effects similar to those of general surgery anesthesia. Common solvents and degreasers present in the aviation environment include toluene isocyanates (found in paints, foams, and adhesives) and methyl ethyl ketone, which is specified for use in aviation maintenance manuals.

COMPOSITE MATERIALS

5-36. Composite materials are used in many Army airframes due to their strength, thermal resistance, and light weight. These composite materials are composed of fibers and resins.

5-37. Fibers include carbon graphite, boron, Kevlar, and fiberglass, which generally are safe as long as they remain intact. Disruption of the fiber matrix occurs with grinding, scraping, sanding, reworking, or burning and during a crash. These disruptions create an inhalation hazard. Particles smaller than 3.5 microns long are more likely to become lodged in the lungs and produce lung disease similar to that caused by asbestos.

5-38. Resins are bonding agents that provide insulation and the physically resistant properties of composites. Epoxy is an example of a resin. The primary hazard posed by resin vapors is inhalation during the curing process. Resins can cause asthma, skin irritation, and nervous system effects.

FIRE EXTINGUISHING AGENTS

5-39. Fire extinguishing agents pose a toxic threat to aircrews fighting fires, especially within enclosed cabins or cockpits. Crewmembers can be exposed to these agents while using portable extinguishers or to gaseous agents in the ventilation system following the discharge of automatic or semiautomatic fire extinguishing systems aboard the aircraft. Ground support personnel are at risk as well, but to a lesser extent because of their nonenclosed environmental conditions. The three chemical classes of fire extinguishing agents in current use are—

- Halogenated hydrocarbons.
- Carbon dioxide.
- Aqueous film forming foam.

HALOGENATED HYDROCARBONS

5-40. The halogenated hydrocarbon group is composed of carbon tetrachloride, chlorobromomethane, dibromodifluoromethane, and bromotrifluoromethane. Because of their toxicity, these halogenated hydrocarbons are no longer used to fight fires. Currently, Halon is the halogenated hydrocarbon most commonly used as a fire extinguishing agent.

5-41. Frequently found on the flight line, Halon is also used in automatic fire suppression systems designed for large electrical and computer areas. It offers excellent fire suppression properties without chemical residuals and is relatively nontoxic to personnel, except when discharged extensively in an enclosed space. Within a confined area, Halon acts as a simple asphyxiant, displacing oxygen from the room upon release. In addition, the discharge of Halon from a compressed state can generate impulse noise levels greater than 160 decibels. Because of its strong tendency to deplete the atmospheric ozone layer, Halon is being removed from all areas except those deemed mission essential. Under extremely high temperatures, Halon can decompose into other, more toxic gases such as hydrogen fluorine, hydrogen chloride, hydrogen bromide, and phosgene analogues.

5-42. Phosgene (a thermal byproduct of Halon) and carbon tetrachloride significantly irritate the lower respiratory tract. Exposure to sublethal concentrations of phosgene can permanently damage the respiratory system.

CARBON DIOXIDE

5-43. Large quantities of carbon dioxide are required to extinguish a fire; therefore, it can be hazardous when used as a fire extinguishing agent. At low concentrations, carbon dioxide acts as a respiratory stimulant. Inhaling a 2- to 3-percent concentration results in discomfort and shortness of breath and is tolerable for approximately 20 to 25 minutes. A person can tolerate a concentration of up to 5 percent for 10 minutes. A concentration above 20 percent can cause unconsciousness within several minutes.

5-44. Initial acute exposure of less than 2 percent carbon dioxide can result in excitement or increases in heart rate, blood pressure, and breathing rate and depth. These effects are followed by—

- Drowsiness.
- Headache.
- Increasing difficulty in respiration.
- Vertigo.
- Indigestion.
- Muscle weakness.
- Lack of coordination.
- Poor judgment.

5-45. At concentrations of 10 percent or above, crewmembers can experience mental degradation, collapse, and death. If the concentration increases slowly, symptoms appear more slowly and have less effect because the body's defenses have time to act. Although the individual is aware of the changes occurring, he or she might be unable to assess the situation and take corrective action.

5-46. Carbon dioxide is heavier than air and accumulates in lower areas of enclosed spaces, causing normal air to become diluted and allowing the carbon dioxide to act as a simple asphyxiant. Because of this risk, crewmembers must be familiar with the hazards and symptoms of carbon dioxide poisoning. The cabin area must be ventilated quickly when initial symptoms are detected, and the crew should use 100-percent oxygen if available.

AQUEOUS FILM FORMING FOAM

5-47. Aqueous film forming foam is a protein-based material used to physically separate a flammable liquid (for example, fuel) from its oxygen source. Even if ingested it is essentially nontoxic, but the foam produces irritation in the eyes and skin similar to that caused by household soaps.

FLUOROCARBON PLASTICS AND POLYURETHANE

5-48. Fluorocarbon plastics are used in all aircraft as corrosion-resistant coatings and insulation for radio wires and other electronic equipment. Polyurethane is used in cockpit and cabin interiors. These materials are chemically inert at ordinary temperatures but decompose at high temperatures and pose a problem in aircraft only when a fire occurs. At about 662 degrees Fahrenheit, these materials release fluorine gas, which then reacts with moisture to form hydrogen fluoride, a highly corrosive acid. Above 700 degrees Fahrenheit, a small quantity of highly toxic perfluoroisobutylene is released. Phosgene and cyanide also are produced through thermal decomposition. Rapid, uncontrolled burning of fluorocarbon plastics yields more toxic products than controlled thermal decomposition. If an aircraft fire occurs, crewmembers must wear oxygen masks (if available) to protect themselves against fumes from fluorocarbon plastics. These agents are very irritating to the eyes, nose, and respiratory tract.

OXYGEN CONTAMINATION

5-49. Perceived oxygen contamination can affect the performance of aircrews that routinely fly high-altitude profiles. Aviators often report objectionable odors in breathing systems using compressed gaseous oxygen. These odors, while not present in toxic concentrations, can produce nausea and vomiting. However, some odors are neither offensive nor disagreeable, as indicated by such descriptive terms as stale, sweet, cool, and fresh. In situations other than accidental or gross contamination, oxygen analysis has indicated the presence of small amounts of a number of contaminants. These contaminants include water vapor, methane, carbon dioxide, acetylene, ethylene, nitrous oxide, traces of hydrocarbons, and other unidentified substances. Odors also have been attributed to trichlorethylene, a solvent that previously was used to clean oxygen tank cylinders. Either singly or in combination, these contaminants seem to never reach concentrations toxic to humans, although distinctive symptoms such as headache, nausea, vomiting, and disorientation have been reported. However, the problem with perceived oxygen contamination is most often psychological rather than physiological. Aviators might become more concerned and apprehensive during flight about their oxygen source. This preoccupation can lead to stress-induced hyperventilation or loss of situational awareness. If pilots are concerned about this issue, they should land as soon as practical and evaluate their oxygen equipment.

This page intentionally left blank.

Chapter 6

Effects of Temperature Extremes on the Human Body

Body temperature must be maintained within narrow limits, usually between 94 and 100 degrees Fahrenheit. However, heat injuries and hypothermia can occur within much narrower limits. Extreme temperatures can have a devastating effect on the body's ability to control its temperature. Exposure to temperature extremes in the aviation environment impairs aircrew efficiency and intensifies other stresses such as hypoxia and fatigue. Extreme climates can cause uncomfortable or unbearable cockpit conditions, as can atmospheric temperature or altitude changes. Interior aircraft ventilation and heating and protective equipment also can create temperature extremes. This chapter briefly covers aviation operations in extreme climates.

SECTION I – HEAT IN THE AVIATION ENVIRONMENT

6-1. Army aviation operations generally take place at low altitudes associated with extremely high temperatures and humidity. Heat can seriously hamper mission requirements and hinder accomplishment of complex tasks. Army aircraft construction and unit locations increase the potential for heat stress problems.

Contents

RADIANT HEAT

6-2. Solar radiant heat is the primary heat stress problem in aircraft. Large expanses of glass or Plexiglas™ produce a greenhouse effect caused by conflicting transmission characteristics for radiation of differing wavelengths, trapping thermal energy within the cockpit. The cockpit temperature of aircraft parked on airfield ramps can be 50 to 60 degrees Fahrenheit higher than those parked in hangars due to the radiation of solar heat through transparent surfaces. This radiation heats objects within the cockpit, which then reradiate the waves at frequencies that cannot penetrate the glass or Plexiglas™. Therefore, heat accumulates within the cockpit and becomes a significant stress factor at altitudes below 10,000 feet.

KINETIC HEAT

6-3. During flight, the aircraft structure is heated by friction between its surface and the air and by the rise in temperature caused by air compression at the aircraft's front. Cockpit insulation and cabin air ductwork can reduce effects of kinetic heating.

ELECTRICAL HEAT LOADS AND COOLING SYSTEMS

6-4. The electrical heat load in cockpits is increasing as new high-performance aircraft are developed and fitted with additional improved avionics equipment. The possibility of degraded performance increases with escalations in cockpit temperature.

6-5. Comfortable limits in the cockpit are between 68 to 72 degrees Fahrenheit and 25 to 50 percent relative humidity. To maintain this temperature and humidity range, aircraft must have extra heating and cooling equipment installed, which is expensive in both cost and performance. In general, 1 pound of extra load on an aircraft requires 9 pounds of structure and fuel to fly it.

HEAT TRANSFER

TEMPERATURE REGULATION

6-6. The body maintains its heat balance with several mechanisms. These mechanisms are radiation, conduction, convection, and evaporation.

Radiation

6-7. Radiation involves the transfer of heat from an object of intense temperature to an object of lower temperature through space by radiant energy. The rate of heat transfer depends primarily on the difference between the objects' temperatures. If body temperature is higher than the temperature of surrounding objects, more heat radiates away from the body than is radiated to it.

Conduction

6-8. Conduction is the transfer of heat between objects, in contact at different temperatures, from heated molecules of the body to cooler molecules of adjacent objects. The objects' proximity determines the overall rate of conduction.

Convection

6-9. Convection is the transfer of heat from the body in liquids or gases where molecules are free to move. During body heat loss, air molecules move as the body heats surrounding air; the heated air expands and rises as it is displaced by denser, cooler air. Respiration, which contributes to body temperature regulation, is a type of convection.

Evaporation

6-10. Evaporative heat loss involves the transformation of a substance from a liquid state (such as sweat) to a gaseous state. Heat is lost when water on the body surface evaporates. Evaporation is the most common and generally the most easily explained form of heat loss.

Limitations

6-11. Radiation, convection, and conduction all suffer one major disadvantage in cooling the body: they become less effective as temperature increases. When the temperature of air and nearby objects exceeds skin temperature, the body gains heat. This gain can be dangerous for aviators.

6-12. When ambient temperature increases to about 82 to 84 degrees Fahrenheit, sweat production increases abruptly to offset the loss of body cooling through radiation, convection, and conduction. At 95 degrees Fahrenheit, sweat evaporation accounts for nearly all heat loss.

6-13. Many factors affect the evaporation process. These factors include—
- Protective clothing.
- Availability of drinking water.
- Relative humidity above 50 percent.
- Environmental temperature above 82 degrees Fahrenheit.

6-14. Relative humidity is the factor that most limits evaporation. At relative humidity of 100 percent, no heat is lost through evaporation. Although the body continues to sweat, it loses only a tiny amount of heat. For example, a person can function all day at a temperature of 115 degrees Fahrenheit with relative humidity of 10 percent if given enough water and salt. If relative humidity rises to 80 percent at the same temperature, that person might be incapacitated within 30 minutes.

HEAT INJURY

6-15. The body undergoes certain physiological changes to counteract heat stress. Cutaneous circulation, or blood flow to the skin, increases tremendously to draw heat from the body's inner core to the surface, where it can be lost to ambient air. Blood flow to other organs such as the kidneys and liver is reduced, and heart rate is increased so the body can maintain adequate blood pressure. As temperature increases, receptors in the skin, brain, and neuromuscular system are stimulated to increase sweat production. Heavy sweating produces 1 pint to 1 quart of sweat per hour; however, heat stress can result in 3 to 4 quarts being produced. If a person does not replace this sweat by drinking liquids, the body rapidly dehydrates, sweat production drops, and body temperature increases, causing further heat injury.

6-16. Individuals vary in their responses to heat stress. Factors that influence physiological responses include the amount of work performed, physical condition, and ability to adapt to the environment. Other factors that might predispose a Soldier to heat injury include—

- Exposure to 2 or 3 days of—
  - Sleep loss.
  - Increased exertion levels.
  - Increased heat exposure.
- Poor fitness.
- Overweight.
- Minor illness (such as cold symptoms).
- Taking prescribed or over-the-counter medications, supplements, or dietary aids.
- Use of alcohol within the last 24 hours.
- Prior history of heat illness (any heat stroke or more than two episodes of heat exhaustion).
- Skin disorders (such as rash or sunburn).
- Age (greater than 40 years).

6-17. Heat injuries, which range from marginal to critical-catastrophic, include—

- Sunburn: red, hot skin that might blister; victim might experience moderate to severe pain and/or fever.
- Heat rash (prickly heat): red, itchy skin that might be bumpy due to blocked pores.
- Heat cramps: painful skeletal muscle cramps or spasms that primarily affect the legs and arms.
- Heat exhaustion: dizziness, headache, nausea, unsteady walk, weakness, fatigue, rapid pulse, and shortness of breath; heat exhaustion is the most common exertional heat illness.
- Heat stroke: same symptoms as heat exhaustion but more severe; elevated temperature, usually above 104 degrees Fahrenheit; altered mental status with confusion, agitation, delirium, and disorientation; nausea and vomiting; can progress to loss of consciousness, coma, and seizures; heat stroke is a medical emergency that can cause death.

6-18. Additional medical considerations in a hot weather environment are—

- Dehydration.
- Over hydration (hyponatremia).

6-19. Additional information on treating and preventing hot weather injuries can be found in Technical Bulletin (Medical) (TB MED) 507.

PERFORMANCE IMPAIRMENT

6-20. Heat stress causes general physiological changes but also results in performance impairment. Even a slight increase in body temperature impairs an individual's ability to perform complex tasks such as those required to fly an aircraft safely. A body temperature of 101 degrees Fahrenheit roughly doubles an aviator's error rate. Increases in body temperature generally have the following effects on an aviator:

- Error rates increase.
- Short-term memory becomes less reliable.

- Perceptual and motor skills slow.
- The capacity to perform aviation tasks decreases.
- Reaction and decision times slow.
- The conduct of routine tasks slows.
- Errors of omission are more common.
- Vigilant task performance degrades slightly after 30 minutes and markedly after 2 to 3 hours.

HEAT STRESS PREVENTION

6-21. Personnel can take preventive measures to avoid heat stress. They can reduce workload, replace water and salt loss, acclimate properly, and wear protective clothing.

REPLACE WATER AND SALT LOSS

6-22. The human body cannot adjust to decreased water intake. Daily water requirements depend on the environment, heat stress, activity level, and duration of exposure. Soldiers must replace water lost through sweating to avoid heat injury. The body normally absorbs water at a rate of 1.2 to 1.5 quarts per hour. Fluid intake should not exceed 1.5 quarts per hour or 12 quarts per day. Conducting activities in the cool early morning or evening hours can minimize water loss.

6-23. Salt loss is high in personnel who either have not acclimated or have acclimated but are subject to strenuous activity under heat stress. Replenishing lost salt is important. Eating all meals (including field rations and meals, ready to eat with salt packet) usually provides the body's salt requirement. Soldiers should not use salt tablets; if larger amounts of salt are required, they should consult their flight surgeon.

ACCLIMATE

6-24. Heat acclimation greatly enhances a Soldier's resistance to heat injury and improves physical work capabilities. A minimum of 2 weeks should be allowed for healthy individuals to acclimate, with progressive increases in heat exposure and physical exertion. Individuals who are less physically fit might require more time to fully acclimate. Significant heat acclimation can be attained in 3 to 5 days. Full heat acclimation takes up to 14 days with 2 to 3 hours per day of carefully supervised exercise in the heat.

WEAR PROTECTIVE CLOTHING

6-25. In direct sunlight, an individual should wear loose clothing to allow adequate ventilation and evaporative cooling. In a hot environment, clothing protects an individual from solar radiation but reduces the loss of body heat from convection and conduction. Dark clothing absorbs radiant heat while light clothing reflects it. Individuals should wear headgear to reduce heat load to the head.

INFLIGHT HEAT STRESS REDUCTION

6-26. Army aviation crewmembers are required to work in hot cockpits. Their ability to handle a particular situation depends on the specific aircraft and problem. If crewmembers will be exposed to heat for an extended period, the only alternative might be to terminate the mission to prevent incapacitation (mission termination should be treated as a last resort, however). Crewmembers can minimize inflight heat stress by increasing ventilation and continually replacing fluids.

INCREASE VENTILATION

6-27. More than any other crewmember, the pilot must guard against heat stress. When speed and altitude permit, the pilot should open a window or canopy and direct cool air onto the head and neck to reduce heat buildup.

CONTINUALLY REPLACE FLUIDS

6-28. Fluid intake during flight helps prevent dehydration and makes up for profuse sweating. Crewmembers should be encouraged to drink fluids as conditions permit, especially in anticipation of physical exertion.

SECTION II – COLD IN THE AVIATION ENVIRONMENT

6-29. Although heat stress causes the most significant problems for crewmembers, cold weather also adversely affects the body. Aircrews must understand how the body reacts to cold temperature extremes.

COLD INJURY

6-30. Many factors influence the incidence of cold injury. If troops are in a static defensive position, the incidence of injury drops as they have time to take care of their bodies. Factors that can increase an individual's susceptibility to cold injury include—

- Previous cold injury or other significant injuries.
- Use of tobacco, nicotine, or alcohol.
- Skipping meals or poor nutrition.
- Low activity.
- Fatigue and sleep deprivation.
- Little experience or training in cold weather.
- Previous cold casualty.
- Over-motivation.

6-31. Cold weather injuries include—

- Chilblain: acutely red, swollen, hot, tender skin, usually accompanied by itching.
- Immersion foot (trench foot): cold, numb feet that might progress to hot with shooting pains; victim might also experience swelling, redness, and bleeding; Soldiers with suspected immersion foot should seek medical attention immediately.
- Frostbite, which can be superficial or deep:
    - Superficial: involves only the skin, which usually appears pale, yellowish, and waxy-looking (grayish in dark-skinned Soldiers); the skin's surface feels very stiff or hard, but underlying tissue is soft.
    - Deep: extends beyond the first layer of skin and can include the bone; discoloration is the same as superficial frostbite but underlying tissue is hard; large areas might appear purple; deep frostbite is a medical emergency that requires immediate evacuation to a medical facility.
- Hypothermia: shivering might or might not be present; victim might exhibit drowsiness, mental slowness, or lack of coordination, which can progress to unconsciousness, irregular heartbeat, and death; hypothermia is the most serious cold injury and victims must be evacuated immediately.
- Snow blindness: a temporary condition that results in pain, redness, or a watery or gritty feeling in the eyes.

6-32. First aid for cold injuries depends on the injury. In frostbite, a superficial cold injury can be adequately treated by warming the affected part with body heat. This warming can be done by covering cheeks with hands, placing hands under armpits, or placing feet under a buddy's clothing next to the abdomen. The injured part should not be massaged, exposed to a fire or stove, rubbed with snow, slapped, chafed, or soaked in cold water. Individuals should avoid walking when they have cold-injured feet. Deep frostbite is very serious and requires more aggressive first aid to avoid or minimize the loss of parts of fingers, toes, hands, or feet. The sequence for treating cold injuries depends on whether the condition is life threatening; the priority is to remove injured Soldiers from the cold. More information on treating and preventing cold weather injuries can be found in TB MED 508.

COLD INJURY PREVENTION

6-33. Some general measures can be taken to prevent all types of cold injury. Individuals can—

- Keep their body dry.
- Limit exposure to the cold.
- Avoid wearing wet clothing.
- Monitor the wind chill factor.
- Keep activity below the perspiration level.
- Avoid direct contact of bare skin and cold metal.
- Use the buddy system to check for early signs of cold injury.
- Wear several layers of loose-fitting clothing to increase insulation and cold weather headgear to prevent loss of body heat.
- Avoid alcohol intake. Alcohol dilates surface blood vessels, a process that initially causes the body to feel warmer but actually chills it through heat loss.

6-34. Wind chill charts provide time limits for cold exposure before an individual suffers injury. These charts correlate wind velocities and ambient air temperature to provide an equivalent temperature based on the wind chill factor. The same data apply when wet boots or wet clothing is worn or flesh is exposed. These charts also indicate the level below which frostbite becomes a real hazard. Immersion (trench) foot can occur at any temperature shown on these charts, given the right combination of wind velocity and ambient air temperature. Figure 6-1 provides an example of a wind chill chart.

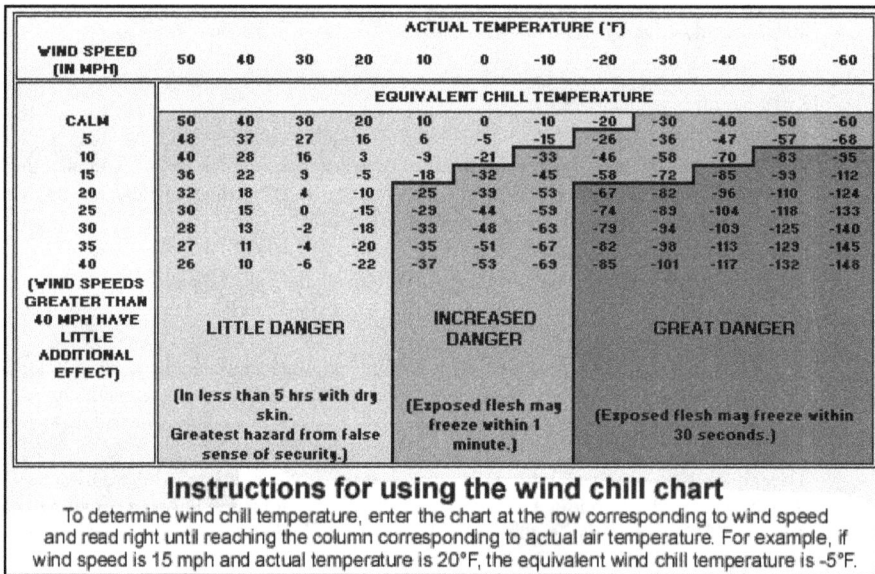

WIND SPEED (IN MPH)	ACTUAL TEMPERATURE (°F)											
	50	40	30	20	10	0	-10	-20	-30	-40	-50	-60
	EQUIVALENT CHILL TEMPERATURE											
CALM	50	40	30	20	10	0	-10	-20	-30	-40	-50	-60
5	48	37	27	16	6	-5	-15	-26	-36	-47	-57	-68
10	40	28	16	3	-9	-21	-33	-46	-58	-70	-83	-95
15	36	22	9	-5	-18	-32	-45	-58	-72	-85	-99	-112
20	32	18	4	-10	-25	-39	-53	-67	-82	-96	-110	-124
25	30	15	0	-15	-29	-44	-59	-74	-89	-104	-118	-133
30	28	13	-2	-18	-33	-48	-63	-79	-94	-109	-125	-140
35	27	11	-4	-20	-35	-51	-67	-82	-98	-113	-129	-145
40	26	10	-6	-22	-37	-53	-69	-85	-101	-117	-132	-148

(WIND SPEEDS GREATER THAN 40 MPH HAVE LITTLE ADDITIONAL EFFECT)

LITTLE DANGER (In less than 5 hrs with dry skin. Greatest hazard from false sense of security.)

INCREASED DANGER (Exposed flesh may freeze within 1 minute.)

GREAT DANGER (Exposed flesh may freeze within 30 seconds.)

Instructions for using the wind chill chart

To determine wind chill temperature, enter the chart at the row corresponding to wind speed and read right until reaching the column corresponding to actual air temperature. For example, if wind speed is 15 mph and actual temperature is 20°F, the equivalent wind chill temperature is -5°F.

Figure 6-1. Wind chill chart

Chapter 7

Noise and Vibration in Army Aviation

Noise levels in both rotary- and fixed-wing aircraft exceed safe noise exposure limits. In addition, crewmembers are subjected to aircraft vibrations that can produce fatigue, degrade comfort, interfere with performance effectiveness, and under severe conditions, influence operational safety and occupational health. Both noise and vibration effects can occur simultaneously with initial exposure or manifest only after the passage of time and repeated exposure. This chapter addresses the physiology of noise and vibration and offers strategies to minimize short- and long-term exposure.

CHARACTERISTICS AND EFFECTS

7-1. Noise is loud, unpleasant, or unwanted sound. Vibration is the motion of objects relative to a reference position, usually an object at rest. In aviation, noise and vibration can cause annoyance, speech interference, fatigue, and hearing loss.

ANNOYANCE

7-2. Noise is undesirable when it warrants unnecessary attention or interferes with routine activities. High-frequency noise and vibration are especially irritating and can cause a subjective sense of fatigue.

SPEECH INTERFERENCE

7-3. When noise and vibration reach a certain loudness or amplitude, they mask normal communication and words become difficult to understand.

HEARING LOSS

7-4. Permanent hearing damage is the most common and significant undesirable effect of noise. The effects of excessive vibration include internal organ malfunctions and skeletal disabilities. Damage can be rapid when noise is extremely intense or prolonged, but it is often subtle in onset and results from continual exposure at lesser intensities. All aviation personnel must understand this damage can become permanent.

SOUND AND VIBRATIONAL MEASUREMENT

7-5. Sound and vibration energy have measurable characteristics. These characteristics are frequency, intensity/amplitude, and duration.

FREQUENCY

7-6. Frequency is the physical characteristic that gives sound pitch. Frequency of periodic motion is the number of times per second air pressure oscillates. The number of oscillations, or cycles per second, is measured in hertz (Hz).

Human Hearing and Speech Range

7-7.   The human ear is very sensitive and can detect frequencies from 20 to 20,000 Hz. Speech involves frequencies from 200 to 6,800 Hz, the range in which the ear is most sensitive.

Speech Intelligibility

7-8.   People must be able to hear in the range of 300 to 3,000 Hz to understand speech communication. Speech outside these ranges can result in incoherence or misinterpretation.

Vibration

7-9.   Vibration most affects the body in low frequencies, usually confined to frequency ranges below 100 Hz to displace body parts. These effects vary greatly with direction, body support, and restraint.

INTENSITY/AMPLITUDE

7-10.   Intensity is a measure that correlates sound pressure to loudness. Amplitude (for vibration) is the maximum displacement about a position of rest.

7-11.   Aviation personnel must understand the relationship of decibels to sound pressure (vibration). For every 20-decibel increase in loudness, sound pressure increases by a factor of 10. At 80 decibels, sound pressure is 10 thousand times greater than at 0 decibels; at 100 decibels, sound pressure is 1 million times greater than at 0 decibels. The sound pressure that moves through air to stimulate hearing also can cause hearing loss under certain conditions. Table 7-1 shows the effects of various sound intensities on listeners.

Table 7-1. Effects of various sound intensities

Frequency (decibels)	Effect
0	Hearing threshold
65	Average human conversation
85	Damage-risk limit
120	Discomfort threshold
140	Pain threshold
160	Eardrum rupture

DURATION

7-12.   Duration is the length of time an individual is exposed to noise or vibration. It is a variable factor that can be measured in seconds, minutes, hours, days, or any other selected unit of time.

NATURAL BODY RESONANCE

7-13.   Natural body resonance is the mechanical amplification of vibration by the body at specific frequencies. Table 7-2 (page 7-3) shows resonant frequencies for various parts of the human body.

Table 7-2. Resonant frequencies and the human body

Body Part	Resonant Frequency (Hz)
Whole body	4–8
Shoulder girdle	4–8
Head	25
Eyes	30–90

DAMPING

7-14. Damping is the loss of mechanical energy in a vibrating system. This loss causes vibration to slow.

NOISE AND HEARING LEVELS

7-15. Army aviation personnel are exposed to two types of sound levels that can impair hearing: steady-state noise and impulse noise.

STEADY-STATE NOISE

7-16. Aviation personnel encounter steady-state noise around operating aircraft. This noise is usually at a high intensity over a wide range of frequencies. The U.S. Surgeon General has established 85 decibels at all frequencies as the maximum permissible sound level for continuous exposure to steady-state noise (damage-risk criteria). There is a direct link between exposure duration and intensity; the louder the sound, the shorter the time required to cause hearing loss. Table 7-3 shows recommended allowable noise exposure levels for various exposure durations. Exposure to noise above recommended duration levels could result in noise-induced hearing loss, which is the primary risk to Army aviation personnel.

Table 7-3. Recommended allowable noise exposure levels

Exposure Duration Per Day (hour)	Maximum Exposure Level (decibel)
8	85
4	90
2	95
1	100
1/2	105
Note: For every 5-decibel noise intensity increase, the exposure time limit is cut in half.	

IMPULSE NOISE

7-17. Weapons fire produces impulse noise, which is an explosive sound that builds quickly to a high intensity but then falls rapidly. Although the entire cycle usually lasts only milliseconds, impulse noise is detrimental to hearing when intensity exceeds 140 decibels.

7-18. In both rotary- and fixed-wing aircraft, overall noise levels generally equal 100 or more decibels and therefore exceed the 85-decibel damage-risk criteria. Table 7-4 (page 7-4) shows estimated noise levels for rotary- and fixed-wing Army aircraft.

Table 7-4. Rotary- and fixed-wing aircraft noise levels

Aircraft	Noise Level (decibels)
OH-58C	103
OH-58D	100
CH-47D	112
UH-60A	108
AH-64	104
TH-67*	102
C-12/RC-12	106**
UC-35	96***

*Based on a Bell 206 helicopter
** Exterior noise level
*** Cabin noise level

7-19. The frequency that generates the most intense noise level is 300 Hz. Low-frequency noise produces high-frequency hearing loss. Providing adequate hearing protection for lower frequencies is very difficult. Exposure to these levels without hearing protection ultimately will result in permanent hearing loss.

VIBRATIONAL EFFECTS

7-20. The human body reacts in various ways to vibration:
- Vibration can cause short-term acute effects due to the body's biomechanical properties.
- The human body acts like a series of objects connected by springs.
- The connective tissue that binds the major organs together reacts to vibration the same way springs do.
- When the body is subjected to certain frequencies, tissue and organs begin to resonate (increase in amplitude).
- Objects create momentum when they reach their resonant frequency, which then increases in intensity with each oscillation.
- Without shock absorption, vibration will damage the mass or organ.

7-21. Helicopters subject crewmembers to vibrations over a frequency range that coincides with the body's resonant frequencies. Prolonged exposure to vibration causes both short- and long-term effects on the body. Vibration can affect the respiratory system, as well as cause—
- Motion sickness.
- Disorientation.
- Pain.
- Microcirculatory effects.
- Visual problems.

HEARING LOSS

7-22. Factors such as age, health, and the noise environment contribute to hearing loss. There are three types of hearing loss: conductive, presbycusis, and sensorineural.

CONDUCTIVE

7-23. Conductive hearing loss occurs when some defect or impediment blocks sound transmission from the external ear to the inner ear. Wax buildup, middle-ear fluid, or ossicle calcification can impede the mechanical transmission of sound. Conductive hearing loss primarily affects low frequencies and, in most cases, can be treated medically. A hearing aid is often beneficial because the inner ear can still detect sounds if they are loud enough. An aviator can fly with a hearing aid if he or she is given a waiver to continue on flight status.

PRESBYCUSIS

7-24. Presbycusis hearing loss usually results from old age. The hair cells of the cochlea become less resilient as people age.

SENSORINEURAL

7-25. Sensorineural hearing loss occurs when the cochlea's hair cells are damaged within the inner ear. This type of hearing loss is caused primarily by noise exposure, but disease or aging can contribute as well. Sensorineural hearing loss caused by noise exposure generally occurs first in the higher frequencies. A hearing aid might be of benefit in some cases, but no known medical cure exists for this type of hearing loss.

MIXED

7-26. A crewmember might have an ear infection that could cause conductive hearing loss but be diagnosed with sensorineural hearing loss. The ear infection is treatable; sensorineural hearing loss is not.

HEARING PROTECTION

INDIVIDUAL RESPONSIBILITY

7-27. Pilots, crewmembers, ground support troops, and passengers should wear hearing protection at all times. Hearing loss is one hazard in the aviation environment that adequate protective measures can minimize. Every individual has a responsibility to use hearing protection.

7-28. The amount of sound protection offered by a protective device is determined first by its fit and condition, but most importantly by the willingness and ability of the individual to use it properly. Using individual devices in combination provides the best hearing protection.

7-29. While individual devices are not foolproof, virtually all noise-induced hearing loss is preventable if the devices fit properly and are worn on all flights. Even if hearing is already affected somewhat, protective devices will help prevent further damage.

PROTECTIVE DEVICES

7-30. Aircraft noise levels interfere with speech communication between crewmembers and pose the risk of hearing loss. Protective measures that can reduce the undesirable effects of noise include—
- Use of personal protective measures.
- Isolation or distance from the noise source.

Helmets

7-31. The HGU-56P aviator helmet (figure 7-1, page 7-6) provides excellent protection in terms of noise and crash attenuation. Designed primarily for noise protection, this helmet also provides exceptional noise attenuation from 3,000 to 8,800 Hz.

Figure 7-1. HGU-56P aviator helmet

7-32. The HGU-56P helmet reduces noise exposure to safe limits for every aircraft in the Army inventory except the UH-60 Black Hawk and CH-47 Chinook. Table 7-5 shows estimated attenuation levels for various helmet types.

Note: Operations in UH-60 and CH-47 aircraft require both helmet and earplug use to attenuate noise and prevent hearing loss.

Table 7-5. Estimated attenuation levels by helmet

Aircraft	Hearing Protector	Effective Exposure Level (decibels)
OH-58D	HGU-56P	81.6
OH-58C	HGU-56P	76.9
UH-60A	HGU-56P	90.6
CH-47D	HGU-56P	86.8
AH-64	IHADSS (Reg and XL)	80.2
C-12	H-157 headset	70.5

7-33. Ancillary devices worn with the aviator's helmet can significantly compromise hearing protection. For example, eyeglass frames break the ear seal and create a leak that produces a sound path from outside to inside the ear cup.

Earplugs

Communications Earplug

7-34. The communications earplug (CEP) (figure 7-2, page 7-7) improves hearing protection and speech communication reception. The CEP includes a miniature transducer that reproduces speech signals from the aircraft's internal communications system (ICS). The foam tip acts as a hearing protector similar to the yellow foam earplugs worn by pilots for double hearing protection. A miniature wire from the CEP connects to the ICS through a mating connector mounted on the rear of the helmet. The CEP was recently issued an airworthiness release (AWR) for all Army aircraft using the HGU-56P helmet and M24 mask.

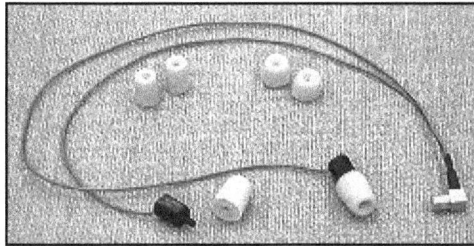

Figure 7-2. Communications earplug

Insert-Type Earplugs

7-35. Insert-type earplugs are a common form of hearing protection. All earplugs tend to loosen with talking or vibration and must be reseated periodically to prevent inadvertent noise exposure. Users' voices sound lower and muffled with properly fitted earplugs, and initial use can diminish the user's ability to hear cockpit communications. Noise protection with earplugs is 18 to 45 decibels across all frequency bands. Three types of earplugs are—

- The E-A-R® foam earplug, which provides excellent noise attenuation, comfort, and ease in maintaining a seal. To ensure maximum attenuation, these plugs should be inserted properly and kept clean.
- The V-51R single-flange earplug, which is available in five different sizes and provides a suitable fit for more than 95 percent of all Army aviation personnel (10 percent of crewmembers need a different size for each ear). These plugs can be cleaned with soap and water.
- The triple-flange earplug, which provides nearly the same attenuation as the V-51R and is available in three sizes (small, medium, and large). These plugs are comfortable for most individuals and can be cleaned with soap and water.

Combined Hearing Protection

7-36. In combination with the HGU-56P and IHADSS helmets, earplugs provide additional protection from noise generated by all aircraft in the U.S. Army inventory. Table 7-6 shows attenuation levels at the pilot's station for crewmembers wearing the HGU-56P helmet with the three earplug types described above.

Table 7-6. Attenuation levels for the HGU-56P with earplugs

Earplug	UH-60A (120 knots)	CH-47D (100 knots)	OH-58 (100 knots)
Triple-flange plug	70.6	75.5	63.7
Single-flange plug	73.3	76.4	65.4
E-A-R® foam plug	68.4	75.3	61.5

Earmuffs

7-37. Several types of earmuffs (figure 7-3, page 7-8) provide adequate sound protection for aviation ground support personnel. When adjusted properly and in good condition, most earmuffs attenuate sound as well as properly fitted earplugs. However, earmuffs tend to provide slightly more high-frequency protection and slightly less low-frequency protection than earplugs.

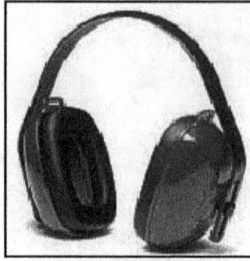
Figure 7-3. Earmuffs

VIBRATION PREVENTIVE MEASURES

7-38. Vibration cannot be eliminated, but its effects on human performance and physiological function can be reduced. Preventive measures include—
- Maintaining good posture during flight.
- Restraint systems provide protection against high-magnitude vibration experienced in extreme turbulence.

> **CAUTION**
>
> Body supports such as lumbar inserts and added seat cushions can reduce discomfort and dampen vibration. However, they might increase the likelihood of injury during a crash sequence due to their compression characteristics. Do not modify aircraft seats for the sake of comfort.

- Maintaining equipment. Proper aircraft maintenance such as blade tracking can reduce unnecessary vibration exposure.
- Isolating crewmembers and passengers. Patients placed on the floor of medical evacuation (MEDEVAC) aircraft experience more vibration than those situated in upper racks.
- Limiting exposure time. Short flights with frequent breaks are preferred over one long flight, mission permitting.
- Letting the aircraft do the work. Crewmembers should not grip controls tightly. Vibration can be transmitted through control linkages during turbulence.
- Maintaining good physical condition. Fat multiplies vibration, but muscle dampens it by reducing the magnitude of oscillations encountered in flight. Good physical condition also lessens the effects of fatigue and allows Soldiers to function during extended combat operations with minimum rest.
- Maintaining sufficient hydration. Crewmembers should drink a minimum of two quarts of water in addition to fluids taken with meals. Coupled with vibration, dehydration can cause fatigue twice as fast and requires double the time needed for recovery.

Chapter 8

Vision

Crewmembers rely more on their vision than any other sense to orient themselves in flight. While vision is the most accurate and reliable sense, visual cues can be misleading and contribute to incidents within the flight environment. Aviation personnel must be aware of and know how to effectively compensate for physical deficiencies and self-imposed stressors as well as visual cue deficiencies and limitations. This chapter discusses visual limitations and compensation techniques.

SECTION I – GENERAL

8-1.   Crewmembers must completely understand eye function and techniques they can employ to overcome visual limitations. It is usually not a lack of visual acuity that causes problems for crewmembers; rather, it is not understanding "how" to see properly.

ANATOMY AND PHYSIOLOGY OF THE EYE

8-2.   Understanding basic anatomy and physiology of the eye enables crewmembers to use their eyes more effectively during flight. Light enters the eye and passes through the cornea, a circular, transparent protective tissue that projects forward

Contents

and protects the eye. From there it enters the pupil, which is the opening (black portion) in the center of the iris. The pupil allows light to enter the eye and stimulate the retina. The iris is the round, pigmented (colored) membrane surrounding the pupil and adjusts pupil size by using ciliary muscles attached to the pupil. The iris adjusts the size of the pupil's exposed portion to regulate the amount of light entering the eye. When the pupil dilates (enlarges) under low light levels, it allows more light to enter the eye to further stimulate the retina. When the pupil constricts (becomes smaller) under high light levels, it decreases the amount of light entering the eye to avoid oversaturation (stimulation) of the retina. Light entering the eye is regulated so the retina is neither undersaturated nor oversaturated with light images, both of which have negative effects on visual acuity.

8-3.   After light travels through the pupil it strikes the lens, a transparent, biconvex membrane located behind the pupil. The lens then directs (refracts) the light to the retina, the posterior or rear portion of the eye. The retina is a complex, structured membrane consisting of 10 layers called the Jacob's membrane. The retina contains many tiny photoreceptor cells known as rods and cones. When light stimulates the retina, it produces a chemical change within the photoreceptor cells that stimulates and transmits nerve impulses to the brain via the optic nerve. The brain deciphers these impulses and creates a mental image that interprets what the individual is viewing. Figure 8-1 (page 8-2) illustrates the basic anatomy of the human eye.

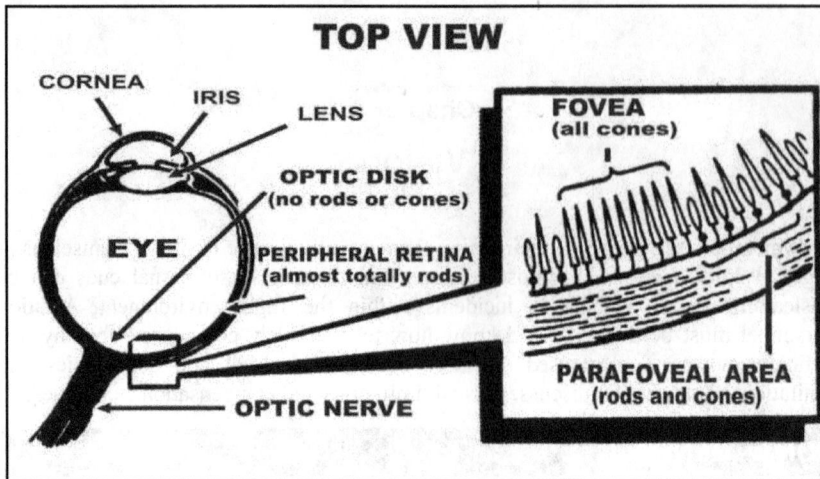

Figure 8-1. Anatomy of the human eye

VISUAL ACUITY

8-4.   Visual acuity measures the eye's ability to resolve spatial detail. The Snellen test is commonly used to measure an individual's visual acuity. Normal visual acuity is 20/20, a value that indicates an individual reads at 20 feet the letters an individual with normal acuity (20/20) reads at 80 feet.

8-5.   The human eye functions like a camera. It has a simultaneous field of view (FOV), which is oval and typically measures 130 degrees vertically by 160 degrees horizontally. When two eyes are used for viewing, overall FOV measures about 120 degrees vertically by 200 degrees horizontally.

RETINAL PHOTORECEPTOR CELLS

Rods and Cones

8-6.   Retinal rod and cone cells are named for their shape. Cone cells are used primarily for day or high-intensity light vision (viewing periods or conditions). The rods are used for night or low-intensity light vision (viewing periods or conditions). Some characteristics of day and night vision are due to the distribution pattern of rods and cones on the retina. The center of the retina, the fovea, contains a very high concentration of cone cells but no rod cells. The concentration of rod cells begins to increase toward the retina's periphery.

Cone Neurology

8-7.   The retina contains seven million cone cells. Each cone cell in the fovea is connected to a single nerve fiber that leads directly to the brain. Each cell generates a nerve impulse under sufficient light levels during daylight or high-intensity light exposure. Cone cells provide sharp visual acuity and color perception. Under low light or dark conditions, cone cells depict shades of black, gray, and white; crewmembers will perceive other colors if light intensity is heightened by artificial sources such as:

- Aircraft position lights.
- Anticollision lights.
- Runway lights.
- Beacon lights.
- Artificial light in metropolitan areas.

Rod Neurology

8-8. There are 120 million rod cells in the retina. There is a 10-to-1 to 10,000-to-1 ratio of rod cells to neuron cells within the retina. Due to the large number of rod cells connected to each nerve fiber outside the fovea, dim light can trigger a nerve impulse to the brain. The periphery of the retina, where the rods are concentrated, is much more sensitive to light than the fovea. This concentration is responsible for night vision, which provides silhouette recognition of objects. It is also why crewmembers' eyes are highly sensitive to light during low ambient light or dark conditions.

Iodopsin and Rhodopsin

8-9. Vision is possible due to chemical reactions within the eye. The chemical iodopsin is always present within cone cells. Iodopsin allows cone cells to immediately respond to visual stimulation regardless the ambient light level. Rod cells, however, contain an extremely light-sensitive chemical called rhodopsin, more commonly referred to as visual purple. Rhodopsin is not always present in the rods because light bleaches it out and renders the rods inactive to stimulation. Rhodopsin is so sensitive that bright light exposure can bleach out all visual purple within seconds.

Night Vision

8-10. Night vision requires a buildup of rhodopsin be present in the rods. The average time required to gain the greatest sensitivity or adaptation to a dark environment is 30 to 45 minutes. When fully adapted, the rod cells become up to 10,000 times more sensitive than at the start of the dark adaptation period. Total light sensitivity can increase 100,000 times through a dilated pupil.

Day Blind Spot

8-11. Since humans have two eyes, they view all images with binocular vision. Each eye compensates for the day blind spot in the optic disk of the opposite eye. The day blind spot covers an area of 5.5 to 7.5 degrees and is located about 15 degrees from the fovea, originating where the optic nerve attaches to the retina. The size of the day blind spot is due to the optic nerve's oval shape combined with its offset position where it attaches to the retina. No cones or rods are present at the attachment point. The day blind spot causes difficulty when individuals do not move their head or eyes but continue to look straight forward while an object is brought into the visual field. Figure 8-2 demonstrates the day blind spot.

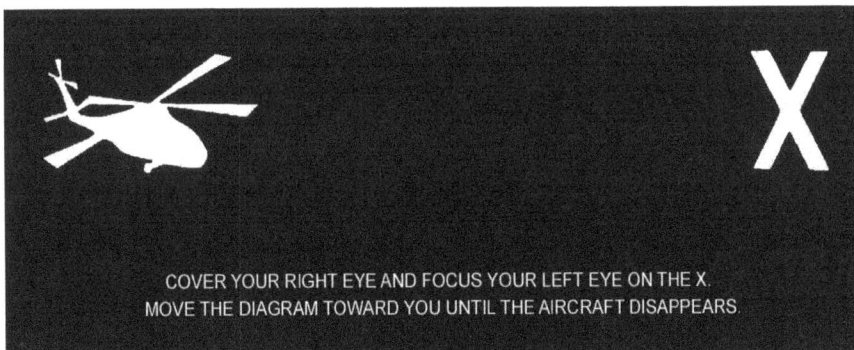

COVER YOUR RIGHT EYE AND FOCUS YOUR LEFT EYE ON THE X.
MOVE THE DIAGRAM TOWARD YOU UNTIL THE AIRCRAFT DISAPPEARS.

Figure 8-2. Day blind spot

SECTION II – TYPES OF VISION

8-12. The three types of vision and viewing periods associated with Army aviation are photopic, mesopic, and scotopic. Each type requires different sensory stimuli or ambient light conditions.

PHOTOPIC VISION

8-13. Photopic vision (figure 8-3) is experienced during daylight or under high levels of artificial illumination. Cones concentrated in the fovea centralis are primarily responsible for vision in bright light. Due to the high-level light condition, rod cells are bleached out and become less effective. Sharp image interpretation and color vision are characteristics of photopic vision. The fovea centralis is automatically directed toward an object by a visual fixation reflex. Therefore, under photopic conditions, the eye uses central vision for interpretation, especially in determining details.

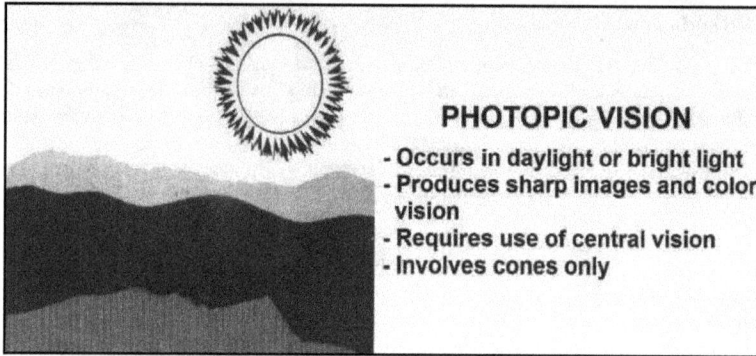

PHOTOPIC VISION
- Occurs in daylight or bright light
- Produces sharp images and color vision
- Requires use of central vision
- Involves cones only

Figure 8-3. Photopic vision

MESOPIC VISION

8-14. Mesopic vision (figure 8-4) is experienced at dawn, dusk, and under full moonlight. Vision is achieved by a combination of rods and cones. Visual acuity steadily decreases with declining light. Color vision is reduced or degraded as light levels decrease and the cones become less effective. Mesopic vision is the most dangerous vision type for crewmembers. How degraded the ambient light condition is determines what type of scanning or viewing technique crewmembers should use to detect objects and maintain safe and incident-free flight. For example, the gradual loss of cone sensitivity might necessitate off-center viewing to detect objects in and around the flight path. Incidents might occur if crewmembers fail to recognize the need to change scanning techniques from central or focal viewing to off-center viewing.

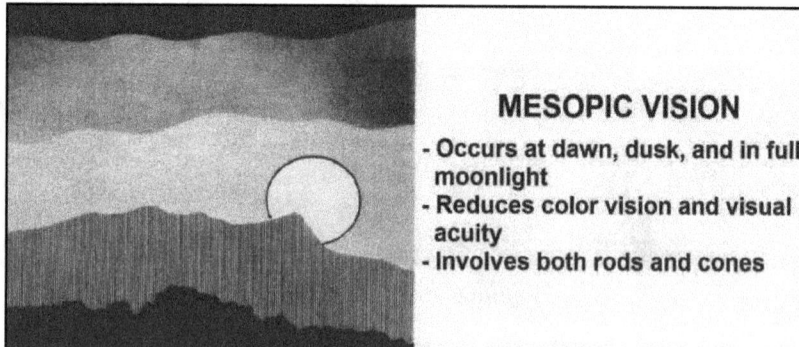

MESOPIC VISION
- Occurs at dawn, dusk, and in full moonlight
- Reduces color vision and visual acuity
- Involves both rods and cones

Figure 8-4. Mesopic vision

SCOTOPIC VISION

8-15. Scotopic vision (figure 8-5, page 8-5) is experienced in low light environments such as partial moonlight and starlight conditions. Cones become ineffective in these conditions, causing poor resolution in detail. Visual acuity decreases to 20/200 or less, and color perception is lost. A central or night blind spot occurs when cone cell sensitivity is lost. Scotopic vision degrades primary color perception to shades of black, gray, and white unless the light source is of adequate intensity to stimulate the cones. Peripheral vision is used primarily while viewing with scotopic vision.

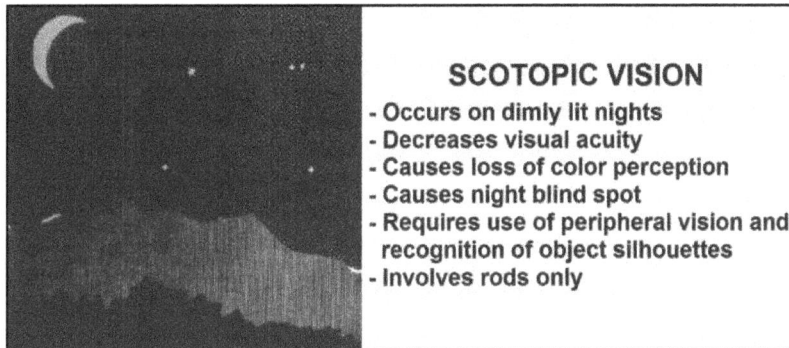

Figure 8-5. Scotopic vision

NIGHT BLIND SPOT

8-16. The night blind spot (figure 8-6) should not be confused with the day blind spot. The night blind spot occurs when the fovea becomes inactive in low light conditions and involves an area from 5 to 10 degrees wide in the center of the visual field. An object viewed directly at night might not be seen due to the night blind spot; if the object is detected, it will fade away when stared at longer than 2 seconds. The size of the night blind spot increases as the distance between the eyes and object increases. Therefore, the night blind spot can hide larger objects as the distance between the observer and object increases. Figure 8-7 (page 8-6) illustrates this effect.

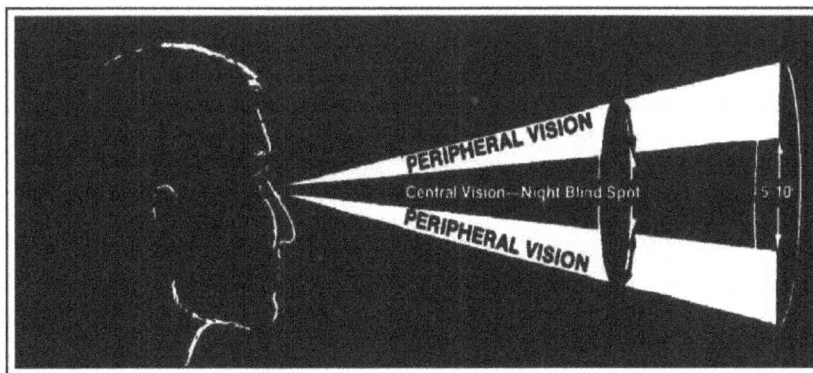

Figure 8-6. Night blind spot

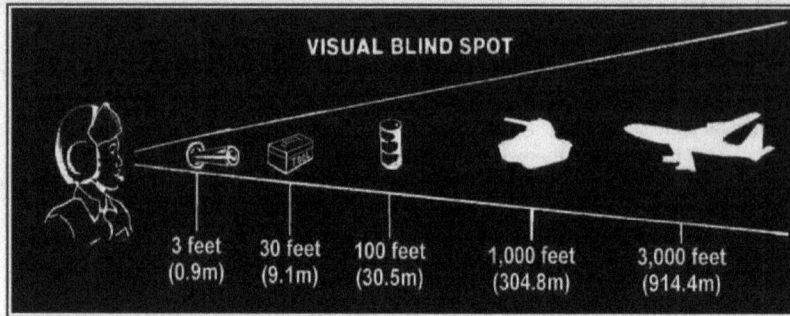

Figure 8-7. Visual blind spot

PERIPHERAL VISION

8-17. Stimulation of only rod cells (peripheral vision) is primary for viewing during scotopic vision. Crewmembers must use peripheral vision to overcome the effects of scotopic vision. Peripheral vision allows crewmembers to see dimly lit objects and maintain visual reference to moving objects. The natural reflex of looking directly at an object must be reoriented through night vision training. To compensate for scotopic vision, crewmembers must use searching eye movements to locate an object and small eye movements to retain sight of the object. Crewmembers also must use off-center viewing; if the eyes are held stationary when focusing on an object for more than 2 to 3 seconds using scotopic vision, images can fade away or bleach out completely.

SECTION III – VISUAL DEFICIENCIES

8-18. Aviation personnel must be able to recognize and understand common visual deficiencies. Important eye problems related to degraded visual acuity and depth perception include myopia, hyperopia, astigmatism, presbyopia, and retinal rivalry. Surgical procedures to sculpt or reshape the cornea also might result in visual deficiencies.

MYOPIA

8-19. Myopia, often referred to as nearsightedness, is caused by an error in refraction where the lens of the eye does not focus an image directly on the retina. When a person with myopia views an image at a distance, the eye's actual focal point is in front of the retinal plane or wall, causing blurred vision. Thus, distant objects are not seen clearly and only nearby objects are in focus. Figure 8-8 depicts this condition.

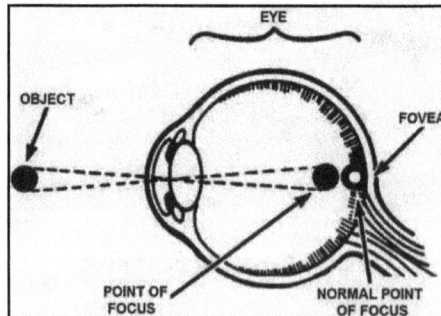

Figure 8-8. Myopia (nearsightedness)

NIGHT MYOPIA

8-20. Blue wavelengths of light prevail in the visible portion of the spectrum at night. Therefore, slightly nearsighted or myopic individuals viewing blue-green light at night might experience blurred vision. Even crewmembers with perfect vision will find image sharpness decreases as pupil diameter increases. For individuals with mild refractive errors, these factors combine to make vision unacceptably blurred unless they wear corrective glasses.

8-21. Another issue crewmembers must consider is "dark focus." When light levels decrease, the eye's focusing mechanism might move toward a resting position, making the eye more myopic. These factors become important when crewmembers rely on terrain features during unaided night flights. Special corrective lenses can be prescribed to correct night myopia.

HYPEROPIA

8-22. Hyperopia, often referred to as farsightedness, also is caused by a refraction error; the eye's lens does not focus images directly on the retina. When a crewmember views a near image in a hyperopic state, the eye's actual focal point is behind the retinal plane or wall, causing blurred vision. Nearby objects are not seen clearly; only more distant objects are in focus. Figure 8-9 depicts this condition.

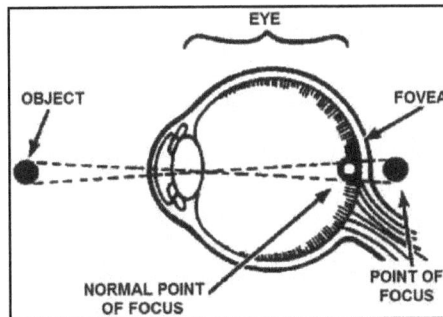

Figure 8-9. Hyperopia (farsightedness)

ASTIGMATISM

8-23. Astigmatism is the inability to focus different meridians simultaneously. It results from an unequal curvature of the cornea or eye lens that causes a ray of light to spread over a diffused area on the retina. In normal vision, a ray of light is sharply focused on the retina. If, for example, an astigmatic individual focuses on power poles (vertical), the wires (horizontal) will be out of focus, as shown in figure 8-10.

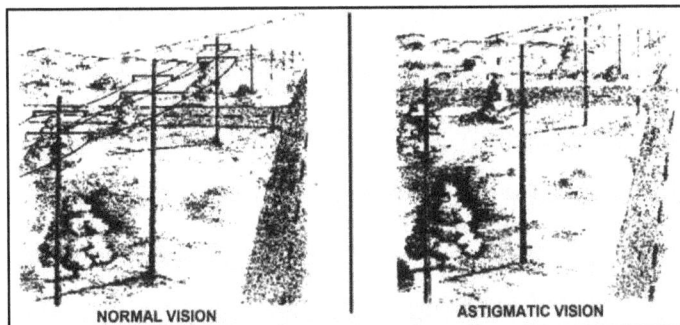

Figure 8-10. Astigmatism

PRESBYOPIA

8-24. Presbyopia, a condition that causes the lenses to harden, is part of the normal aging process. Beginning in the early teens, the human eye gradually loses the ability to accommodate for and focus on nearby objects. When people are about 40 years old, their eyes are unable to focus at normal reading distances without reading glasses. Reduced illumination interferes with focus depth and accommodation ability.

8-25. Lens hardening can result in clouding of the lenses, a condition known as cataracts. Aviators with early cataracts might see a standard eye chart clearly in normal daylight but have difficulty under bright light conditions due to the light scattering as it enters the eye. This glare sensitivity is disabling under certain circumstances. Glare disability, related to contrast sensitivity, is the inability to detect objects against varying shades of backgrounds. Other visual functions that decline with age and affect crewmember performance include:

- Dynamic acuity.
- Glare recovery.
- Function under low illumination.
- Information processing.

RETINAL RIVALRY

8-26. Retinal rivalry might be experienced when the eyes attempt to simultaneously perceive two dissimilar objects independently. This phenomenon can occur when pilots view objects through the heads-up display in the AH-64. Conflict in total perception arises when one eye views one image and the other eye views another image. Quite often, the dominant eye overrides the nondominant eye, possibly causing information delivered to the nondominant eye to be missed. Additionally, this rivalry can lead to ciliary spasms and eye pain. Mental conditioning and practice appear to alleviate this condition; therefore, retinal rivalry becomes less of a problem as crewmembers gain experience.

SURGICAL PROCEDURES

8-27. Various surgical procedures are available to correct visual deficiencies. The most common procedures are described below, but this list is not inclusive of all available options. AR 40-501 states all corrective eye surgeries involving laser-assisted in-situ keratomileusis (LASIK), photorefractive keratectomy (PRK), or other forms of corrective eye surgery disqualify Army crewmembers from flight duty. Crewmembers must consult their flight surgeon before undergoing these procedures.

PHOTOREFRACTIVE KERATECTOMY

8-28. PRK is a procedure that corrects corneal refractive errors through a series of fine laser ablations that resculpt the cornea. This procedure flattens the cornea, which then bends or refracts light properly on the retina and corrects myopic deficiency. Some studies suggest there is increased risk of haze at the treated interface with increased ultraviolet exposure due to the destruction of the corneal membrane, even years after surgery.

LASER EPITHELIAL KERATOMILEUSIS

8-29. Laser epithelial keratomileusis (LASEK) is similar to PRK in its depth of corneal involvement but utilizes a flap technique similar to LASIK. An epithelial flap is made and removed mechanically, followed by laser sculpting of the corneal stroma. One benefit to this procedure is that postsurgical flap displacement, while more likely to occur due to the thinness of the flap, is less likely to cause permanent vision change as compared to the thicker and deeper LASIK flap.

LASER-ASSISTED IN-SITU KERATOMILEUSIS

8-30. LASIK is the procedure surgeons use to carve and reshape the cornea. A laser is used to shave the anterior half of the cornea, creating a flap that is then retracted. The inner side of the cornea is then reshaped with the laser, causing the cornea to flatten. The flap is replaced in its original position when reshaping is complete. After surgery, the flatter cornea properly bends and refracts light on the retina. Unlike PRK, this technique can correct for severe myopia and hyperopia. LASIK's primary adverse effect is astigmatism caused by irregularities in the corneal surface. In addition, permanent damage to the cornea and severely degraded visual acuity will result if the flap becomes suddenly detached in an accident.

SECTION IV – FACTORS AFFECTING OBJECT VISIBILITY

8-31. The ease with which an object can be seen depends on various factors. Each factor can either increase or decrease the object's visibility. Object visibility increases as—

- Object angular size increases and distance between the object and viewer decreases.
- Ambient light illumination (overall brightness) increases.
- Degree of retinal adaptation increases.
- Color and contrast between the object and background increase.
- Object position within the visual field (visibility threshold) increases.
- Eye focus and viewing time increase.
- Atmospheric clarity increases; ND-15 sunglasses can aid visibility in excessive light or bright conditions.

8-32. Interference in the perception of instantaneous visual pictures occurs as aircraft speed increases. In some cases, it might take 1 to 2 seconds or longer to recognize and consciously assess a complex situation. By the time an object is eventually perceived, it might already have been overtaken. The time it takes to perceive an object is significant for crewmembers. Perception time includes the time it takes—

- The message indicating an image has been identified within the visual field to travel from the eye to the brain, including the time it takes the brain to receive, comprehend, and identify the information.
- The eye to turn toward and focus on an unknown object.
- An individual to recognize the object and determine its importance.
- To transmit a decision to move muscles and cause the aircraft to respond to control inputs.

SECTION V – NIGHT VISION

8-33. Crewmembers should achieve maximum dark adaptation in the least time possible. Crewmembers also must protect themselves against the loss of night vision. There are several methods for accomplishing these requirements.

DARK ADAPTATION

8-34. Dark adaptation is the process by which the eyes become more sensitive to low levels of illumination. Rhodopsin (visual purple) is the substance in the rods responsible for light sensitivity. The degree of dark adaptation increases as the amount of visual purple in the rods increases through biochemical reaction. Each person adapts to darkness in varying degrees and at different rates. For example, a person in a darkened movie theater adapts more quickly to the prevailing illumination level. However, compared to a moonless night, the light level within a movie theater is high. Additionally, a person in a darkened theater requires less time to adapt to complete darkness than an individual in a lighted hangar. The lower the starting illumination level, the less time required for adaptation.

8-35. Dark adaptation for optimal night vision acuity approaches its maximum level in about 30 to 45 minutes under minimal lighting conditions. If the eyes are exposed to bright light after dark adaptation, their sensitivity is temporarily impaired. The degree of impairment depends on the intensity and duration of the exposure. Brief flashes from high-intensity, white xenon strobe lights commonly used as aircraft anticollision lights have little effect on night vision because the energy pulses are of such short duration, lasting only milliseconds. Exposure of 1 second or longer to a flare or searchlight, however, can seriously impair night vision. Depending on brightness (intensity) and exposure duration or after repeated exposures, complete dark adaptation recovery time can range from several minutes to 45 minutes or longer.

8-36. Exposure to bright sunlight also has a cumulative and adverse effect on dark adaptation. Reflective surfaces such as sand, snow, water, and manmade structures intensify this condition. Exposure to intense sunlight for 2 to 5 hours decreases visual sensitivity for up to 5 hours and also decreases the rate of dark adaptation and degree of night visual acuity. These cumulative effects can persist for several days.

8-37. Retinal rods are least affected by the wavelength of a dim red light. Figure 8-11 compares rod and cone cell sensitivities. Since rods are stimulated by low ambient light levels, red lights do not significantly impair night vision if proper techniques are used. To minimize the adverse effects of red lights on night vision, crewmembers should adjust light intensity to the lowest usable level and view instruments only briefly.

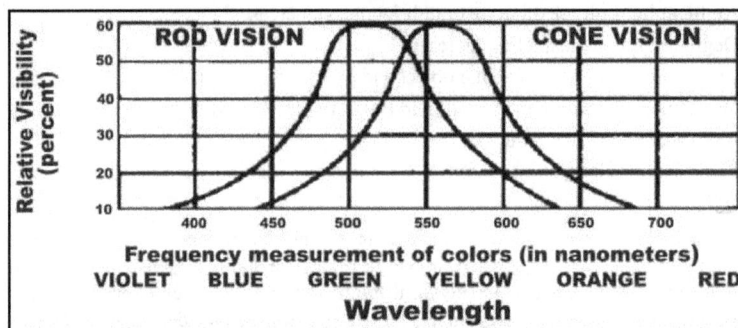

Figure 8-11. Rod and cone cell sensitivities

8-38. Illness adversely affects dark adaptation. Individuals with high body temperatures consume oxygen at a higher-than-normal rate, causing oxygen depletion that can induce hypoxia and degrade night vision. In addition, the unpleasant feelings associated with sickness are distracting and can restrict a crewmember's ability to concentrate on flight duties and responsibilities.

PROTECTIVE EQUIPMENT

SUNGLASSES

8-39. When exposed to bright sunlight for prolonged periods, crewmembers anticipating night flight should wear military-issued, neutral-density sunglasses (ND-15) or equivalent filter lenses. This precaution minimizes the negative effects of sunlight and solar glare on rhodopsin production, which maximizes the rate of dark adaptation and improves night vision sensitivity and acuity.

RED-LENS GOGGLES

8-40. If possible, crewmembers should wear approved red-lens goggles or be exposed to red lighting to achieve complete dark adaptation before executing night-flying operations. These procedures allow crewmembers to begin dark adaptation in an artificially illuminated room before flight. Red-lens goggles and red lighting reduce dark adaptation time and can preserve up to 90 percent of dark adaptation in both eyes. Red lighting and red-lens goggles do not significantly interfere with rhodopsin production and decrease the possibility of undesirable effects from accidental exposure to bright lights, especially as crewmembers transition from the briefing room to the flight line. Exposure to bright lights does, however, lengthen the time crewmembers wearing red-lens goggles need to achieve dark adaptation. Crewmembers wearing red-lens goggles will not achieve complete dark adaptation if the light source is intense enough and exposure is prolonged.

8-41. Crewmembers must not use red lighting or red-lens goggles when viewing inside or outside the aircraft during flight. Red lighting is a longer nanometer, which is very fatiguing to the eyes. In addition, the reds and browns found on nontactical maps not constructed for red light use bleach out when viewed under red lighting.

SUPPLEMENTAL OXYGEN EQUIPMENT

8-42. When flying at or above 4,000 feet pressure altitude, crewmembers should use pressure-altitude supplemental oxygen if available. Adverse effects on night vision begin at 4,000 feet pressure altitude. Effective night vision depends on the optimal function and sensitivity of the retinal rods. A lack of oxygen (hypoxia) significantly reduces rod sensitivity, increases dark adaptation time, and decreases night vision. AR 95-1 describes the requirements for supplemental oxygen use related to pressure altitudes.

PROTECTIVE MEASURES

COCKPIT LIGHT ADJUSTMENT

8-43. Instrument, cockpit, and rear cargo area overhead lights should be adjusted to the lowest readable level that allows instruments, charts, and maps to be interpreted without prolonged staring or exposure. Although blue-green lighting at low intensities can be used in cockpits without significantly disrupting unaided night vision and dark adaptation, items printed in blue-green might wash out. However, the use of blue-green lighting has several benefits. Blue-green light falls naturally on the retinal wall and allows the eye to focus easily on maps, approach plates, and instruments, thereby decreasing eye fatigue. In addition, the intensity necessary for blue-green lighting is less than that for red lighting, resulting in decreased infrared signature and less glare. When blue-green lighting is used properly, the decrease in light intensity and ease of focusing make it more effective for night vision.

EXTERIOR LIGHT ADJUSTMENT

8-44. If possible, exterior lights should be dimmed or turned off, mission permitting. Aviators should consult command policy for local procedures.

LIGHT FLASH COMPENSATION

8-45. The pilot should turn the aircraft away from a light source if a high-intensity flash is expected from a specific direction. When flares illuminate a viewing area or are inadvertently ignited nearby, the pilot should maneuver the aircraft away from the flares to a position along the illuminated area's periphery. To minimize exposure, the pilot should turn the aircraft so vision is directed away from the light source. When lightning or other unexpected conditions occur, crewmembers can preserve dark adaptation by covering or closing one eye while using the other eye to observe. The covered eye provides the night vision capabilities required for flight after the light source has passed. Time spent expending ordnance should be limited to decrease the effects of flash from aerial weapons systems and keep light levels low. Similarly, crewmembers firing automatic weapons should use short bursts of fire. If direct view of a light source cannot be avoided, crewmembers should cover or close one eye because dark adaptation occurs independently in each eye. Depth perception is severely degraded or lost, however, if both eyes are exposed to a light source since neither remains completely dark adapted.

NIGHT VISION TECHNIQUES

8-46. The human eye functions less efficiently at reduced ambient light levels. This reduction limits a crewmember's visual acuity. Normal color vision decreases and finally disappears as the cones become inactive and the rods begin to function. Tower beacons, runway lights, and other colored lights still can be identified if the light is of sufficient intensity to activate the cones. Normal central daylight vision also decreases due to the night blind spot that develops in low illumination or dark viewing conditions. Therefore, proper techniques for night vision viewing must be used to overcome reduced visual acuity at lower light levels.

OFF-CENTER VISION

8-47. There are no limitations to viewing an object with central vision during daylight. If this same technique is used at night, however, the viewer might not see the object due to the night blind spot that exists under low light illumination. To compensate for this limitation, crewmembers must use the off-center vision technique (figure 8-12). This technique requires crewmembers to view an object by looking 10 degrees above, below, or to either side rather than directly at the object. The eyes maintain visual contact with the object via peripheral vision.

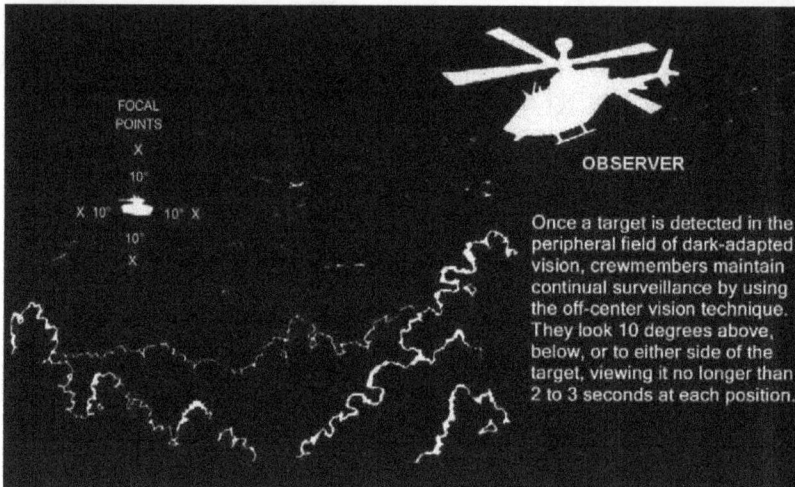

Figure 8-12. Off-center vision technique

8-48. Rapid head or eye movement and fixation decrease the integrating capability of dark-adapted eyes. A steady fixation lasting .5 second to 1 second achieves maximum sensitivity.

8-49. Objects viewed longer than 2 to 3 seconds tend to bleach out and become one solid, invisible tone, resulting in a potentially unsafe operating condition. Crewmembers must be aware of this phenomenon and avoid viewing objects longer than 2 to 3 seconds. By shifting their eyes from one off-center point to another, crewmembers can continue to see objects in their peripheral field of vision.

SCANNING

8-50. During daylight, objects can be perceived at great distances with good detail. At night, however, range is limited and detail is poor. Objects along the flight path can be more readily identified at night when crewmembers use proper techniques to scan the terrain. Effective scanning requires crewmembers to look from right to left or left to right. They should begin scanning at the greatest distance at which an object can be perceived (top) and move inward toward the aircraft's position (bottom). Figure 8-13 (page 8-13) illustrates this scanning pattern.

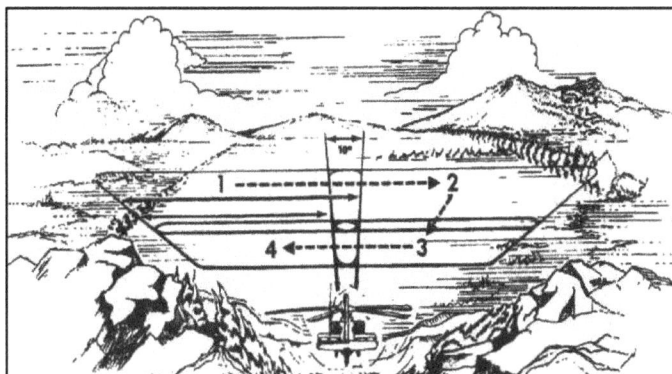

Figure 8-13. Right-to-left or left-to-right scanning pattern

8-51. The retina's light-sensitive elements are unable to perceive images in motion, so crewmembers should use a stop-turn-stop-turn scanning pattern to compensate. For each stop, crewmembers should scan an area about 30 degrees wide, to include an area about 250 meters wide at a distance of 500 meters. Each stop's duration is based on the degree of detail required, but no stop should last more than 2 to 3 seconds. When moving from one viewing point to the next, crewmembers should overlap the previous field of view by 10 degrees. This scanning technique allows greater clarity in observing the periphery. Other scanning techniques, as illustrated in figure 8-14, may be developed to fit the situation.

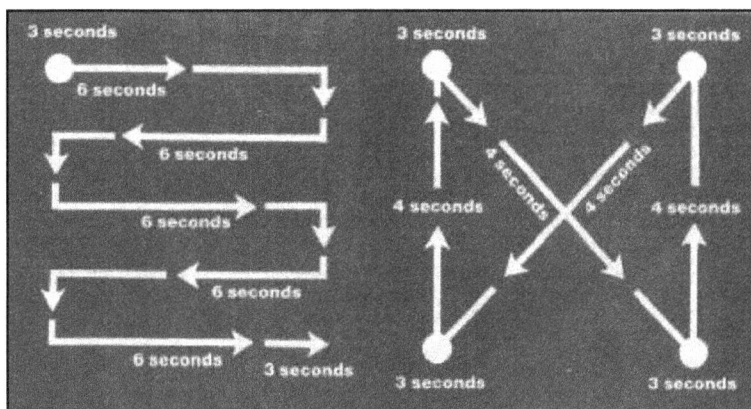

Figure 8-14. Stop-turn-stop-turn scanning pattern

SHAPES OR SILHOUETTES

8-52. Since visual acuity is reduced at night, objects must be identified by their shapes or silhouettes. Therefore, crewmembers must be familiar with the architectural design of structures in the area covered by the mission. A building silhouette with a high roof and steeple is easily recognized as a church in the United States. However, religious buildings in other parts of the world might have low-pitched roofs with no distinguishing features, including cylinder-shaped structures. For example, minarets attached to mosques or religious temples are similar in shape to barn silos in the United States. Features depicted on maps assist crewmembers in recognizing silhouettes.

DISTANCE ESTIMATION AND DEPTH PERCEPTION

8-53. Distance estimation and depth perception cues are easy to recognize when crewmembers use central vision under good illumination. As light levels decrease, however, the ability to accurately judge distance degrades and the eyes become vulnerable to illusions. Crewmembers can better judge distance at night if they understand the mechanisms of distance estimation and depth perception cues. Distance can be estimated using individual cues or a variety of cues. Crewmembers usually use subconscious factors to determine distance. They can more accurately estimate distance if they understand these factors and learn to look for or be aware of other distance cues. Distance estimation and depth perception cues can be binocular or monocular.

BINOCULAR CUES

8-54. Binocular cues depend on the slightly different view each eye has of an object. Thus, binocular perception is of value only when the object is close enough to make a perceptible difference in the viewing angle of both eyes. However, since most distances outside the cockpit are so great, binocular cues are of little to no value to crewmembers. Binocular cues also operate on a more subconscious level than monocular cues and are not greatly improved through study and training. Therefore, these cues are not covered further in this publication.

MONOCULAR CUES

8-55. Several monocular cues assist crewmembers with distance estimation and depth perception. These cues are geometric perspective, retinal image size, aerial perspective, and motion parallax and can be remembered by the mnemonic acronym GRAM.

Geometric Perspective

8-56. An object appears to have a different shape when it is viewed at varying distances and from different angles. As illustrated in figure 8-15, the types of geometric perspective include linear perspective (A), apparent foreshortening (B), and vertical position in the field (C) and can be remembered by the mnemonic acronym LAV.

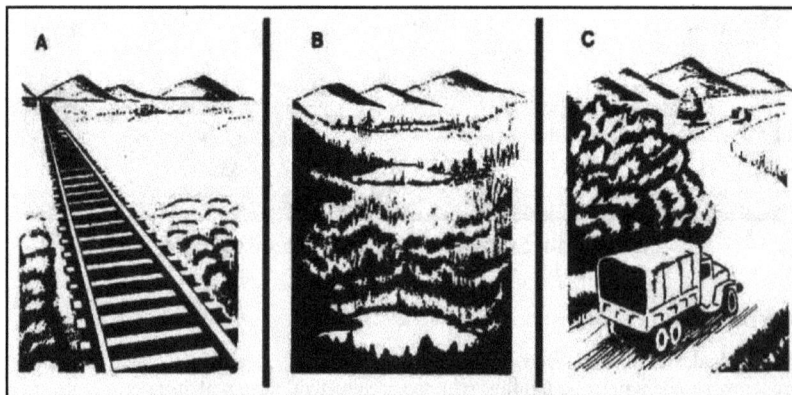

Figure 8-15. Geometric perspective

Linear Perspective

8-57. Parallel lines such as railroad tracks tend to converge as distance from the observer increases, as illustrated in part A of figure 8-15.

Apparent Foreshortening

8-58. The shape of an object or terrain feature appears elliptical (oval and narrow) when viewed from a distance at both higher and lower altitudes. As the distance to the object or terrain feature decreases, the apparent perspective changes to its true shape or form. When flying at lower altitudes and at greater distances, crewmembers might not see objects clearly. If the mission permits, pilots should gain altitude and decrease distance from the viewing area to compensate for this perspective. Once altitude increases and distance between the aircraft and viewing area decreases, the viewing field widens and enlarges so objects become apparent. Part B of figure 8-15 illustrates how the shape of a body of water changes when viewed at different distances while the aircraft maintains the same altitude.

Vertical Position in the Field

8-59. Objects or terrain features at greater distances from the observer appear higher on the horizon than those closer to the observer. In part C of figure 8-15, the higher vehicle appears closer to the top and at a greater distance from the observer. Before flight, crewmembers should already be familiar with the actual sizes, heights, and altitudes of known objects or terrain features within and around the planned flight route. If the situation and time permit, crewmembers can reference published information to verify actual sizes and heights of objects and terrain features within their flight path. In addition, crewmembers should cross-reference the aircraft altitude indicator to confirm actual aircraft altitude is adequate to safely negotiate the object or terrain feature without prematurely changing aircraft heading, altitude, attitude, or a combination thereof.

Retinal Image Size

8-60. Retinal image size is used in distance estimation. An image focused on the retina is perceived by the brain to be of a given size. The factors that aid in determining distance using the retinal image are known size of objects, increasing and decreasing size of objects, terrestrial association, and overlapping contours or interposition of objects. These factors can be remembered by the mnemonic acronym KITO.

Known Size of Objects

8-61. The nearer an object is to the observer, the larger its retinal image. By experience, the brain learns to estimate the distance of familiar objects by the size of their retinal image. Figure 8-16 shows how this method works. A structure projects a specific angle on the retina based on its distance from the observer. If the angle is small, the observer judges the structure to be a great distance away, while a larger angle indicates the structure is close. To use this cue, the observer must know the object's actual size and have prior visual experience with it. If no experience exists, the observer determines the distance to an object primarily by motion parallax (discussed in paragraph 8-69 below).

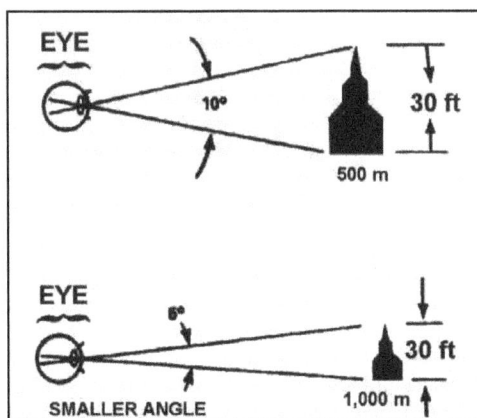

Figure 8-16. Known size of objects

Increasing or Decreasing Size of Objects

8-62. If the retinal image of an object increases in size, the object is moving closer to the observer. If the retinal image decreases, the object is moving further away. If the retinal image is constant, the object is at a fixed distance.

Terrestrial Association

8-63. Comparison of one object such as an airfield with another object of known size such as a helicopter helps in determining the relative size and apparent distance of the object from the observer. Figure 8-17 shows that objects ordinarily associated together are judged to be at about the same distance. For example, a helicopter observed near an airport is judged to be in the traffic pattern and, therefore, at about the same distance as the airfield.

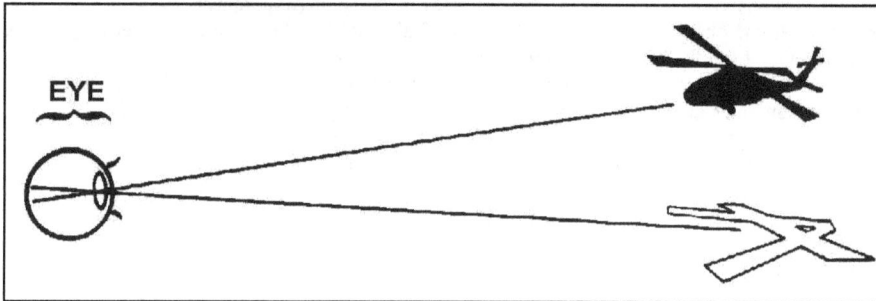

Figure 8-17. Terrestrial association

Overlapping Contours or Interposition of Objects

8-64. When objects overlap, the overlapped object is further away. For example, an object partially concealed by another object is behind the object concealing it. Crewmembers must be especially conscious of this cue when making an approach for landing at night. Lights disappearing or flickering in the landing area should be treated as barriers and the flight path adjusted accordingly. Figure 8-18 illustrates overlapping contour.

Figure 8-18. Overlapping contour

Aerial Perspective

8-65. An object's clarity and its shadow are perceived by the brain and cues for estimating distance. Crewmembers must use the factors discussed below to determine distance with aerial perspective.

Fading of Colors or Shades

8-66. An object viewed through haze, fog, or smoke appears less distinct and at a greater distance than it actually is. Conversely, if atmospheric transmission of light is unrestricted, the object appears more distinct and closer than it actually is. For example, the cargo helicopter in figure 8-19 is larger than the observation helicopter but, due to the difference in viewing distance and size, they both project the same angle on the observer's retina. Assuming the observer has no previous experience with either aircraft's appearance, this cue causes both helicopters to appear the same size. However, if the observer knows the cargo helicopter is the larger aircraft but sees it less distinctly because of visibility restrictions, he or she will judge it to be further away and larger than the observation helicopter. Another example: crewmembers might not be able to distinguish green and red anticollision lights nor the actual interval between aircraft when an additional aircraft is operating at a distance. Both lights can appear white and even blend in with the surrounding foreground.

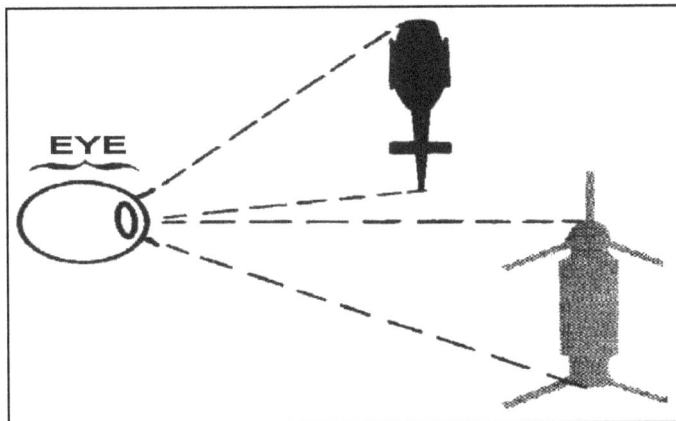

Figure 8-19. Fading of colors or shades

Loss of Detail or Texture

8-67. The further an observer is from an object, the less apparent discrete details become. For example, at a distance a cornfield appears to be a solid color, tree leaves and branches appear to be a solid mass, and objects appear to be at a great distance. When an aircraft is operating on the ground, crewmembers can see the grass or gravel immediately below, in front of, and alongside the aircraft. If they maintain that view as the aircraft slowly ascends, the crewmembers will notice the clarity and detail of the surface fades and eventually blends in with the terrain as a whole, making identification of individual blades or stones impossible. Environmental factors increase the effects of degraded texture and detail throughout the visual field, an issue that severely decreases depth perception. This issue is a contributing factor to crewmember misjudgments of what they do or do not see and the occurrence of incidents related to those misjudgments.

Position of Light Source and Direction of Shadow

8-68. Every object casts a shadow in the presence of a light source. The direction in which the shadow is cast depends on the position of the light source. If an object's shadow is cast toward an observer, the object is closer to the observer than the light source. Figure 8-20 (page 8-18) illustrates how light and shadow help determine distance.

Figure 8-20. Position of light source and direction of shadow

Motion Parallax

8-69. Motion parallax is often considered the most important depth perception cue. Motion parallax refers to the apparent relative motion of stationary objects as viewed by an observer moving across the landscape. Near objects appear to move past or opposite the path of motion; far objects appear to move in the direction of motion or remain fixed. The rate of apparent movement depends on the distance the observer is from the object. Objects near an aircraft appear to move rapidly, while distant objects appear to be almost stationary. Thus, objects that appear to be moving rapidly are judged to be nearby while those moving slowly are judged to be at a greater distance. Motion parallax can be apparent during flight. One example is an aircraft flying at 5,000 feet above ground level. At this altitude distant terrain appears stationary, while the terrain immediately below and to either side of the aircraft appears to be moving slowly (depending on forward airspeed). The opposite is true when an aircraft descends to 80 feet above highest obstacle with a forward airspeed of 120 knots. Terrain and objects in the horizon appear to move at a faster rate, while the terrain and objects underneath and to either side of the aircraft appear to pass at a high rate of speed.

VISUAL ILLUSIONS

8-70. The probability of SD increases as visual information decreases. Reduced visual references create several illusions that can cause SD. Chapter 9 discusses these illusions in more detail.

METEOROLOGICAL CONDITIONS AND NIGHT VISION

8-71. Although a mission might begin with clear skies and unrestricted visibility, meteorological conditions can deteriorate rapidly during flight. Clouds can appear gradually and, due to reduced visibility at night, easily go undetected by crewmembers. Aircraft can enter clouds inadvertently and without warning. Fog and haze can be encountered at low altitudes. Visibility can deteriorate gradually or suddenly. It is difficult to detect adverse weather at night, and crewmembers must constantly be aware of changing weather conditions. The following paragraphs discuss adverse weather indicators crews might encounter at night.

8-72. Ambient light levels gradually decrease as cloud coverage increases, causing a loss of visual acuity and terrain contrast even to the point of complete obscurity. Should this condition occur, pilots must initiate inadvertent instrument meteorological conditions (IMC) procedures. Crewmembers also must follow local standing operating procedures and command directives. Inadvertent IMC at night is one of the leading causes of Class A aviation mishaps.

8-73. Clouds are present if the moon and stars are not visible. The less visible the moon and stars, the heavier the cloud coverage.

8-74. Clouds obscuring moon illumination create shadows. Crewmembers can detect these shadows by observing the varying levels of ambient light along the flight route.

8-75. The halo effect observed around ground lights indicates the presence of moisture and possible ground fog. As fog and moisture increase, the intensity of these lights decrease. This same effect is apparent during flight. As moisture increases, light emitted from the aircraft is reflected back on the aircraft. This reflection makes it possible for crewmembers to misjudge critical factors such as the layout and height of terrain features and manmade structures, as well as actual position, heading, and altitude of other aircraft.

8-76. The presence of fog over water indicates the temperature and dew point are equal and that fog might soon form over ground areas.

SECTION VI – SELF-IMPOSED STRESS AND VISION

8-77. Crewmembers experience stressors such as altitude during flight. These stressors might not be controllable and can affect mission performance. Crewmembers also must cope with self-imposed stress but, unlike aviation stress, this type can be controlled. Factors leading to self-imposed stress include drugs, exhaustion, alcohol, tobacco, and hypoglycemia/nutritional deficiency. These factors (figure 8-21) can be remembered by the mnemonic acronym DEATH (more information can be found in AR 40-8).

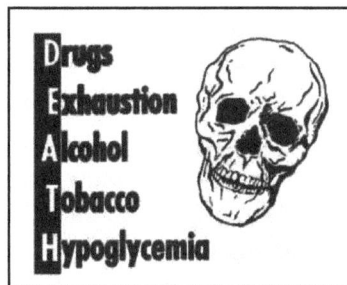

Figure 8-21. Self-imposed stress factors

DRUGS

8-78. Adverse side effects associated with drug use are illness and decreases in motor skill function, awareness level, and reaction time. Crewmembers who become ill should consult their flight surgeon and avoid self-medicating, which is unauthorized for flight personnel. AR 40-8 contains restrictions on drug use while on flight status.

EXHAUSTION

8-79. A combination of multiple factors causes exhaustion; it rarely stems from one factor alone. Contributing factors include poor diet habits and dehydration; poor sleep patterns and lack of rest; poor physical condition and inadequate exercise; various environmental factors; and combat stress. Common side effects of exhaustion include altered levels of concentration, awareness, and attentiveness; increased drowsiness (nodding off or falling asleep); and ineffective night-vision viewing techniques (staring rather than scanning).

8-80. Exhaustion reduces mental alertness and causes crewmembers to respond more slowly to situations that require immediate reaction. Exhausted crewmembers tend to concentrate on one aspect of a situation rather than consider the total environment. They also are prone to staring instead of practicing proper scanning techniques, a mistake that can cause incidents.

8-81. Good physical conditioning should decrease fatigue and improve night scanning efficiency. However, excessive exercise in a given day can lead to increased fatigue. Night flight is more stressful than day flight, and crewmembers must follow prescribed crew rest policies.

ALCOHOL

8-82. Alcohol impairs a person's judgment and causes him or her to become uncoordinated. It also hinders a crewmember's ability to view properly. Crewmembers under the influence of alcohol are more likely to stare at objects and neglect proper scanning techniques, particularly at night. The effects of alcohol are long lasting, as evidenced by the body's physiological response to a hangover.

8-83. Alcohol causes histotoxic hypoxia, a poisoning of the bloodstream that interferes with oxygen use by body tissues. At sea level, every ounce of alcohol in the bloodstream increases the body's physiological altitude. For example, 1 ounce of alcohol in an individual's bloodstream at sea level has an equivalent physiological altitude of 2,000 feet. An individual who consumes 3 ounces of alcohol at sea level and is then placed at 4,000 feet has an equivalent physiological altitude of 10,000 feet. Hypoxic hypoxia combines with histotoxic hypoxia at these higher altitudes, and the individual's time of useful consciousness is severely diminished. If a flight lasts longer than 60 minutes, the individual can become unconscious or even die from a lack of oxygen (see paragraph 8-7, AR 95-1).

8-84. Guidance for performing or resuming crewmember duties after alcohol consumption is 12 hours after the last drink with no residual physiological effects present. Crewmember duties consist of preflight and postflight actions including maintenance and are not limited to actual aircraft operation or flight. Detrimental effects associated with alcohol consumption include poor judgment, decision making, perception, reaction time, coordination, and scanning techniques (staring).

TOBACCO

8-85. Of all self-imposed stressors, cigarette smoking most impairs visual sensitivity at night. Hemoglobin in the red blood cells has a 200 to 300 times greater affinity for carbon monoxide than oxygen, meaning it accepts carbon monoxide far more rapidly than oxygen. When an individual exhales, the process of pulmonary perfusion (gas exchange within the lungs) releases carbon dioxide from the bloodstream. When an individual inhales, oxygen is usually absorbed into blood through hemoglobin in the red blood cells. These processes maintain normal levels of oxygen and other gases within the bloodstream.

8-86. Smoking increases carbon monoxide, which in turn reduces blood's capacity to carry oxygen. Hypemic hypoxia, a condition that negatively affects an individual's peripheral vision and dark adaptation, results from this increase in carbon monoxide. For example, if an individual smokes three cigarettes in rapid succession or 20 to 40 cigarettes within a 24-hour period, blood carbon monoxide content increases by 8 to 10 percent. The resulting physiological effects at sea level are the same as flying at 5,000 feet but, more importantly, the individual loses about 20 percent of his or her night vision capability. Table 8-1 compares night vision reduction rates at varying altitudes for smokers and nonsmokers.

Table 8-1. Night vision reduction rates for
smokers and nonsmokers

Altitude (feet)	Nonsmoker (%)	Smoker (%)
4,000	Sea level	20
6,000	5	25
10,000	20	40
14,000	35	55
16,000	40	50

HYPOGLYCEMIA AND NUTRITIONAL DEFICIENCY

8-87. Aviation personnel must not skip or postpone meals and should avoid supplementing primary meals with fast sugars such as sodas and candy bars. These foods and beverages can cause hypoglycemia, a condition that results in hunger pangs, distraction, habit pattern breakdown, shortened attention span, and other physiological changes. Supplementing meals with fast sugars sustains an individual for 30 to 45 minutes on average, followed by an increase in the intensity of negative effects. Hypoglycemia is not the only adverse effect of an improper diet; a diet deficient in vitamin A can impair night vision. Vitamin A is an essential element in the buildup of rhodopsin (visual purple), which stimulates rod cells. Nigh vision is severely degraded without this buildup. A balanced diet that includes foods such as eggs, butter, cheese, liver, carrots, and most green vegetables provides adequate vitamin A intake and helps maintain visual acuity. Crewmembers must consult a flight surgeon before consuming vitamin A supplements not organic to these foods.

SECTION VII – OTHER VISION CONSIDERATIONS

NERVE AGENTS AND NIGHT VISION

8-88. Night vision is adversely affected by minute amounts of nerve agents. When direct contact occurs, the pupils constrict and do not dilate in low ambient light, resulting in a condition known as miosis. Currently available automatic chemical alarms are not sensitive enough to detect low agent concentrations.

8-89. The exposure time required to cause miosis depends on agent concentration. Miosis can occur gradually as the eyes are exposed to low concentrations over a long period. However, exposure to high concentrations can cause miosis in the few seconds it takes to put on a protective mask. Repeated exposure over a period of days is cumulative.

8-90. Symptoms of miosis range from minimal to severe, depending on dosage to the eye. Severe miosis, which is characterized by a reduced ability to see in low ambient light, persists about 48 hours after onset. The pupil gradually returns to normal over several days, but full recovery can take up to 20 days. Repeated exposure within the affected time is cumulative.

8-91. The onset of miosis is insidious since it is not always immediately painful. Miotic Soldiers might not recognize their condition even as they carry out tasks requiring vision in low ambient light. After a nerve agent attack (especially with the more persistent types), commanders should assume some night vision loss has occurred among personnel otherwise fit for duty and consider grounding crewmembers until they fully recover. All exposed crewmembers and maintenance personnel must consult their flight surgeon and local medical personnel immediately after exposure.

FLIGHT HAZARDS

8-92. Solar glare, bird strikes, nuclear flash, and lasers are possible hazards crewmembers might encounter during low-level flight.

SOLAR GLARE

8-93. Glare from direct, reflected, and scattered sunlight causes discomfort and reduces visual acuity. To reduce or eliminate discomfort, all crewmembers should use their helmets' tinted visor or wear ND-15 sunglasses with the clear visor. Day blindness can occur in areas with extreme solar glare such as snowy terrain, bodies of water, or desert environments.

BIRD STRIKES

8-94. Bird strikes can occur anytime, day or night, during low-level flight. Cockpit windshields are designed to withstand impacts but the potential for shattering exists. According to the Federal Aviation Administration, if an aircraft traveling at an airspeed equivalent to a 120-mile per hour ground speed strikes a 2-pound seagull, the force exerted would be equal to 4,800 pounds (some antiaircraft rounds exert less force). Therefore, if the viewing environment permits, crewmembers should wear or lower the clear visor for night flights and tinted visor for day flights. These visors also protect the eyes from glass fragments should the windshield shatter.

NUCLEAR FLASH

8-95. A fireball from a nuclear explosion can cause flash blindness and retinal burns. By day, the optical blink reflex should prevent retinal burns from distances where survival is possible. When the pupil is dilated at night, however, retinal burns are possible and indirect flash blindness can deprive crewmembers of all useful vision for periods exceeding 1 minute. No practical protection against nuclear flash has been developed.

LASERS

8-96. Mobile military lasers currently work by converting electrical and chemical energy into light. This light can be either continuously emitted or collected over time and suddenly released. A laser is light amplified by a stimulated emission of radiation through one prism or a series of multiple prisms, which increases light frequency and intensity. The beam of light produced is usually less than 1 inch in diameter and might or might not be visible to the naked eye (ultraviolet, infrared, and thermal lasers).

8-97. Laser range finders and target designators (except thermal infrared lasers) operate by accumulating and suddenly releasing light energy in the form of a crystal rod about the size of a cigarette. The laser pulse is controlled by an electrical signal that turns the laser on and off. Laser pulses travel at the speed of light—300,000 kilometers per second. When a laser emits light during a pulse, the power output averages about 3 megawatts (3 million watts) along a narrow beam. About 90 percent of emitted energy is contained in this beam. This characteristic makes lasers useful as range finders and target designators but renders them dangerous to human eyes.

8-98. Lasers can damage eyes from a considerable distance, although a beam's energy level decreases as its diameter widens with increasing distance. Therefore, distance is the best protection against lasers. If distance is not possible, protective ballistic and laser protective eyewear goggles or visors might offer limited protection. Ballistic limit protections (BLPs) are specific to laser frequency. Crewmembers must identify the type of laser frequency threats they might encounter to ensure they receive the correct BLP eyewear from the unit aviation life support equipment technician.

8-99. Smoke, fog, and dust weaken laser light, but even in these conditions lasers present a real danger to crewmembers. A useful rule is if a target can be seen through smoke, laser energy can hit the target and also strike the eyes. In daylight, even visual-light lasers are virtually invisible unless there is smoke, mist, or fog in the air.

8-100. The four major classes of directed-energy laser systems are high-energy lasers, low-energy lasers, radio-frequency lasers, and particle-beam lasers.

Class 1 (Low Energy)

8-101. Class 1 laser devices do not emit hazardous laser radiation in any operating or viewing condition. Class 1 lasers include fully enclosed lasers such as the PAQ-4A/B/C infrared aiming light and many laser marksmanship trainers.

Class 2 (Low-to-Medium Energy)

8-102. Class 2 laser devices usually include continuous-wave visible laser devices. Crewmembers must take precautions to prevent staring into the direct beams of these devices. Momentary exposure (greater than 0.25 second) is not considered hazardous; for example, current laser pointers, construction lasers, and alignment lasers.

Class 3a (Medium Energy)

8-103. Class 3a lasers generally are not hazardous unless crewmembers view them with magnifying optics from within the beam. Class 3a lasers include visible and invisible frequency lasers such as the miniature eye-safe laser infrared observation set (MELIOS).

Class 3b (Medium-to-High Energy)

8-104. Class 3b lasers are potentially hazardous if a direct or specularly reflected beam is viewed by unprotected eyes. Care must be taken to prevent intrabeam (within the beam) viewing and control specular reflections from surfaces such as mirrors and still water. Class 3b lasers include many rangefinders and the AIM-1, GCP-1, and AN/PEQ-2A laser pointers.

Class 4 (High Energy)

8-105. Class 4 lasers are pulsed, visible, near-infrared lasers that produce diffuse reflections, fire, and skin and eye hazards, with the eyes being especially vulnerable. These lasers have an average output of 500 milliwatts or greater. Safety precautions generally consist of using door interlocks to protect personnel entering a laser facility from exposure, baffles to terminate primary and secondary beams, and use of protective eyewear and clothing. Crewmembers inadvertently or suddenly exposed to these lasers will receive serious retinal burns within tenths of a second if their eyes are unprotected. During peacetime military operations, these lasers typically are operated only on cleared, approved laser ranges or while personnel are using appropriate eye and skin protection. Actual enemy forces, however, might intentionally expose crewmembers to deplete their fighting capability. Class 4 lasers include industrial welders and target designator lasers.

PROTECTIVE MEASURES

BUILT-IN PROTECTIVE MEASURES

8-106. Filters constructed of glass or plastic can stop laser light. These filters absorb or reflect light of a given color or wavelength. Sunglasses are specially created to filter visual light, but an infrared or ultraviolet laser will penetrate the lenses and damage the eyes. The Army currently provides protective eyewear such as ballistic-laser protective spectacles (B-LPS) that help prevent eye injuries from certain types of lasers.

8-107. Crewmembers can take active and passive protective measures to protect themselves from laser injury. Passive protective measures include—

- Taking cover.
- Getting out of the laser's path.
- Using available protective gear.
- Keeping all exposed skin covered to prevent burns.

8-108. Active protective measures include—

- Using countermeasures as taught or directed by the unit commander.
- Applying evasive action.
- Scanning the battlefield with one eye or monocular optics.
- Minimizing the use of binoculars in areas where lasers could be in use.

8-109. If actively engaged by lasers, crewmembers should deploy smoke and use hardened optical systems and built-in or clip-on filters such as the B-LPS. FM 8-50 contains information regarding laser injury prevention and medical management.

This page intentionally left blank.

Chapter 9

Spatial Disorientation

SD is a contributing factor in more aircraft accidents than any other physiological problem in flight. Regardless of their flight experience, all crewmembers are subject to disorientation. The human body is structured to perceive changes in movement on land in relation to the Earth's surface. In aircraft, the visual, vestibular, and proprioceptive sensory systems can provide the brain erroneous orientation information. This misinformation can cause sensory illusions that lead to SD.

COMMON TERMS OF SPATIAL DISORIENTATION

SPATIAL DISORIENTATION

9-1.   SD is an individual's inability to determine his or her position, attitude, and motion relative to the Earth's surface. When SD occurs, pilots are unable to see, believe, interpret, or prove information derived from their flight instruments. They instead rely on false information provided by their senses.

SENSORY ILLUSION

9-2.   A sensory illusion is a false perception of reality caused by the conflict of orientation information derived from one or more equilibrium mechanisms. Sensory illusions are a major cause of SD.

TYPES OF SPATIAL DISORIENTATION

TYPE I (UNRECOGNIZED)

9-3.   In type I SD, an aviator does not perceive any indication of SD or think anything is wrong. What the aviator sees—or thinks he or she sees—is corroborated by other senses. The pilot might see the instruments functioning properly and have no suspicion of instrument malfunction. Likewise, the aircraft might be performing normally with no indication of aircraft control malfunction. Unaware of a problem, the pilot fails to recognize or correct the SD, a mistake that usually results in a fatal aircraft mishap. Type I SD is the most dangerous type of disorientation. An example is the height/depth perception illusion, where a pilot descends into the ground or some obstacle above the ground due to a lack of situational awareness.

TYPE II (RECOGNIZED)

9-4.   In type II SD, the pilot perceives a problem resulting from SD but might not recognize it as SD. The pilot might feel a control is malfunctioning or perceive an instrument failure as in the graveyard spiral, a classic example of type II SD. The pilot will not correct aircraft roll as indicated by the attitude indicator because his or her vestibular indications of straight-and-level flight are so strong.

TYPE III (INCAPACITATING)

9-5.   In type III SD, the pilot experiences such an overwhelming sensation of movement that he or she cannot orient using visual cues or the aircraft instruments. Type III SD is not fatal if the copilot can gain control of the aircraft.

EQUILIBRIUM MAINTENANCE

9-6.   The visual, vestibular, and proprioceptive sensory systems (figure 9-1) are especially important in maintaining equilibrium and balance. The combined functioning of these senses usually maintains equilibrium and prevents SD. The visual system is the most reliable of the three systems during flight. The vestibular and proprioceptive systems are unreliable in flight without the visual system.

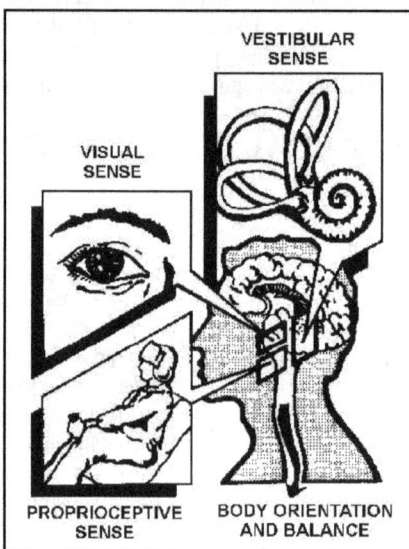

Figure 9-1. The three equilibrium systems

VISUAL SYSTEM

9-7.   Of the three sensory systems, the visual system is the most important in maintaining equilibrium and orientation. To some extent, the eyes can help determine the speed and direction of flight by comparing aircraft position relative to some fixed reference point. The visual system provides 80 percent of orientation in humans (chapter 8 contains more information about the eyes).

9-8.   Under IMC, crewmembers lose fixed reference points outside the aircraft and the pilot must rely on visual sensory input from the instruments for spatial orientation. Relying on the visual sense and believing the instruments rather than the input of the other senses requires disciplined training.

9-9.   The eyes allow the pilot to scan sensitive flight instruments that provide accurate spatial orientation information. These instruments indicate unusual aircraft attitudes resulting from turbulence, distraction, inattention, mechanical failure, or SD.

VESTIBULAR SYSTEM

9-10. The vestibular system is located within the inner ear, which contains the sense organs that detect motion and gravity. This system is located in the temporal bone on each side of the head. Each vestibular apparatus consists of two distinct structures, the semicircular canals and vestibule proper, which contains the otolith organs. Both the semicircular canals and otolith organs sense changes in aircraft attitude. The semicircular canals also sense changes in angular acceleration and deceleration. Figure 9-2 depicts the vestibular system.

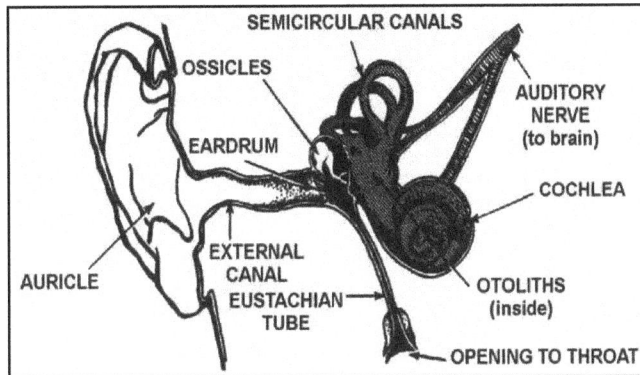

Figure 9-2. Vestibular system

Otolith Organs

9-11. The otolith organs are small sacs located in the vestibule. Sensory hairs project from each macula into the otolithic membrane, an overlying, gelatinous membrane that contains chalklike crystals called otoliths. The otolith organs (figure 9-3) respond to gravity and linear acceleration and deceleration. Changes in head position relative to gravitational force cause the otolithic membrane to shift position on the macula. The sensory hairs then bend, signaling a change in head position.

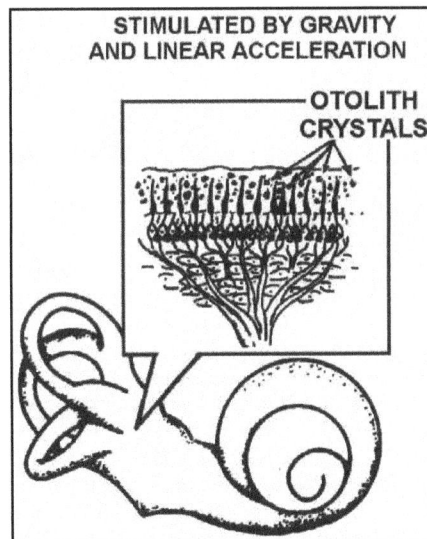

Figure 9-3. Otolith organs

9-12. When the head is upright, the hair cells generate a "resting" frequency of nerve impulses (figure 9-4, page 9-4).

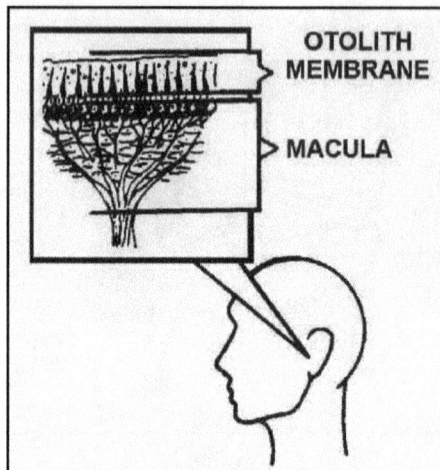

Figure 9-4. Position of hair cells when head is upright

9-13. The resting frequency is altered when the head is tilted, and the brain is informed of the new position. The position of the hair cells when the head is tilted forward and backward is illustrated in figure 9-5.

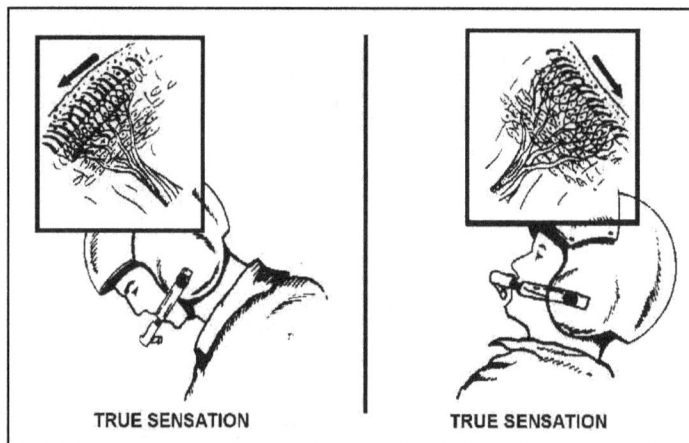

TRUE SENSATION   TRUE SENSATION

Figure 9-5. Position of hair cells when head is tilted forward and backward

9-14. Linear acceleration and deceleration stimulates the otolith organs. The body cannot physically distinguish between the inertial forces resulting from linear acceleration and the force of gravity. Forward acceleration results in backward displacement of the otolithic membrane. When an adequate visual reference is not available, crewmembers might experience a false sensation of backward tilt (figure 9-6, page 9-5).

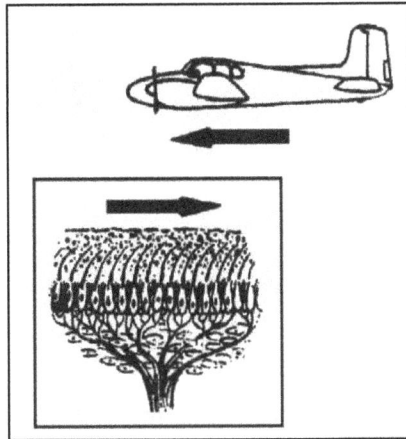

Figure 9-6. False sensation of backward tilt

SEMICIRCULAR CANALS

9-15. The semicircular canals sense changes in angular acceleration and react to any changes in roll, pitch, or yaw attitude. Figure 9-7 shows where these changes are registered in the semicircular canals.

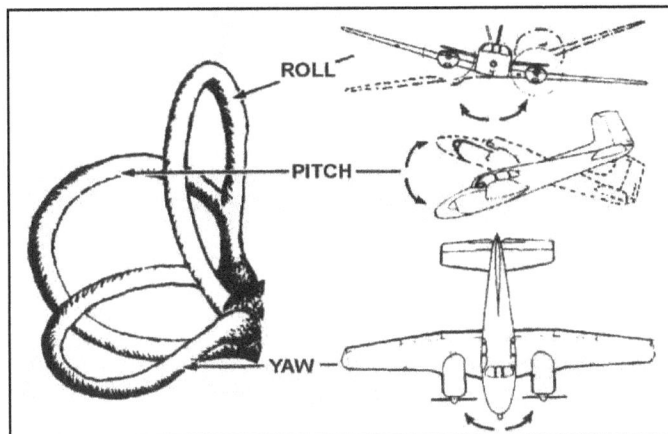

Figure 9-7. Reactions of semicircular canals to changes in angular acceleration

9-16. The semicircular canals are situated in three planes perpendicular to each other and filled with a fluid called endolymph. The inertial torque resulting from angular acceleration in the canal plane puts this fluid into motion. This motion bends the cupula, a gelatinous structure located in the ampulla of the canal. This bending then moves the hair cells situated beneath the cupula, stimulating the vestibular nerve. These nerve impulses are then transmitted to the brain, where they are interpreted as rotation of the head. Figure 9-8 (page 9-6) shows a cutaway section of the semicircular canal.

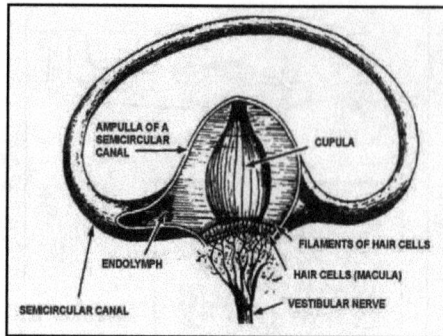

Figure 9-8. Cutaway view of the semicircular canal

9-17. When no acceleration takes place, the hair cells are upright. The body senses that no turn has occurred. The position of the hair cells and the actual sensation correspond, as shown in figure 9-9.

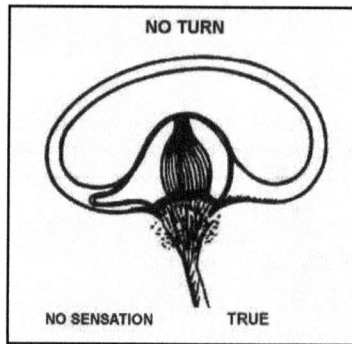

Figure 9-9. Position of hair cells during no acceleration

9-18. When the semicircular canal is stimulated during clockwise acceleration, fluid within it lags behind the accelerated canal walls. The lag creates a relative counterclockwise movement of this fluid. The canal wall and cupula move in the direction opposite the fluid motion. The brain interprets movement of the hairs to be a turn in the same direction as the canal wall, and the body correctly senses a clockwise turn is being made. Figure 9-10 shows the position of the hair cells and resulting true sensation during a clockwise turn.

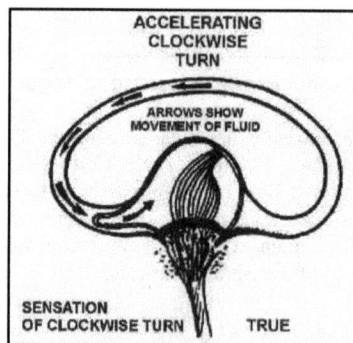

Figure 9-10. Sensation during a clockwise turn

9-19. If a clockwise turn continues at a constant rate for several seconds or longer, the motion of the fluid within the canals catches up with the canal walls. At this point the hairs are no longer bent, and the brain receives the false impression that turning has stopped. A prolonged constant turn in either direction results in a false sensation of no turn. The position of the hair cells and resulting false sensation during a prolonged clockwise turn is shown in figure 9-11.

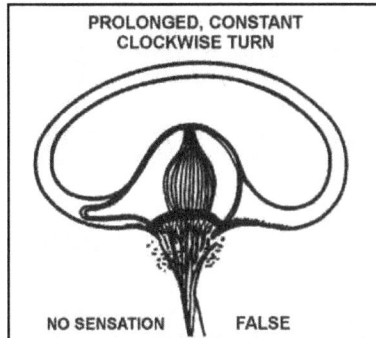

Figure 9-11. Sensation during a prolonged clockwise turn

9-20. When the aircraft's clockwise rotation slows or stops, fluid within the canal moves briefly in a clockwise direction. This movement sends a signal to the brain that is falsely interpreted as body movement in the opposite direction. In an attempt to correct the falsely perceived counterclockwise turn, the pilot might turn the aircraft in the original clockwise direction. Figure 9-12 shows the position of the hair cells and resulting false sensation when a clockwise turn slows or stops.

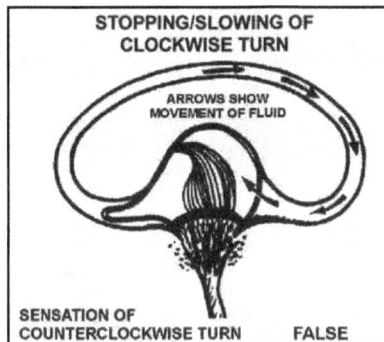

Figure 9-12. Sensation during slowing or stopping of a clockwise turn

PROPRIOCEPTIVE SYSTEM

9-21. The proprioceptive system reacts to sensations resulting from pressure on sensors in the joints, muscles, and skin and from slight changes in the position of internal organs. The proprioceptive system is closely associated with the vestibular system and, to a lesser degree, the visual system.

9-22. Forces act upon seated pilots in flight. With training and experience, pilots can easily distinguish the most discrete aircraft movements by gauging the pressure of the seat against their bodies. Recognition of these movements led to the term "seat of the pants" flying.

VISUAL ILLUSIONS

9-23. Visual illusions give false impressions or misconceptions of actual conditions. Therefore, crewmembers must understand the types of illusions that can occur and disorientation resulting from each.

9-24. Although the visual system is the most reliable of the senses, some illusions can result from misinterpreting what is seen; what is perceived is not always accurate. Even with references outside the cockpit and instrument displays inside, crewmembers must be vigilant to interpret information correctly.

RELATIVE MOTION ILLUSION

9-25. Relative motion is falsely perceived self-motion in relation to another object's motion. The most common example is when an individual in a car is stopped at a traffic light and another car pulls alongside. The individual stopped at the light perceives the second car's forward motion as his or her own rearward motion, resulting in the individual applying more pressure to the brakes than necessary. This illusion can be encountered during flight in situations such as formation flight, hover taxi, or hovering over water or tall grass.

CONFUSION WITH GROUND LIGHTS

9-26. Confusion with ground lights occurs when a pilot mistakes ground lights for celestial lights. The illusion prompts the pilot to place the aircraft in an unusual attitude to keep the misperceived ground lights above the aircraft. Isolated ground lights can appear as celestial lights, which could lead to the illusion the aircraft is in a nose-high or one-wing-low attitude (part A, figure 9-13). When no celestial lights are visible because of overcast conditions, unlighted terrain can blend with the dark overcast to create the illusion the unlighted terrain is part of the sky (part B, figure 9-13). This illusion can be avoided by referencing the flight instruments and establishing true horizon and attitude.

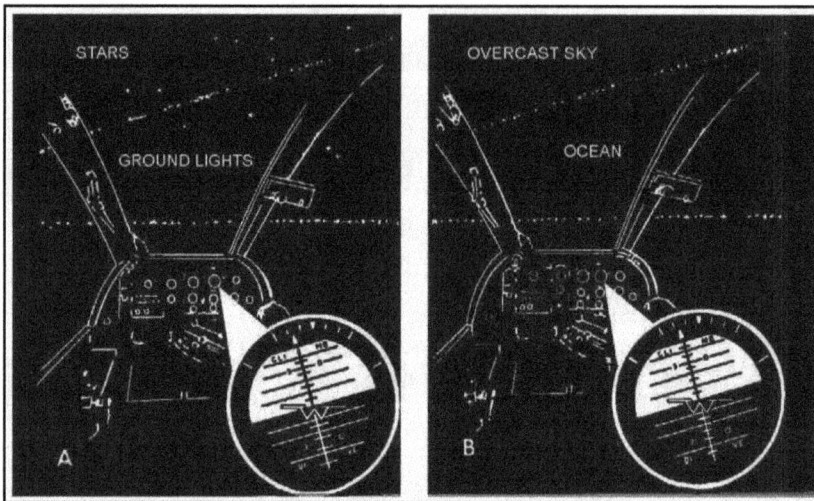

Figure 9-13. Confusion of ground lights and stars at night

FALSE HORIZON ILLUSION

9-27. False horizon illusions (figure 9-14, page 9-9) occur when a pilot confuses cloud formations with the horizon or ground. A sloping cloud deck can be difficult to perceive as anything but horizontal if it extends any great distance in the pilot's peripheral vision. The pilot might perceive the cloudbank to be horizontal even if it is not horizontal to the ground, causing he or she to fly the aircraft in a banked attitude. This condition is often insidious and goes undetected until the pilot recognizes it, transitions to instruments, and makes necessary corrections. This illusion also might occur if the pilot looks outside after having given prolonged attention to a task inside the cockpit. Confusion can result in the pilot placing the aircraft parallel to the cloudbank.

Figure 9-14. False horizon illusion

HEIGHT-DEPTH PERCEPTION ILLUSION

9-28. Height-depth perception illusions are due to a lack of sufficient visual cues and causes crewmembers to lose their depth perception. Flying over areas devoid of visual references such as desert, snow, or water deprives crewmembers their perception of height. Misjudging the aircraft's true altitude, the pilot might fly the aircraft dangerously low to the ground or other obstacles above the ground. Flight in an area where visibility is restricted by fog, smoke, whiteout, brownout, or haze can produce the same illusion.

CRATER ILLUSION

9-29. Crater illusions occur when crewmembers land at night under night vision device (NVD) conditions and the infrared searchlight is directed too far under the aircraft's nose. This combination creates the illusion of landing with upsloping terrain in all directions or landing in a crater. This illusionary depression lulls the pilot into continually lowering the collective and could result in the aircraft prematurely impacting the ground, causing damage to both aircraft and crew. If observing another aircraft during hover taxi, the pilot might perceive the crater is moving with the aircraft being observed.

STRUCTURAL ILLUSION

9-30. Structural illusions are caused by the effects of rain, snow, sleet, heat waves, or other visual obscurants. A straight line can appear curved when viewed through heat waves in the desert. A single wingtip light might appear as a double light or in a different location when viewed through rain. Curvature of the aircraft windscreen also can cause structural illusions due to the refraction of light rays as they pass through the windscreen (figure 9-15, page 9-10). Pilots must remain aware of the potential for false perceptions when operating in environments containing these obscurants.

Figure 9-15. Structural illusion

SIZE-DISTANCE ILLUSION

9-31. Size-distance illusions (figure 9-16) are false perceptions of distance from an object or the ground, created when a crewmember misinterprets an unfamiliar object's size to be the same as an object they are accustomed to viewing. These illusions can occur if visual cues such as a runway or trees are of a different size than expected. A pilot making an approach to a larger, wider runway might perceive the aircraft is too low, while a pilot making an approach to a smaller, narrower runway might perceive the aircraft is too high. A pilot making an approach 25 feet above the trees in Washington State, where the average tree is 100 feet tall, might fly the aircraft dangerously low if trying to make the same approach at Fort Rucker, AL, where the average tree height is 30 feet. This illusion also can occur when a crewmember views another aircraft's position lights at night. The observed aircraft will appear further away than before if it suddenly flies into smoke or haze.

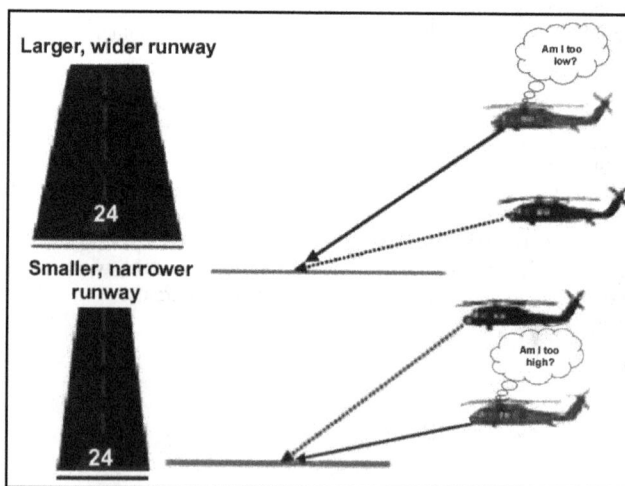

Figure 9-16. Size-distance illusion

FASCINATION (FIXATION) IN FLYING

9-32. Fascination or fixation in flying can be separated into two categories: task saturation and target fixation. Task saturation occurs when crewmembers become so engrossed with a problem or task within the cockpit they fail to properly scan outside the aircraft. Target fixation, commonly referred to as target hypnosis, occurs when crewmembers ignore orientation cues and focus their attention on an object or goal. For example, an attack pilot on a gunnery range might become so intent on hitting a target that he or she forgets to fly the aircraft, causing it to strike the ground, target, or shrapnel.

REVERSIBLE PERSPECTIVE ILLUSION

9-33. Reversible perspective illusions occur at night when a crewmember perceives another aircraft to be moving away as it is actually approaching. If each aircraft's pilot has the same assumption and the rate of closure is significant, by the time both pilots recognize their misperception it might be too late to avoid a mishap. This illusion is often experienced when a crewmember observes another aircraft flying a parallel course. Aircrew coordination is paramount in these situations, and crewmembers must observe the other aircraft's position lights to determine the direction of flight. "Red on right returning" is an easy way to remember this principle; if the other aircraft's red position light is on the right and its green position light on the left, it is traveling in the opposite direction of the observing aircraft's flight path.

ALTERED PLANES OF REFERENCE

9-34. Altered planes of reference (figure 9-17) create an inaccurate sense of altitude, attitude, or flight path position in relation to an object so great in size it replaces the horizon as the plane of reference. For example, a pilot approaching a line of mountains might feel the need to climb even though the aircraft's altitude is adequate. The pilot comes to this mistaken conclusion because he or she subconsciously moves the horizon, which helps maintain orientation, to the top of the ridgeline. Without an adequate horizon, the brain attempts to fix a new horizon. Conversely, an aircraft entering a valley that contains a slowly increasing upslope condition might become trapped because the slope can quickly increase and exceed the aircraft's ability to climb above the hill, causing it to crash into the surrounding hills.

Figure 9-17. Altered planes of reference

AUTOKINESIS

9-35. Autokinesis occurs primarily at night when ambient visual cues are minimal and a small, dim light is seen against a dark background. After about 6 to 12 seconds of visually fixating on the light, an individual perceives movement at up to 20 degrees in any particular direction or in several directions in succession, although there is no actual object displacement. This illusion can cause a pilot to mistake the fixated object for another aircraft. In addition, a pilot flying at night might perceive a relatively stable lead aircraft to be moving erratically when, in fact, it is not. The unnecessary and undesirable control inputs the pilot makes to compensate for the illusory movement result in increased workload and wasted motion at best and an operational hazard at worst.

FLICKER VERTIGO

9-36. Flicker vertigo (figure 9-18) is not technically an illusion. However, as most people are aware from personal experience, viewing a flickering light can be both distracting and annoying. Flicker vertigo is created by helicopter rotor blades or airplane propellers interrupting direct sunlight at a rate of 4 to 20 cycles per second. Flashing anticollision strobe lights can produce this effect, especially when an aircraft is in the clouds. Though rare, crewmembers should be aware that photic stimuli (flickering light) at certain frequencies can cause seizures in individuals susceptible to flicker-induced epilepsy.

Figure 9-18. Flicker vertigo

VESTIBULAR ILLUSIONS

9-37. The vestibular system provides accurate information as long as an individual is on the ground. Once the individual is airborne, however, the vestibular system might malfunction and cause illusions that pose the greatest problem with SD. Aviators must understand vestibular illusions and the conditions in which they occur and be able to distinguish between accurate vestibular system inputs and those that cause SD.

SOMATOGYRAL ILLUSIONS

9-38. Somatogyral illusions occur when angular acceleration and deceleration stimulates the semicircular canals. Some types of somatogyral illusions that might be encountered in flight are the leans, graveyard spin, and Coriolis illusion.

Leans

9-39. Leans is the most common form of SD. This illusion occurs when a pilot fails to perceive angular motion. During continuous straight-and-level flight, the pilot correctly perceives that he or she is straight and level (part A, figure 9-19, page 9-13). However, if the pilot were to roll into or out of a bank, he or she might experience perceptions that contradict the reading on the attitude indicator. In a slow roll, for instance, the pilot might fail to perceive the aircraft is no longer vertical or feel the aircraft is still flying straight and level although the attitude indicator shows it is in a bank (part B, figure 9-19). Once the pilot detects the slow roll, he or she will make a quick recovery and resume straight-and-level flight. However, the pilot might perceive the aircraft is banking in the opposite direction even though the attitude indicator shows it is flying straight and level (part C, figure 9-19). The pilot might then feel it is necessary to turn the aircraft so it aligns with the falsely perceived vertical position. Instead, the pilot should maintain straight-and-level flight as shown by the attitude indicator. To counter the falsely perceived vertical position, the pilot must lean his or her body in the original direction of the subthreshold roll until the false sensation subsides (part D, figure 9-19).

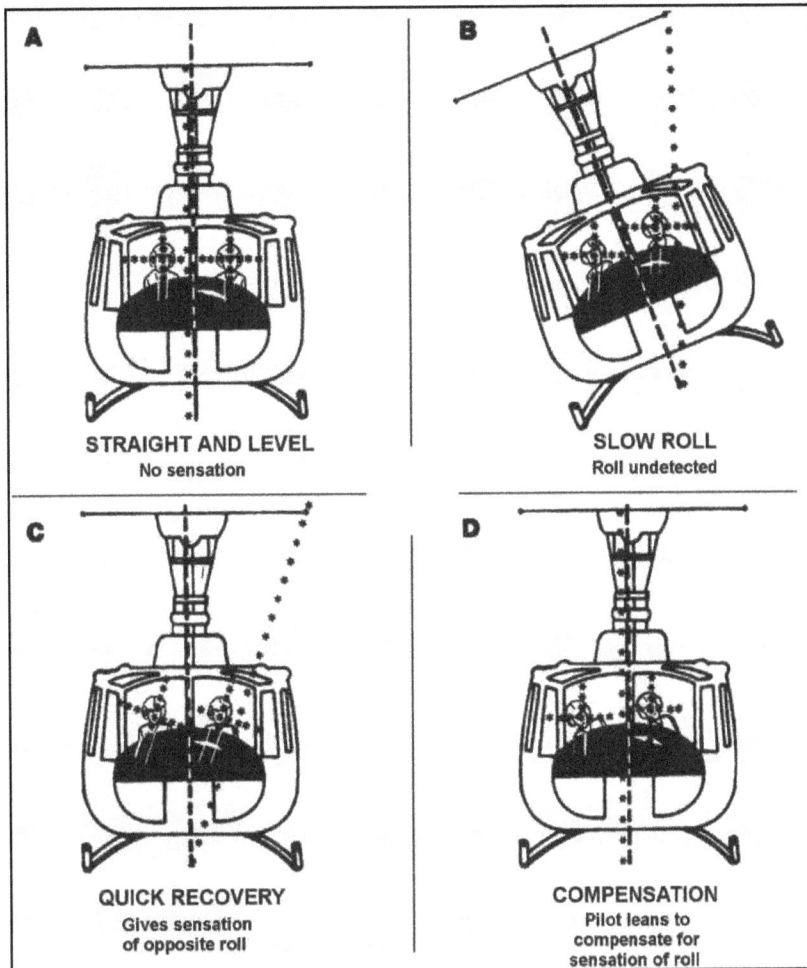

Figure 9-19. Leans

Graveyard Spin

9-40. The graveyard spin, shown in figure 9-20 (page 9-14), usually occurs in fixed-wing aircraft. For example, if a pilot enters a spin and remains in it for several seconds, the semicircular canals will reach equilibrium and no motion will be perceived. Upon recovering from the spin, the pilot will undergo deceleration, which is sensed by the semicircular canals. He or she will have a strong sensation of being in a spin in the opposite direction even if the flight instruments contradict that perception. If deprived of external visual references, the pilot might disregard the instruments and make control corrections against the falsely perceived spin, causing the aircraft to reenter a spin in the original direction.

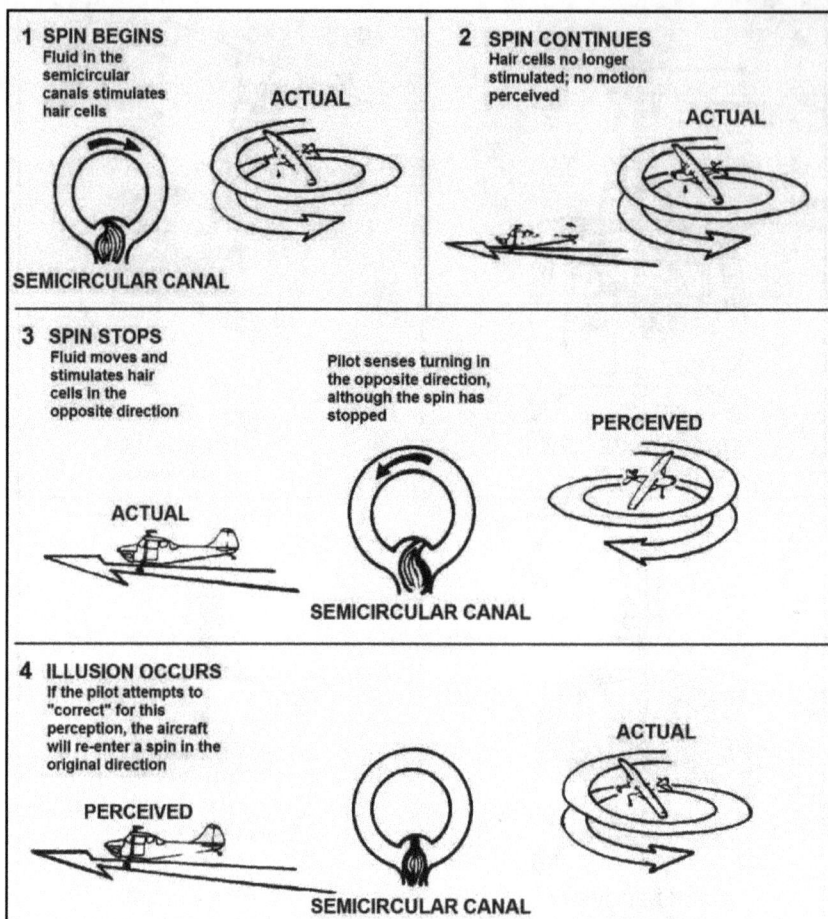

Figure 9-20. Graveyard spin

9-41. A pilot, noting a loss of altitude as the spin develops, might apply back pressure on the controls and add power in an attempt to gain altitude. This maneuver will tighten the spin and possibly cause the pilot to lose control of the aircraft.

Coriolis Illusion

9-42. Regardless of aircraft type, Coriolis illusions are the most dangerous of all vestibular illusions and cause overwhelming disorientation.

9-43. These illusions occur during prolonged turns when a pilot makes a head motion in a different geometrical plane. When the pilot enters and remains in a turn, the semicircular canal corresponding to the yaw axis equalizes and the endolymph fluid no longer deviates or bends the cupula. Figure 9-21 (page 9-15) illustrates fluid movement in the semicircular canals during a turn.

9-44. If the pilot moves his or her head in a geometrical plane different from the turn, the yaw axis semicircular canal moves from a plane of rotation to a new plane of nonrotation. Fluid in that canal then slows, resulting in a sensation of turning in the direction opposite the original turn. The other two canals are simultaneously brought within a plane of rotation, and fluid stimulates the other two cupulas. The combined effects of coupler deflection (fluid movement) in all three canals creates a new perception of motion in three different planes of rotation—yaw, pitch, and roll—and causes the pilot to experience an overwhelming head-over-heels tumbling sensation.

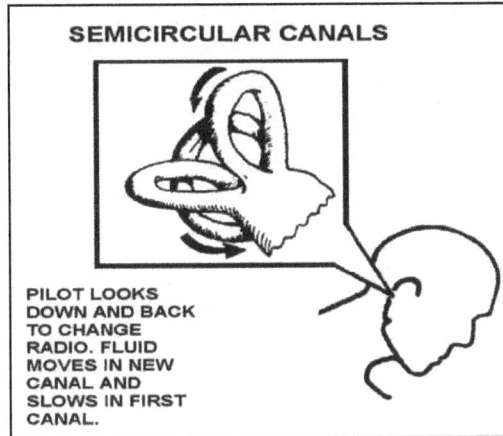

Figure 9-21. Fluid movement in the semicircular canals during a turn

SOMATOGRAVIC ILLUSION

9-45. Somatogravic illusions are caused when changes in gravity or linear acceleration and deceleration stimulate the otolith organ. The three types of somatogravic illusions encountered in flight are oculogravic, elevator, and oculoagravic.

Oculogravic Illusion

9-46. Oculogravic illusions occur when inertia from an aircraft's linear acceleration and deceleration causes the otolith organ to sense a nose-high or nose-low attitude. During linear acceleration, the gelatinous layer that contains the otolith organ is shifted aft, resulting in a false perception that the aircraft is in a nose-high attitude. Intuitive reactions to this false perception can have catastrophic results. For example, a pilot correcting for this illusion without a through instrument cross-check will most likely dive the aircraft.

9-47. These illusions do not occur if adequate outside references are available. A pilot making an instrument approach in inclement weather or darkness is considerably more susceptible to oculogravic illusions.

Elevator Illusion

9-48. Elevator illusions occur during upward acceleration. Inertia causes the eyes to track downward as the body tries, through inputs supplied by the inner ear, to maintain visual fixation on the environment or instrument panel. With his or her eyes tracked downward, the pilot senses the aircraft's nose is rising. This illusion is common among aviators flying aircraft that encounter updrafts.

Oculoagravic Illusion

9-49. Oculoagravic illusions result from downward movement of an aircraft. Inertia causes the pilot's eyes to track upward, resulting in a false sensation that the aircraft is in a nose-low attitude. This illusion is commonly encountered as a helicopter enters autorotation. The usual intuitive response is to add aft cyclic, which decreases airspeed below desired levels.

PROPRIOCEPTIVE ILLUSIONS

9-50. Proprioceptive illusions rarely occur alone. They are closely associated with the vestibular system and, to a lesser degree, the visual system. Proprioceptive information input to the brain can lead to false perceptions of true vertical. During turns, banks, climbs, and descending maneuvers, proprioceptive information is fed into the central nervous system. A properly executed turn vectors gravity and centrifugal force through the aircraft's vertical axis. Without visual references, the body senses only being pressed firmly into the seat. Because this sensation is usually associated with climbs, a pilot might falsely interpret it as such. Conversely, recovering from turns lightens pressure on the seat and creates an illusion of descending. This false perception might cause the pilot to pull back on the stick and reduce airspeed. Figure 9-22 illustrates a proprioceptive illusion.

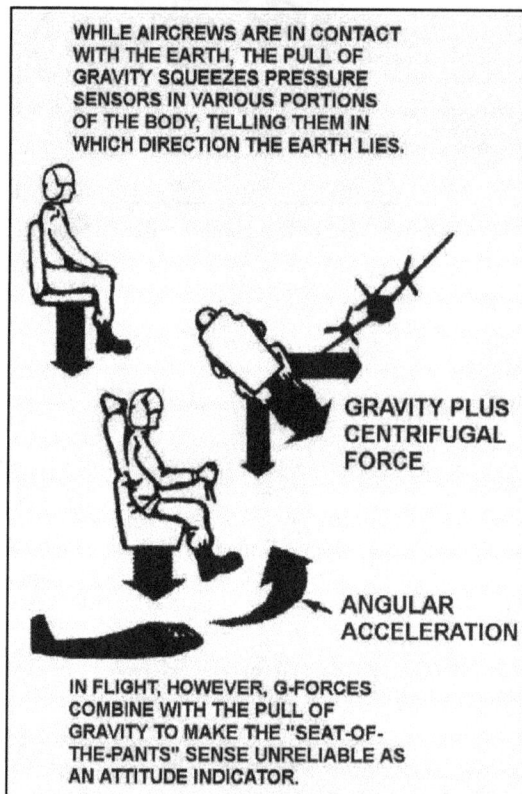

Figure 9-22. Proprioceptive illusion

PREVENTION OF SPATIAL DISORIENTATION

9-51. SD cannot be eliminated, but crewmembers must remember the misleading sensations from sensory systems are predictable. Due to normal functioning and limitations of the senses, all pilots, regardless of experience level, can suffer the effects of SD. As such, crewmembers must be aware of SD's potential hazards, understand their significance, and learn to overcome them. Training, instrument proficiency, good health, maintaining situational awareness, and aircraft design all help to minimize SD. Additional measures pilots should take to prevent SD include—

- Never fly without visual reference points (either the actual horizon or artificial horizon provided by the instruments).

- Trust the instruments. Pilots must never try to fly visual meteorological conditions and IMC at the same time.
- Avoid fatigue, smoking, hypoglycemia, hypoxia, and anxiety, all of which intensify illusions.

TREATMENT OF SPATIAL DISORIENTATION

9-52. SD can easily occur in the aviation environment. If SD occurs, pilots should—

- Refer to the instruments and develop a good cross-check.
- Delay intuitive actions long enough to check both visual references and the instruments.
- Transfer control to the other pilot (if two pilots are in the aircraft); rarely will both pilots experience SD at the same time.

This page intentionally left blank.

Chapter 10

Oxygen Equipment and Cabin Pressurization

With the technological advances of today's Army aircraft and the increase in operational requirements at altitudes exceeding 10,000 feet mean sea level (MSL), oxygen equipment and cabin pressurization are crucial. Without supplemental oxygen and cabin pressurization, crewmembers are at increased risk of hypoxia, evolved-gas disorders, and DCS. This chapter explains cabin pressurization and oxygen equipment and their use in Army aviation.

OXYGEN SYSTEMS

10-1. Aircraft oxygen systems consist of containers that store oxygen in a gaseous, liquid, or solid state; tubing to direct the flow; devices that control oxygen pressure and percentage; and a mask to deliver oxygen to the user. Oxygen systems exist in many forms throughout the military, but the following equipment is used in Army aircraft.

GASEOUS OXYGEN

10-2. Aviator's gaseous oxygen is the most common breathing oxygen found in Army aircraft. It is classified as Type I, Grade A, and meets MIL-O-27210E military specifications. Gaseous oxygen is 99.5 percent pure by volume and contains no more than 0.005 milligrams of water vapor per liter at 760mm/Hg pressure and 15 degrees Celsius. Gaseous oxygen is odorless and contaminant free.

10-3. Oxygen used for medical purposes is classified as Type I, Grade B, and is not acceptable for use by aviators because of its high moisture content. Temperatures at high altitudes can cause freezing in the oxygen-delivery system and restrict oxygen flow.

ONBOARD OXYGEN-GENERATING SYSTEM

10-4. The onboard oxygen-generating system (OBOGS) is the primary method of oxygen delivery for patients aboard the UH-60Q Black Hawk. Use of this system reduces many of the potential hazards associated with gaseous high-pressure systems and offers the added benefits of simpler service and maintenance. Various OBOGS have been tested and some show great potential for future military use. The applicable aircraft technical manual contains specific OBOGS capabilities.

STORAGE SYSTEMS

GASEOUS LOW-PRESSURE SYSTEM

10-5. Low-pressure oxygen is commonly used during emergencies. This system's breathing oxygen is stored in yellow, lightweight, shatterproof cylinders with a maximum charge pressure of 400 to 450 pounds per square inch. The low-pressure system is not very effective because the volume of oxygen that can be stored is limited. In addition, if system pressure falls below 50 pounds per square inch, the system must be recharged within 2 hours to prevent moisture condensation within the cylinders. If not recharged within this timeframe, the system must be purged before refilling.

GASEOUS HIGH-PRESSURE SYSTEM

10-6. The gaseous high-pressure system is in use aboard most Army aircraft with internal storage systems. Breathing oxygen is stored in green heavyweight cylinders that contain a maximum charge pressure of 1,800 to 2,200 pounds per square inch. This system allows the safe storage of large amounts of oxygen to meet mission requirements of Army fixed-wing aircraft.

10-7. The H-2 bailout bottle is an example of a gaseous high-pressure system. The H-2 provides crewmembers with an emergency oxygen source should their aircraft oxygen system fail and also supplies oxygen to high-altitude parachutists during jumps. This system is automatically activated during an ejection sequence or manually activated by pulling the ball handle ("green apple"). The H-2 provides about 10 minutes of breathing oxygen and cannot be stopped once activated.

10-8. The helicopter oxygen system (HOS), pictured in figure 10-1, is a self-contained portable oxygen system that supplies oxygen to crewmembers on missions requiring oxygen at altitude. The HOS is tailored for use in the UH-60, CH-47 (forward or aft), and the UH-1 but can be used in other aircraft, although additional supply hoses might be required. Each HOS can provide 100-percent oxygen to six personnel for 1 hour at altitudes up to 25,000 feet MSL. Oxygen is stored in two tandem-connected storage cylinders that must be recharged by an oxygen servicing unit.

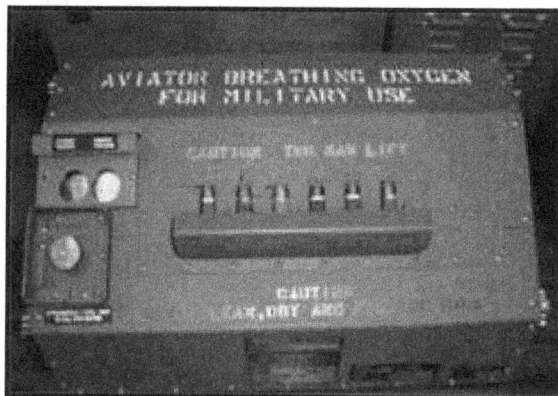

Figure 10-1. Helicopter oxygen system

OXYGEN REGULATORS

10-9. The flow of oxygen into a mask must be controlled whenever oxygen systems are used onboard aircraft. Two types of oxygen regulators, diluter demand and continuous flow, are currently used in Army aircraft.

DILUTER-DEMAND REGULATOR

10-10. A diluter-demand oxygen regulator fits better, wastes less oxygen, and provides a higher percentage of oxygen than a continuous-flow regulator. A mask-regulator makes up the self-contained, quick-donning unit available to pilots who encounter cabin pressurization problems (figure 10-2, page 10-3).

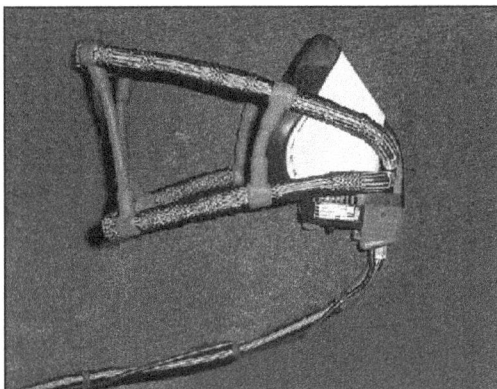

Figure 10-2. Quick-donning mask-regulator assembly unit

10-11.   During each inhalation, negative pressure closes the one-way exhaust valve in the mask and opens the demand valve in the regulator, thereby providing oxygen flow only on demand. The regulator can mix suitable amounts of ambient air and oxygen to prolong the oxygen source. When the diluter level is placed in the NORMAL position, the breathing mixture at ground level is primarily ambient air with very little added oxygen. During ascent, an air inlet is partially closed by an aneroid pressure valve to provide a higher concentration of oxygen. This inlet valve closes completely at 34,000 feet MSL, and the regulator then delivers 100-percent oxygen. On descent, this process reverses.

10-12.   The regulator can also provide 100-percent oxygen at any altitude when the diluter lever is placed in the 100% OXYGEN position. The diluter level should be set on NORMAL for routine operations and placed on 100% OXYGEN when hypoxia is suspected or prebreathing is required.

CONTINUOUS-FLOW REGULATOR

10-13.   Continuous-flow regulators provide protection at altitudes up to 25,000 feet MSL and supply a continuous flow of 100-percent oxygen to the user. The three major types of regulators are manual, automatic, and automatic with manual override.

OXYGEN MASKS

10-14.   The three oxygen masks primarily used in the Army aviation community are the passenger, MBU-12/P or MBU-20/P, and diluter-demand quick-don masks. The passenger mask is a continuous-flow device, while the MBU-12/P and diluter-demand quick-don masks are pressure-demand devices. The continuous-flow mask supplies the user with continuous oxygen; the pressure-demand masks provide oxygen when the user inhales. Oxygen in the mask is then maintained at a positive pressure until the regulator pressure is overcome during exhalation.

PASSENGER OXYGEN MASK

10-15.   The passenger oxygen mask found onboard Army fixed-wing aircraft supplies a continuous flow of oxygen to the user regardless of inhalation. The mask, pictured in figure 10-3 (page 10-4), plugs into receptacles within the passenger compartment.

Figure 10-3. Passenger oxygen mask

MBU-12/P Oxygen Mask

10-16. The MBU-12/P oxygen mask (figure 10-4) is available in four sizes: short, regular, long, and extra long. To ensure a proper fit, crewmembers should wear a mask in the size that most closely matches their facial measurements.

10-17. The MBU-12/P oxygen mask consists of a silicone-rubber inner facial piece bonded to a hard shell to form a one-piece assembly. The MBU-12/P mask offers several improvements over previous masks, including greater comfort, better fit, and increased downward vision.

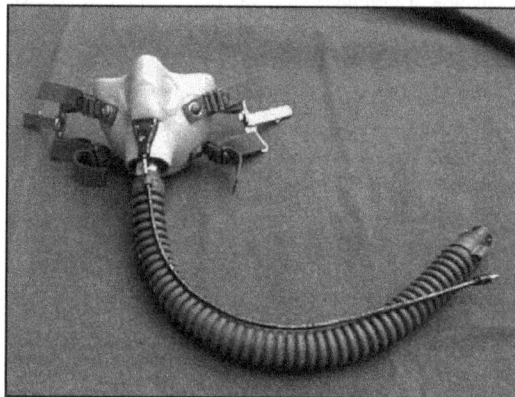

Figure 10-4. MBU-12/P oxygen mask

MBU-20/P Oxygen Mask

10-18. Used for flights up to 50,000 feet MSL, the MBU-20/P oxygen mask (figure 10-5, page 10-5) is available in four sizes: small narrow, medium narrow, medium wide, and large wide. The mask assembly allows for communication and integrates with HGU-series flight helmet assemblies.

10-19. The MBU-20/P oxygen mask consists of a hard shell, upper and lower strap assemblies, breathing hose, inhalation valve elbow, and inhalation and exhalation valves.

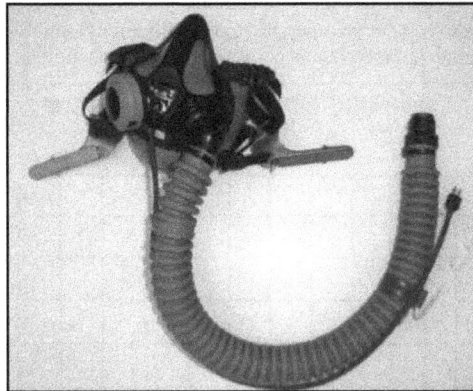

Figure 10-5. MBU-20/P oxygen mask

OXYGEN EQUIPMENT CHECKLIST

10-20. Since oxygen equipment can malfunction easily, it must be checked continually. Crewmembers must check their oxygen equipment using the appropriate checklist or technical manual.

CABIN PRESSURIZATION

10-21. The Army's fixed-wing aircraft can fly at higher altitudes than crewmembers can physiologically tolerate. Therefore, cabin pressurization was developed to ensure the safety and comfort of crewmembers and passengers.

CABIN PRESSURIZATION SYSTEM

10-22. The most efficient method for protecting crewmembers flying at altitude is to increase barometric pressure inside the cabin so it is greater than ambient pressure outside. In high-altitude flight without pressurization, crewmembers require continuous use of oxygen equipment, which increases crew fatigue. Pressurization has some disadvantages, however. Crewmembers encountering problems with cabin pressurization can suffer serious physiological impairment.

10-23. Because greater pressure must exist inside the cabin than outside, aircraft walls must be structurally reinforced to contain this pressure. This reinforcement increases design and maintenance costs and also reduces aircraft performance due to added weight and increased power requirements.

10-24. Cabin pressurization is achieved by extracting outside ambient air, forcing it through compressors, cooling it, and maintaining it at a given cabin altitude. Pressurization is maintained by controlling the amount of air allowed to escape in relation to compressed air. In a typical cabin pressurization system, controls sense changes in cabin and outside ambient air pressure and make adjustments necessary to maintain cabin pressure at a fixed pressure differential, determined by the difference between cabin and outside ambient air pressure. A cabin altimeter, usually part of the pressurization system, allows the pilot to observe cabin altitude and make required pressure changes.

10-25. On most aircraft, cabin altitude usually increases with aircraft altitude up to 5,000 to 8,000 feet MSL. Barometric control maintains the cabin at that set altitude until the maximum pressure differential is reached.

10-26. From sea level to 20,000 feet MSL, a barometric controller modulates the outflow of air from the cabin to maintain a selected cabin rate of climb. Cabin altitude increases until the maximum cabin pressure differential of 6.0 pounds per square inch is reached. Thus, below an altitude of 20,000 feet MSL, cabin pressure altitude is maintained at 3,870 feet MSL.

10-27. The maximum pressure differential is maintained from 20,000 to 31,000 feet MSL (the service ceiling of the C-12D); however, cabin altitude increases with aircraft altitude (figure 10-6). At 31,000 feet MSL and a pressure differential of 6.0 pounds per square inch, cabin altitude reaches 9,840 feet MSL.

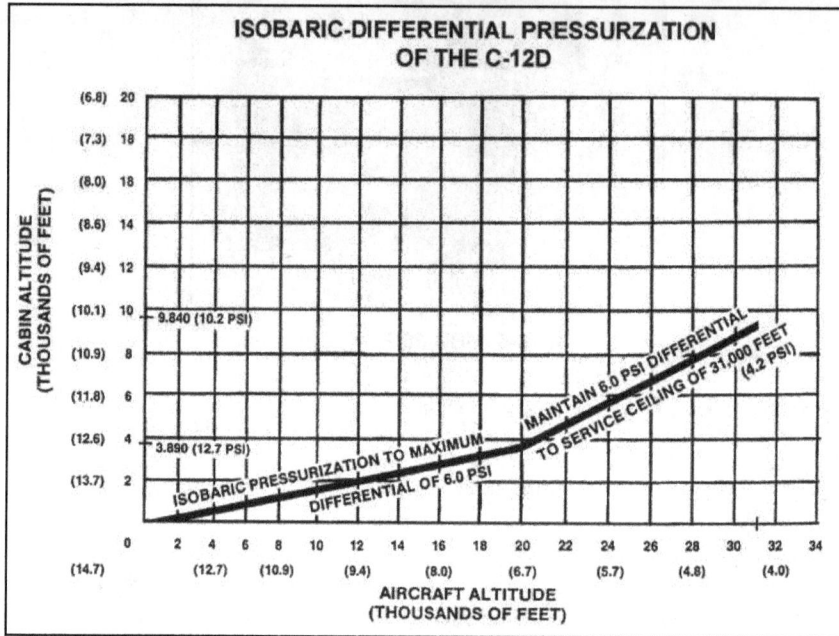

ISOBARIC-DIFFERENTIAL PRESSURZATION OF THE C-12D

Figure 10-6. C-12D cabin pressurization changes with altitude changes

10-28. The cabin pressurization selected for a particular aircraft is usually a compromise among physiological requirements, engineering capabilities, overall aircraft performance, and cost.

ADVANTAGES OF CABIN PRESSURIZATION

10-29. Cabin pressurization offers several advantages for aircraft capable of flight above 20,000 feet MSL. In general, pressurization—

- Eliminates the need for supplemental oxygen equipment.
- Significantly reduces the occurrence of hypoxia and DCS.
- Minimizes trapped gas expansion.
- Reduces crew fatigue since cabin temperature and ventilation can be controlled within desired ranges.

LOSS OF CABIN PRESSURIZATION

10-30. Pressurization system failure and resulting decompression can produce significant physiological problems in crewmembers. Slow cabin decompression, while dangerous because of the slow and insidious onset of hypoxia, is not as physiologically dangerous as rapid decompression. Rapid decompression occurs when the fuselage or pressure vessel is compromised and cabin pressure equalizes almost instantaneously with outside ambient pressure.

10-31. The following factors control the rate and time of decompression:

- Volume of the pressurized cabin. The larger the cabin area, the slower the decompression time.
- Size of the opening. The larger the opening, the faster the decompression time.

- Pressure differential. The larger the pressure differential between outside absolute pressure and interior cabin pressure, the more severe the decompression.
- Pressure ratio. The greater the difference between inside and outside cabin pressure, the longer the time for air to escape and the longer the decompression time.

10-32.   The physiological effects of rapid decompression range from trapped gas expansion within the ears, sinuses, lungs, and abdomen to hypoxia. Gas expansion disorders can be painful and might become severe, but they are temporary. Crewmembers might also experience DCS and adverse effects from cold and wind chill. Hypoxia, however, poses the most serious hazard to crewmembers; its onset can be rapid, depending on cabin altitude after decompression. An average individual's EPT is decreased by half following rapid decompression.

INDICATIONS OF RAPID DECOMPRESSION

10-33.   The rapidity of decompression determines the magnitude of observable decompression characteristics. The earlier crewmembers detect a loss of pressure, the quicker they can take appropriate emergency measures to increase survival. The following observable characteristics indicate pressure loss.

Noise

10-34.   A loud popping noise is produced whenever two different air masses make contact. This explosive sound is often called "explosive decompression."

Flying Debris

10-35.   Crewmembers must be aware of the possibility of flying debris during rapid decompression. The rush of air from inside to outside an aircraft is so forceful that unsecured items might be ejected from the aircraft.

Fogging

10-36.   A sudden loss of pressure causes condensation and a resulting fog effect. Fogging is one of the primary characteristics of decompression because air at a given temperature and pressure holds only so much water vapor.

Temperature

10-37.   A loss of pressurization causes cabin temperature to equalize with outside ambient temperature, significantly decreasing temperature inside the cabin. The amount of temperature decrease depends on altitude.

IMMEDIATE ACTIONS FOLLOWING DECOMPRESSION

10-38.   All crewmembers and passengers must breathe supplemental oxygen after cabin decompression occurs. The crew must also initiate immediate descent to an altitude that minimizes the physiological effects of pressure loss.

This page intentionally left blank.

Appendix A

Hypobaric Chamber Flight Profiles

MEDICAL CLEARANCE

A-1. All personnel must have a current flight physical and DA Form 4186 indicating full flying duty before participating in any hypobaric chamber exercise.

PURPOSE OF HYPOBARIC CHAMBER TRAINING

A-2. The purpose of hypobaric chamber training is to safely demonstrate—

- Crewmember limitations associated with hypoxia at altitude.
- Effects of trapped gas on the body.
- Effects of hypoxia on night vision.
- Capabilities of oxygen equipment.

CHAMBER PROFILES AND APPLICABILITY OF TRAINING

A-3. Figures A-1 through A-5 show the standard hypobaric chamber profiles. For information regarding nonstandard profiles, contact the U.S. Army School of Aviation Medicine, ATTN: MCCS-HA, Fort Rucker, AL 36362-5377.

A-4. Procedures for the U.S. Air Force (USAF) Type I profile in figure A-1 (page A-2) are as follows:

- Begin 30-minute denitrogenation.
- Perform 5,000-feet ear and sinus check by 2,500 feet per minute.
- Ascend main accumulator and lock to 8,000 feet by 2,500 feet per minute.
- Ascend main accumulator and lock to 18,000 feet by 5,000 feet per minute.
- Perform running break of main accumulator and lock; maintain lock at 18,000 feet.
- Continue main accumulator ascent to 35,000 feet by 5,000 feet per minute.
- Descend main accumulator to 30,000 feet for 90-second hypoxia demonstration.
- Descend main accumulator and lock to 25,000 feet by 5,000 feet per minute.
- Begin 5-minute hypoxia demonstration.
- Descend lock to ground level by 5,000 feet per minute.
- Descend main accumulator to 18,000 feet by 5,000 feet per minute for night vision demonstration.
- Descend main accumulator from 18,000 feet to ground level by 2,500 feet per minute.
- Terminate chamber flight.

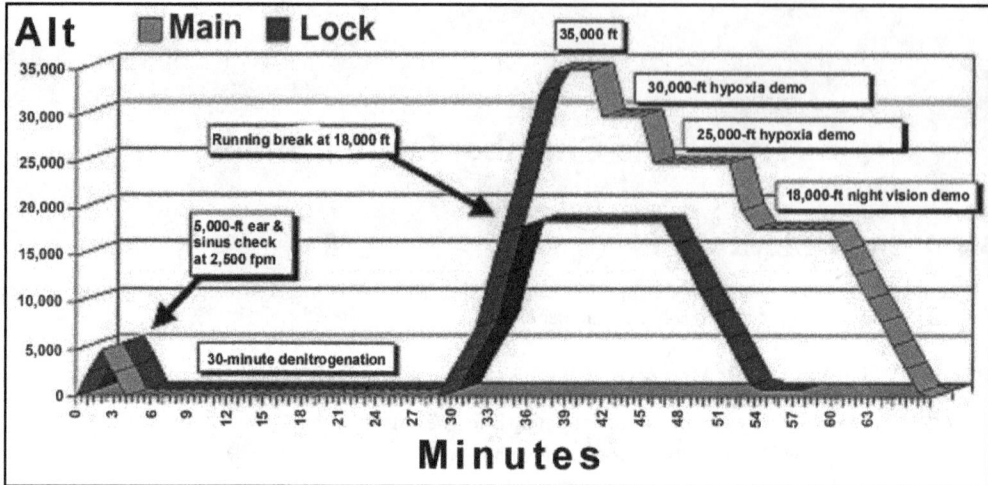

Figure A-1. Type I 35,000-foot U.S. Air Force original training profile

A-5. Procedures for the USAF Type II profile in figure A-2 are as follows:
- Begin 30-minute denitrogenation.
- Perform 5,000-feet ear and sinus check by 2,500 feet per minute.
- Ascend main accumulator from ground level to 8,000 feet by 2,500 feet per minute.
- Ascend main accumulator from 8,000 feet to 25,000 feet by 5,000 feet per minute.
- Begin 5-minute hypoxia demonstration.
- Descend main accumulator from 25,000 feet to 18,000 feet by 5,000 feet per minute for night vision demonstration.
- Descend main accumulator from 18,000 feet to ground level by 2,500 feet per minute.
- Terminate chamber flight.

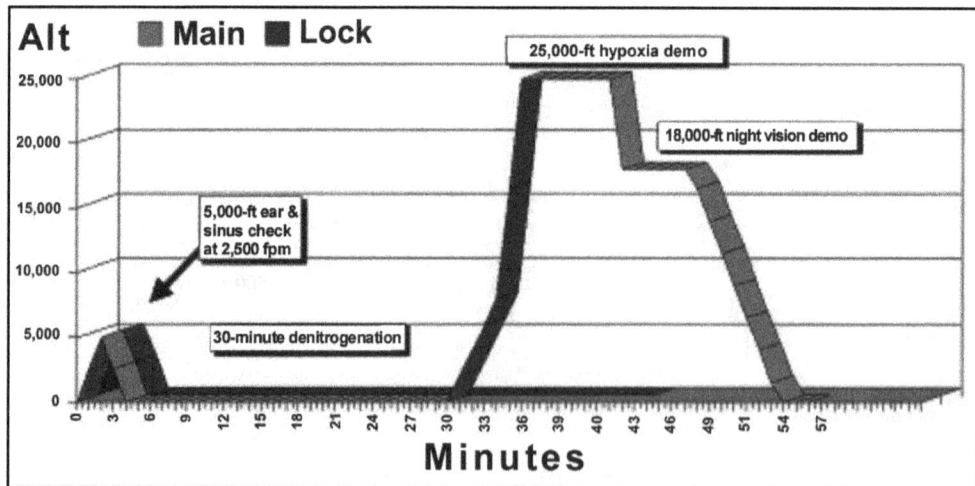

Figure A-2. Type II 25,000-foot U.S. Air Force refresher training profile

A-6. Procedures for the U.S. Army Type IV profile in figure A-3 are as follows:
- Begin 30-minute denitrogenation.
- Perform 5,000-feet ear and sinus check by 5,000 feet per minute.
- Ascend main accumulator from 8,000 feet to 25,000 feet by 5,000 feet per minute.
- Begin 5-minute hypoxia demonstration.
- Descend main accumulator from 25,000 feet to 18,000 feet by 5,000 feet per minute for night vision demonstration.
- Descend main accumulator from 18,000 feet to ground level by 2,500 feet per minute.
- Terminate chamber flight.

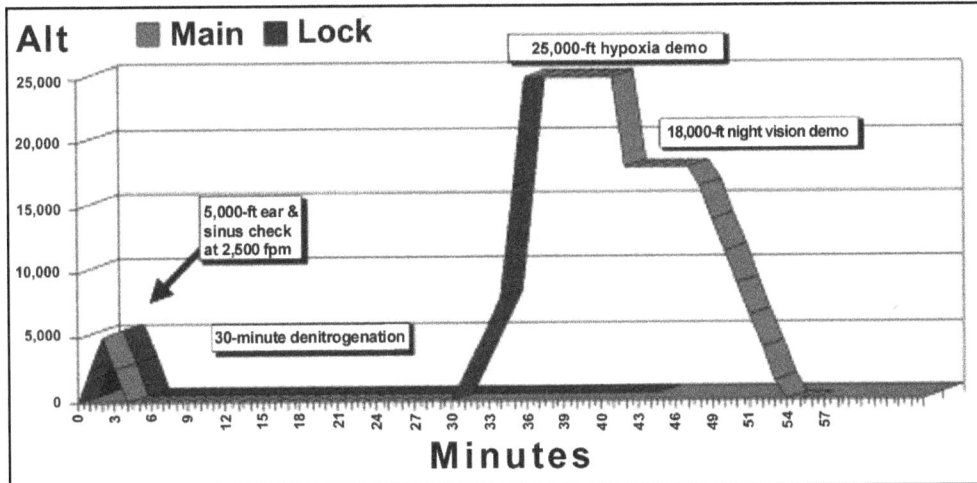

Figure A-3. Type IV 25,000-foot U.S. Army profile

A-7. Procedures for the U.S. Army/USAF Type V profile in figure A-4 (page A-4) are as follows:
- Begin 30-minute denitrogenation.
- Perform 5,000-feet ear and sinus check by 5,000 feet per minute.
- Ascend main accumulator and lock to 18,000 feet by 5,000 feet per minute.
- Perform running break of main accumulator and lock; maintain lock at 18,000 feet.
- Continue main accumulator ascent to 35,000 feet by 5,000 feet per minute.
- Ascend main accumulator to 30,000 feet for 90-second hypoxia demonstration.
- Descend main accumulator to 15,000 feet by 10,000 to 12,000 feet per minute with lock joining descent at 18,000 feet.
- Descend main accumulator and lock to 8,000 feet by 5,000 feet per minute.
- Ascend main accumulator to 25,000 feet by maximum rate of ascent.
- Begin 5-minute hypoxia demonstration.
- Descend lock to ground level by 5,000 feet per minute.
- Descend main accumulator to 18,000 feet by 5,000 feet per minute for night vision demonstration.
- Descend main accumulator from 18,000 feet to ground level by 5,000 feet per minute.
- Terminate chamber flight.

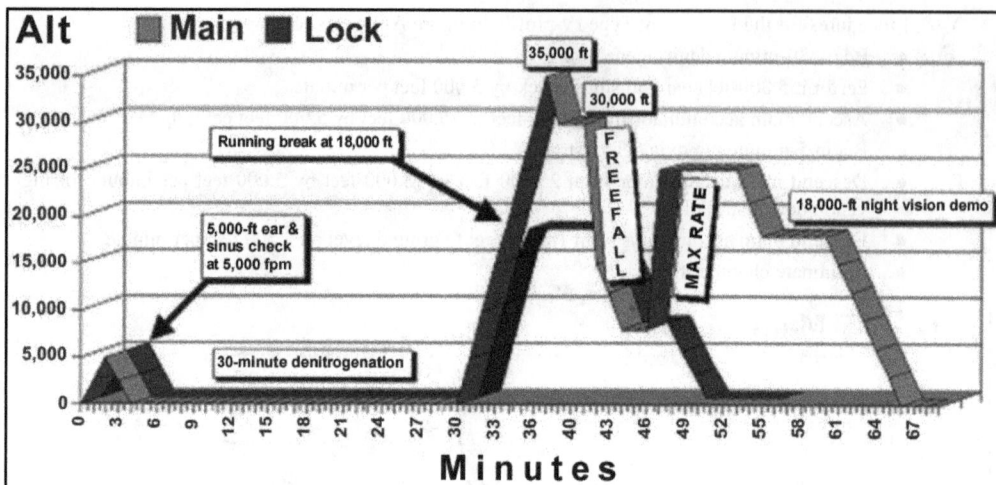

Figure A-4. Type V 35,000-foot U.S. Army/U.S. Air Force profile

A-8. Procedures for the military rapid decompression profile in figure A-5 are as follows:
- Ascend main accumulator to 12,500 feet by maximum rate.
- Ascend lock to 1,500 feet by 2,500 feet per minute.
- Perform rapid decompression.
- Equalize main accumulator and lock at 8,500 feet.
- Descend main accumulator and lock from 8,000 feet to ground level by 2,500 feet per minute.

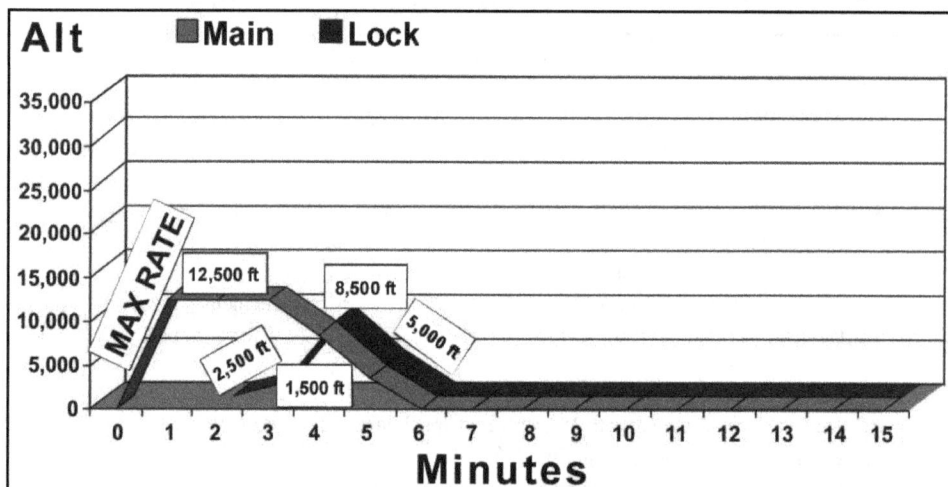

Figure A-5. Military rapid decompression profile

Glossary

AFI	Air Force Instruction
AGSM	anti-G straining maneuver
AR	Army Regulation
Ar	argon
ATM	aircrew training manual
ATP	aircrew training plan
AWR	airworthiness release
BLP	ballistic limit protection
C	Celsius
CBRN	chemical, biological, radiological, and nuclear
CEP	communications earplug
CoHb	carboxyhemoglobin (found in blood as a result of carbon monoxide inhalation)
CO$_2$	carbon dioxide
CREEP	container, restraint system, environment, energy absorption, postcrash protection (aircraft design features that aid crash survival)
DAC	Department of the Army civilian
DCS	decompression sickness
DEATH	drugs, exhaustion, alcohol, tobacco, hypoglycemia
EPT	expected performance time
F	Fahrenheit
Fe$_2$	iron content within hemoglobin
FFD	full flying duty
FOV	field of view
G	unit of acceleration
GRAM	Geometric perspective, retinal image size, aerial perspective, motion parallax
He	helium
Hg	mercury
H$_2$	hydrogen
HOS	helicopter oxygen system
ICS	internal communication system
IMC	instrument meteorological conditions
in/Hg	inches of mercury
JP	Joint Publication
JP-4	jet propulsion fuel, type 4
JP-5	jet propulsion fuel, type 5
JP-8	jet propulsion fuel, type 8

KITO	Known size of objects, increased and decreased size of objects, terrestrial association, and overlapping contours or interposition of objects
LASEK	laser epithelial keratomileusis
LASIK	laser-assisted in-situ keratomileusis
LAV	linear perspective, apparent foreshortening, and vertical position
MEDEVAC	medical evacuation
mm	millimeter
mm/Hg	millimeters of mercury
MOPP	mission-oriented protective posture
MSL	mean sea level
N_2	nitrogen
ND	neutral density
Ne	neon
NOE	nap-of-the-earth
NVD	night vision device
O_2	oxygen
OBOGS	onboard oxygen-generating system
PAO_2	alveolar partial pressure of oxygen
pH	relative acidity of blood: chemical balance (the symbol for the logarithm of the reciprocal of hydrogen ion concentration in gram atoms per liter, used to express the acidity or alkalinity of a solution on a scale of 0 to 14, where less than 7 represents acidity, 7 neutrality, and more than 7 alkalinity)
PCO_2	partial pressure of carbon dioxide
PO_2	partial pressure of oxygen
POI	program of instruction
ppm	parts per million
PRK	photorefractive keratectomy
psi	pounds per square inch
PVO_2	venous pressure of oxygen
RBC	red blood cell
REM	rapid eye movement
ROBD	reduced oxygen breathing device
scuba	self-contained underwater breathing apparatus
SD	spatial disorientation
SF	standard form
STANAG	standardization agreement
STEL	short-term exposure limit
TB MED	Technical Bulletin Medical
TLV	threshold limit values
TRADOC	United States Army Training and Doctrine Command
TUC	time of useful consciousness

USAACE	United States Army Aviation Center of Excellence
USASAM	United States Army School of Aviation Medicine
WBC	white blood cell

SECTION II – TERMS

absorption

A process in which an object collects other materials within itself. Two examples of absorption are a sponge absorbing water and the tissues of the middle ear absorbing oxygen from the middle ear cavity.

acceleration

A change of velocity in magnitude or direction expressed in feet per second squared, or fps^2. The most common accelerative force is gravity. The acceleration produced by gravity is a constant and has a value of 32.2 fps^2.

acclimatization

The physiological adjustment of an organism to a new and physically different environment. An example would be the adaptation of valley dwellers to life in a mountainous region where ambient pressures are relatively low. In this example, acclimatization would occur through a temporary adjustment in cardiac and respiratory rates and an increase in the number of red blood cells.

acute

An incident or disease characterized by sharpness or severity that has a sudden onset, sharp rise, and short course. In physiological training, this term usually describes a severe chamber reaction in which the onset is rapid and immediate aid is required.

alkalosis

The term used by physiological training personnel to refer to a respiratory condition in which there is an increase in blood's basicity produced by abnormally rapid respiration and elimination of excessive amounts of carbon dioxide.

altimeter

An instrument used to measure the altitude of an aircraft or chamber. By making appropriate adjustments and pressure settings, the altimeter can be set to indicate the pressure altitudes used in chamber operations or the true altitudes used during most Army aircraft flights.

altitude sickness

In acute cases, the symptoms of hypoxia seen especially in flying personnel and individuals new to mountainous regions of high altitude; in chronic cases, the symptoms of hypoxia usually seen in individuals who have been at high altitudes in mountainous regions for long periods. Apparently, these individuals' physiological compensatory processes for hypoxia become inadequate. Descent to lower altitudes usually brings relief.

alveoli

The saclike, extremely thin-walled tissues of the lungs in which the flow of inspired gases terminates and across the walls of which gas diffusion takes place between the lungs and blood.

ambient

The existing and adjacent environment. Ambient air pressure is the pressure of the immediate environment.

angular acceleration

Acceleration that results in a simultaneous change in both speed and direction.

anoxia

A total absence of oxygen in blood presented to the tissues or the inability of the tissues to use oxygen delivered to them. Anoxia is an extremely severe and morbid condition. The lack of oxygen with which physiological training personnel are concerned is, strictly speaking, hypoxia, not anoxia.

arterial saturation

The hemoglobin in arterial blood containing as much oxygen as it can hold, giving an arterial oxygen concentration of about 20 milliliters of oxygen per 100 milliliters of blood.

arteries

The blood vessels that possess relatively thick, muscular walls that transport oxygenated blood from the left ventricle to the body tissues. Arteries also transport poorly oxygenated blood from the right ventricle to the lungs.

arterioles

The smaller extensions of the arteries. The muscular walls of these arterial extensions are responsive to nerve and chemical control by the body and thereby regulate the amount of blood presented to the capillaries.

astigmatism

A visual problem caused by an unequal curvature of the cornea or lens of the eye.

atmosphere

The gaseous layer surrounding the earth that is composed primarily of oxygen and nitrogen.

attenuation

The amount of noise protection provided by a specific protective device. The attenuation of any given noise protective device is the number of decibels it reduces the total energy reaching the eardrum.

auricles (atria)

The upper two chambers of the heart, designated the right and left auricles. These chambers receive blood from the vessels and force it into the ventricles.

autokinesis

An illusion in which a single, stationary point of light seen against a dark background appears to move erratically. The illusion is probably caused by involuntary movement of the eyeballs because relative points of reference are missing.

barodontalgia (aerodontalgia)

A toothache that occurs during ascent to altitude or during descent. Causes for this painful condition include poor or loose restorations; presence of decay, infection, or abscess; or gritting of the teeth in times of stress.

barometer

An instrument used to measure atmospheric pressure based on the principle that the pressure exerted by ambient air is sufficient to hold up a column of mercury. The height to which this column is held varies directly with air pressure. The aneroid barometer operates on the principle that the volume of gas in a flexible, enclosed space increases when the pressure on it decreases; for example, during ascent to altitude.

barometric pressure

The pressure of air in a particular environment as measured by the barometer. For example, at 18,000 feet in an altitude chamber, barometric pressure should be 380 mm/Hg.

barotitis media

A condition that develops when equalization of pressure in the middle ear cannot be accomplished during changes in barometric pressure.

bends

A form of decompression sickness that can be produced by the liberation of gaseous emboli (bubbles), primarily nitrogen, in body tissues. This condition is characterized by mild to incapacitating pains in the joints. Pain might be localized to a single area (for example, knee or joint) or generalized in severe cases.

blackout

Temporary blindness caused by an extinguished blood supply to the retina. Blackouts are usually seen during +Gz maneuvers. In such cases, force exerted on the column of blood traveling to the eyes reduces effective blood pressure in the vessels going to the eyes, thereby reducing bloodflow to the eyes. If continued, the force will actually stop bloodflow to the retina.

Boyle's Law

The physical law that states the volume of a gas is inversely proportional to the pressure exerted upon it.

bronchi

The two main tubes leading to the lungs from the trachea. The bronchi are part of the conducting portion of the respiratory system.

bronchioles

The smaller tubules extending from each bronchus. Two types of bronchioles can be distinguished: the *conducting* bronchioles that provide the air passageway into the portion of the lungs where diffusion occurs; and the *respiratory* bronchioles that contain some alveoli in their walls through which the diffusion of gases occurs.

calorie

The amount of heat needed to raise the temperature of 1 gram of water from 250 degrees Celsius to 260 degrees Celsius.

capillaries

The most minute blood vessels. Capillaries have walls of one-cell thickness. These vessels link the arteries and veins; through them, gas diffusion takes place between body tissues and blood.

cardiac arrhythmia

Any variation in the heart's normal rhythm.

cataract formation

A clouding or opacification of the lens resulting from hardening that usually occurs during the aging process.

centrifugal force

The force exerted on an object moving in a circular pattern that causes the object to break away and move outward in a straight line.

centripetal force

The force acting on an object moving in a circular pattern that holds the object on its circular path.

chemoreceptors

The receptors adapted for excitation by chemical substances; for example, aortic and carotid bodies that sense reduced oxygen content in blood and automatically send signals to the cardiovascular and respiratory systems to make necessary adjustments.

chill factor

The temperature decrease resulting from wind velocity. An increased cooling of exposed skin occurs when the skin is subjected to wind.

chloride shift

The passage of chloride ions from plasma into red blood cells when carbon dioxide enters the plasma from the tissues, and the return of these ions to the plasma when carbon dioxide is discharged in the lungs.

chokes

A form of decompression sickness that can occur at altitude and is believed to be caused by gases evolving in the lung tissue. This condition is characterized by a deep substernal pain or burning sensation, difficulty breathing, and nonproductive cough.

chronic

A continued or prolonged condition; for example, a chronic illness is an illness that continues for several years.

cilium

A minute, vibratile, hairlike structure attached to the free surface of a cell.

circadian rhythm

The rhythmic biological functions geared to an internal "biological clock." Circadian rhythm affects processes such as the sleep-wake cycle, hormone production, and body temperature.

circadian desynchronization (jet lag)

Rapid travel from one time zone to another causes the body to resynchronize its diurnal rhythms to the local geophysical and social time cues. Until intrinsic rhythms are reset, sleep disorders and fatigue will prevail. Traveling eastward shortens the day; westward travel lengthens the day. Consequently, resynchronization occurs much more rapidly when traveling west. Shift work can produce effects similar to crossing time zones because of changes in light exposure and activity times.

circulation

Blood movement throughout the body.

coma

A state of complete loss of consciousness from which a patient cannot be aroused despite the use of powerful stimulants.

combustion

An act or instance of burning; a chemical process (as in oxidation) accompanied by the emission of heat and light.

conduction

Heat transfer between molecules of adjacent bodies or in a single body. Heat flows from a body or body portion with a lower heat content; for example, heat transfer from the hand to an ice cube. Physical contact is necessary for heat transfer by conduction.

cones

Nerve cells in the central portion of the retina, with the greatest concentration at the fovea. These cells are used for day vision and allow a person to see detail and distinguish between various colors.

conjunctiva

The mucous membrane lining the inner surface of the eyelids and covering the front part of the eyeball.

continuous flow

The earliest supplementary oxygen breathing system designed for use in aircraft, still used today in certain transport aircraft and for air evacuation. This system provides a constant flow of oxygen to the mask.

contrast sensitivity

The ability to detect objects on varying shades of backgrounds.

convection

A form of heat transfer effected by the flow of fluid across an object of a different temperature. If the object is warmer, the heat will transfer from the object to the liquid or gas; if the object is cooler, the heat will transfer from the liquid or gas to the object.

convulsion

A violent, involuntary contraction or series of contractions of voluntary muscles. Convulsions can occasionally be seen in hypoxic individuals or in people who have hyperventilated.

coriolis illusion

A condition that exists when the head is moved from one plane to another while the body is in rotation, causing an illusion of moving in a plane or rotation in which no angular motion exists.

cornea

The transparent part of the eyeball coat that covers the iris and pupil and admits light to the interior.

counterpressure

The pressure exerted on the outside of the body to balance the high pressure of gases in the lungs.

cyanosis

Blueness of the skin caused by insufficient oxygenation of blood. Blood that has most of its hemoglobin combined with oxygen appears bright red, whereas blood with low oxygenated hemoglobin appears reddish blue or cyanotic.

Dalton's Law of Partial Pressures

The physical law that states the total pressure of a mixture of gases is equal to the sum of the partial pressures of each gas in the mixture.

dark adaptation

The process by which the retinal cells (rods) increase their concentration of the chemical substance (rhodopsin) that allows them to function optimally in twilight or in dimly illuminated surroundings. The process takes between 30 and 45 minutes in a darkened room.

deceleration (negative acceleration)

Any reduction in the velocity of a moving body.

decibel

An arbitrary unit for measuring the relative intensity of a sound.

decompression

Any reduction in the pressure of one's surroundings. A chamber is decompressed each time it ascends.

decompression sickness

The effects produced by the evolvement of body gases or expansion of trapped body gases when ambient pressure is decreased, as in ascent to altitude.

denitrogenation

The reduction of nitrogen concentration in the body. Nitrogen concentration can be reduced by breathing 100-percent oxygen over a period of time. This process diffuses nitrogen from blood to the lungs and eliminates much of the nitrogen dissolved in body tissues.

diffusion

The process through which a substance moves from a place of high concentration to a new location of lower concentration. An example is the diffusion of carbon dioxide from the tissue (with a partial pressure of 50 mm/Hg) to blood (with a partial pressure of 40 mm/Hg).

diluter-demand oxygen regulator

A supplementary oxygen delivery system in which a dilution of pure oxygen (with ambient air) is provided automatically to an individual with each inhalation. At 34,000 feet, the system automatically delivers 100-percent oxygen with each inhalation.

ejection

A method of emergency escape in which a pilot's or crewmember's seat is propelled out of the aircraft by an explosive catapult or rocket charge.

endolymph

The watery fluid contained in the ear's membranous labyrinth.

erythrocytes

Red blood cells.

euphoria

A feeling of well-being.

eustachian tube

The passage leading from the middle ear to the pharynx. The eustachian tube provides the only means by which equalization can be maintained between pressure in the middle ear and ambient pressure during flight.

evaporation

The process by which a liquid changes to a gaseous state and, in doing so, increases its temperature. For example, when sweat evaporates (changes from a liquid to a vapor), it takes heat from the body and increases its own temperature.

expiration

The act of exhaling or breathing outward. Expiration usually involves contraction of certain abdominal muscles and relaxation of the diaphragm.

explosive decompression

A collision of two air masses that produces an explosive sound. A decompression that occurs in about 1 second or less is termed an "explosive decompression."

external respiration

The movement of air into and out of the lungs, ventilation of the lung passages and alveoli, and diffusion of gas across the alveolar-capillary membrane.

flatus

Gas or air in the gastrointestinal tract.

frequency

The measurable characteristic of a noise that gives it a distinctive pitch, measured in cycles per second or hertz.

G-force (+Gx)

The positive accelerative force that acts to move the body at a right angle to the long axis in a back-to-chest direction.

G-force (–Gx)

The negative accelerative force that acts to move the body at a right angle to the long axis in a chest-to-back direction.

G-force (+Gy, –Gy)

The positive or negative accelerative force that acts to move the body at a right angle to the long axis in a shoulder-to-shoulder direction.

G-force (+Gz)

The positive accelerative force that acts to move the body in a headward direction.

G-force (–Gz)

The negative accelerative force that acts to move the body in a footward direction.

glare

A bright light that enters the eye and causes a rapid loss of sensitivity.

glottis

The vocal apparatus of the larynx.

gravity

The force of attraction between the Earth and all bodies on Earth by which each body is held to the Earth's surface. The normal force that acts on all bodies at all times is 1 G.

headward direction

Movement toward the head.

heat

In the absolute sense, the motion of any substance's molecules. The greater the motion, the higher the heat content. The heat content of any object is measured in calories.

heat cramps

A condition marked by sudden development of cramps in skeletal muscles. Heat cramps result from prolonged work in high temperatures and are accompanied by profuse perspiration with loss of sodium chloride (salt) from the body.

heat exhaustion

A condition marked by weakness, nausea, dizziness, and profuse sweating. Heat exhaustion results from physical exertion in a hot environment.

heatstroke

An abnormal physiological condition produced by exposure to intense heat and characterized by hot, dry skin (caused by cessation of sweating), vomiting, convulsions, and collapse. In severe cases, the body's heat control mechanism can be disturbed, causing body temperature to rise to morbid levels.

hemoglobin

An organic chemical compound contained within red blood cells that combines with oxygen to form oxyhemoglobin. In this combination, oxygen is transported within the body.

Henry's Law

The physical law that states the amount of gas that can be dissolved in a liquid is directly proportional to the pressure of that gas over the liquid.

hyperbaric dive

Exposure to increased air pressure by insertion of compressed air into a metal chamber to simulate the pressure found in underwater diving. This exposure to increased pressure is also used as therapy for certain illnesses such as evolved-gas disorders and decompression sickness.

hyperventilation

An abnormally rapid rate of respiration that can lead to an excessive loss of carbon dioxide from the lungs, resulting in alkalosis. Hyperventilation is characterized by dizziness, tingling of the extremities, and, in acute cases, collapse.

hypoxia

Any condition in which the body's oxygen concentration is below normal limits or in which oxygen available to the body cannot be used because of some pathological condition.

hypoxia (histotoxic)

Hypoxia caused by the inability of body tissues to accept oxygen from blood. An example of this type of hypoxia is cyanide or alcohol poisoning.

hypoxia (hypemic)

Hypoxia caused by a reduced capacity of blood to carry oxygen. Two examples of hypemic hypoxia are anemia caused by iron deficiency or a reduction in red blood cells, and carbon monoxide poisoning caused by carbon monoxide combining with hemoglobin, a condition that reduces hemoglobin's oxygen-carrying capacity.

hypoxia (hypoxic)

Hypoxia caused by a decrease in the partial pressure of respired oxygen or the inability of oxygen in the air to reach the alveolar-capillary membrane due to conditions such as strangulation, asthma, and pneumonia. Hypoxic hypoxia is also known as altitude hypoxia.

hypoxia (stagnant)

A condition that results from blood's failure to transport oxygen rapidly enough due to conditions such as shock or heart attack, in which blood moves sluggishly.

illusion

A false impression or misconception with respect to actual conditions or reality.

inertial force

Resistance to change in a state of rest or motion. A body at rest tends to remain at rest, while a body in motion tends to remain in motion.

inspiration

The act of drawing air into the lungs.

intensity

The loudness or pressure produced by a given noise, measured in decibels.

internal respiration

The transport of oxygen and carbon dioxide by blood and the diffusion of these gases into and out of body tissues. Internal respiration also includes oxygen use in metabolism and the elimination of carbon dioxide and water as waste products.

iodopsin

A photosensitive, violet retinal pigment found in retinal cones and important for color vision.

iris

The opaque, contractile diaphragm perforated by the pupil that forms the colored portion of the eye.

isobaric control

The cabin altitude control achieved by maintaining constant pressure as ambient barometric pressure decreases.

isobaric differential

A system built into certain aircraft to control the pressurized environment at a predetermined level.

jet stream

A relatively narrow band of high-velocity winds located between 35,000 and 55,000 feet at approximate north and south latitudes of 30 and 60 degrees.

jolt

The rate of change of acceleration or rate of onset of accelerative forces.

lens

The portion of the eye located behind the pupil that focuses light rays on the retina.

leukocytes

White blood cells.

linear acceleration

Any change in an object's speed without a change in direction; for example, increasing the speed of an automobile from 40 to 65 miles per hour while driving down a straight-and-level highway.

L-1 maneuver

A physiological maneuver that increases G tolerance.

mesopic vision

A combination of cone and rod vision used at dawn or twilight wherein both rod cells and cone cells are used but not to their maximum point of efficiency.

metabolism

The chemical changes in living cells by which energy is provided for vital processes and activities and new material is assimilated.

miosis

Contraction of the eye's pupil.

otolith organs

The small sacs located in the vestibule of the inner ear.

oxidation

The act of oxidizing or state of being oxidized; to combine with oxygen. Chemically, oxidation consists of an increase in positive charges on an atom or a loss of negative charges.

oxygen flow indicator

An instrument connected directly to an oxygen regulator that indicates oxygen flow through the regulator during a user's respiratory cycle. This flow is manifested by the movement of shutters on the indicator's face.

pallor

A paleness or absence of skin coloration.

paresthesia

A form of decompression sickness characterized by abnormal skin sensations; for example, itching and hot and cold sensations. Paresthesia can be caused by the formation of gas bubbles in the layers beneath the skin.

partial pressure

The pressure exerted by any single constituent of a mixture of gases.

photopic

Vision in the daytime or in bright light in which the retinal cones are primarily used.

pitch

Rotation of an aircraft about its lateral axis.

plasma

The fluid portion of blood containing many dissolved compounds including proteins, carbon dioxide, bicarbonates, sugar, and sodium.

platelets

Disk-shaped structures found in blood and known primarily for their role in blood coagulation.

presbycusis

Hearing loss attributed to old age and the aging process in general. Presbycusis can be conductive or sensorineural in nature and is commonly referred to as "senile deafness."

presbyopia

A visual condition that becomes apparent in middle age in which the eye's lens loses elasticity, causing defective accommodation and an inability to focus sharply for near vision.

pressure altitude

Pressure expressed in feet of altitude. Pressure altitude can be obtained by reading the altitude indicated on the altimeter set at 29.92 in/Hg (the standard datum plane).

pressure breathing

Breathing in which the gases respired are at a pressure greater than the ambient pressure. The normal respiratory cycle is reversed during pressure breathing; that is, inhalation is the passive phase of respiration and exhalation is the active phase.

pressure demand

A type of oxygen-delivery system (mask and regulator) that incorporates both the standard demand mechanism and a mechanism for delivering oxygen under a positive pressure. This process necessitates pressure breathing.

pressure differential

The difference in pressure, usually expressed in pounds per square inch, that exists between one or more objects or parts of the same object. This term also refers to a system of pressurizing aircraft cabins in which cabin pressure is kept uniformly higher than ambient pressure.

pressure gauge

An instrument used to measure the air or oxygen pressure in any given system. The dial on the gauge face indicates pressure within the system in pounds per square inch.

pressure suit (full)

A specially designed suit that protects an individual by surrounding the body with a pressurized gas envelope.

pressurized cabin

Any aircraft interior that is maintained at a pressure greater than ambient pressure.

proprioceptive system

A combination of the vestibular, subcutaneous, and kinesthetic sensors that enables an individual to determine body position and its movement in space.

radial acceleration

Any change in the direction of a moving body without a change in its speed.

radial keratotomy

A surgical procedure that creates multiple, radial, spokelike incisions on the eye's cornea to produce better visual acuity.

radiation (heat)

The transfer of heat in the form of wave energy from a relatively warmer body to a cooler body.

rapid decompression

A sudden loss of pressure from an area of relatively high pressure to one of lower pressure. Conventionally, a decompression that occurs in 3 seconds or less is termed a "rapid decompression."

red blood cells

Blood cells that contain, among several other components, the hemoglobin necessary for oxygen transport.

redout

A phenomenon in which individuals lose their vision (and sometimes consciousness). Individuals suffering from redout see nothing but red in their field of vision, often when experiencing –Gz. Redout is believed to be the result of engorgement of the facial blood vessels and movement of the lower eyelid over the eye.

relative gas expansion

The number of times a given volume of gas will expand when the pressure surrounding it is reduced. Relative gas expansion is conventionally determined for body gases by dividing initial gas pressure by estimated final gas pressure. These pressures must be corrected for the constant water vapor pressure of 47 mm/Hg at normal body temperature.

relative humidity

The amount of water vapor in a given air sample at a given temperature. Relative humidity is expressed as a percentage of the maximum amount of water vapor the same sample could contain at that temperature.

residual volume

The volume of air always present in the lungs.

respiration

The process of pulmonary ventilation. Respiration involves gas diffusion between the lungs and blood, gas transport by blood between the lungs and body tissues, the diffusion of gas between blood and body tissues, the use of oxygen within cells, and the elimination of carbon dioxide and water as the cells' chief waste products.

retina

The sensory membrane that lines the eye and receives images formed by the lens. The retina is the immediate instrument of vision and connects to the brain via the optic nerve.

retinal rivalry

The difficulty of the eyes in simultaneously perceiving two dissimilar objects independent of each other due to the dominance of one eye.

rhodopsin

A photosensitive, purple-red chromoprotein in the retinal rods that enhances night vision and is commonly referred to as visual purple.

rods

Nerve endings located in the retina's periphery that are sensitive to the lowest light intensities. Rods respond to faint light at night and in poor illumination but cannot discern color or perceive detail.

roll

Rotation of an aircraft about its longitudinal axis.

speed

The magnitude of an object's motion and rate of change. Speed is expressed as distance covered per unit of time such as miles per hour.

velocity

Speed in a given direction. Velocity describes the magnitude and direction of motion and is measured in distance per unit of time such as feet per second.

vestibule

The oval cavity in the middle of the bony labyrinth in the ear.

yaw

Rotation of an aircraft about its vertical axis.

This page intentionally left blank.

References

These publications are sources for additional information on the topics in this FM. Most joint publications can be found at http://www.dtic mil/doctrine/doctrine htm. Most Army doctrinal publications are available online at http://www.army mil/usapa. Most Air Force and Navy publications and forms are available online at http://www.e-publishing.af mil/ and https://navalforms.daps.dla.mil/web/public/forms, respectively.

SOURCES USED

These documents are the sources quoted or paraphrased in this publication.

AFJMAN 44-151/ NAVMED-P-5059. *NATO Handbook on the Medical Aspects of NBC Defensive Operations, A Med P-6(B).* 1 February 1996.

AR 40-8. *Temporary Flying Restrictions Due to Exogenous Factors Affecting Aircrew Efficiency.* 16 May 2007.

AR 40-501. *Standards of Medical Fitness.* 14 December 2007.

AR 50-5. *Nuclear Surety.* 1 August 2000.

AR 50-6. *Nuclear and Chemical Weapons and Material Chemical Surety.* 28 July 2008.

AR 95-1. *Flight Regulations.* 12 November 2008.

AR 95-27. *Operational Procedures for Aircraft Carrying Hazardous Materials.* 11 November 1994.

AR 385-10. *The Army Safety Program.* 27 August 2007.

FM 3-04.301. *Aeromedical Training for Flight Personnel.* 29 September 2000.

FM 3-11.5. *Multiservice Tactics, Techniques, and Procedures for Chemical, Biological, Radiological, and Nuclear Decontamination.* 4 April 2006.

FM 8-50. *Prevention and Medical Management of Laser Injuries.* 8 August 1990.

MIL-0-27210E. Amendment 1 - *Oxygen, Aviator's Breathing, Liquid and Gas.* Note: This military specification is available from Commanding Officer, Naval Publications and Forms Center, ATTN: NPFC 105, 5801 Tabor Avenue, Philadelphia, PA 19120.

Selye, Hans. *Stress Without Distress.* Philadelphia: Lippincott Publishing Company, 1974.

Selye, Hans. *The Stress of Life.* New York: McGraw-Hill Publishing Company, 2nd Edition, 1978.

STANAG 3114 (Edition 8). *Aeromedical Training of Flight Personnel.* 22 November 2006.

TB MED 507. *Heat Stress Control and Heat Casualty Management.* 7 March 2003.

TB MED 508. *Prevention and Management of Cold-Weather Injuries.* 1 April 2005.

TC 1-210. *Aircrew Training Program Commander's Guide to Individual, Crew, and Collective Training.* 20 June 2006.

TM 3-4240-280-10. *Operator's Manual for Mask, Chemical-Biological: Aircraft, ABC-M24 and Accessories and Mask, Chemical-Biological, Tank, M25A1 and Accessories.* 15 March 1988.

TM 38-250. *Preparing Hazardous Materials for Military Air Shipments.* 15 April 2007.

DOCUMENTS NEEDED

These documents must be available to the intended users of this publication.

AF Form 702. *Individual Physiological Training Record (DD Form 2005, Privacy Act Statement Serves).*

AF Form 1274. *Physiological Training.*

DA Form 759. *Individual Flight Record and Flight Certificate-Army.*

DA Form 2028. *Recommended Changes to Publications and Blank Forms.*

DA Form 3444. *Inpatient Treatment Records and Dental Records (Orange).*

DA Form 4186. *Medical Recommendation for Flying Duty.*

NAVMED 6150/2. *Special Duty Medical Abstract.*

READINGS RECOMMENDED

These sources contain relevant supplemental information for the intended users of this publication.

AFI 11-403. *Aerospace Physiological Training Program*. 20 February 2001.

AGARD 154. *Aeromedical Handbook for Aircrew*.

AR 25-52. *Authorized Abbreviations, Brevity Codes, and Acronyms*. 4 January 2005.

AR 40-5. *Preventive Medicine*. 25 May 2007.

Ellis, Albert and Harper, Robert. *A New Guide to Rational Living*. Hollywood: Wilshire Book Company, 1979.

FM 1-02. *Operational Terms and Graphics*. 21 September 2004.

FM 3-04.203. *Fundamentals of Flight*. 7 May 2007.

FM 3-11. *Multiservice Tactics, Techniques, and Procedures for Nuclear, Biological, and Chemical Defense Operations*. 10 March 2003.

FM 4-25.11. *First Aid*. 23 December 2002.

FM 21-10. *Field Hygiene and Sanitation*. 21 June 2000.

JP 1-02. *Department of Defense Dictionary of Military and Associated Terms*. 12 April 2001.

TM 10-8400-202-13. *Maintenance Instructions for NOMEX Flight Gear Coveralls, Types CWU-27/P and CWU-28/P; Gloves, Type GS-FRP-2; Jacket, Flyer's, Summer, Type CWU-36/P and Winter, Type CWU-45/P; Hood, Winter, Flyer's (CWU-17/P JACKET); Trousers, Flyer's, Extreme Cold Weather, CWU-18/P*. 15 October 1972.

TM 10-8415-206-12&P. *Operator's and Organizational Maintenance Manual Including Repair Parts and Special Tools List for Helmet, Flyer's, Protective, Model SPH-4 Regular (NSN 8415-00-144-4981) and Extra Large (8415-00-144-4985)*. 5 May 1986.

TM 55-1680-351-10. *Operator's Manual for SRU-21/P Army Vest, Survival (NSN 8465-00-177-4819) (LARGE) (8465-01-174-2355) (SMALL)*. 22 April 1987.

TRADOC Program of Instruction 2C-IERW (Common Core). *Initial Entry Rotary-Wing Aviator Common Core*. This POI is available from Commander, U.S. Army Aviation Center of Excellence, ATTN: ATZQ-OP, Fort Rucker, AL 36362-5000.

USAF Special Report, AL-SR-1992-0002. *Night Vision Manual for the Flight Surgeon*. August 1992.

Index

This page intentionally left blank.

By order of the Secretary of the Army:

GEORGE W. CASEY, JR.
General, United States Army
Chief of Staff

Official:

JOYCE E. MORROW
Administrative Assistant to the
Secretary of the Army
0922203

DISTRIBUTION:

Active Army, Army National Guard, and U.S. Army Reserve: To be distributed in accordance with the initial distribution number (IDN) 110725, requirements for TC 3-04.93.